Nieuport

The first plane built by Edouard NIEUPORT.

Edouard NIEUPORT with his first plane.

Nieuport

A Biography of Edouard Nieuport

1875-1911

Gérard & Bertrand Pommier

Schiffer Military History
Atglen, PA

DEDICATION

We dedicate this book to our mother,
as a tribute to the father she never knew.

Book Design by Ian Robertson.
Translated by Rebecca Howell Balinski.

Library of Congress Control Number: 2002107675

Printed in China.
ISBN: 0-7643-1624-9

We are interested in hearing from authors with book ideas on related topics.

Published by Schiffer Publishing Ltd.
4880 Lower Valley Road
Atglen, PA 19310
Phone: (610) 593-1777
FAX: (610) 593-2002
E-mail: Schifferbk@aol.com.
Visit our web site at: www.schifferbooks.com
Please write for a free catalog.
This book may be purchased from the publisher.
Please include $3.95 postage.
Try your bookstore first.

In Europe, Schiffer books are distributed by:
Bushwood Books
6 Marksbury Avenue
Kew Gardens
Surrey TW9 4JF
England
Phone: 44 (0) 20 8392-8585
FAX: 44 (0) 20 8392-9876
E-mail: Bushwd@aol.com.
Free postage in the UK. Europe: air mail at cost.
Try your bookstore first.

Contents

Prototype of NIEUPORT 11.

Foreword

When we were children we heard a great deal from the grownups in our family about our grandfather, who flew airplanes that he had himself dreamt up and then built with his own hands.

Today, as mature adults, we often hear our mother speak of her father, who in his all too fleeting existence as a pioneer in aviation was the only *constructeur pilote* in the world to have produced the airframe, engine, magneto, sparkplugs, and propeller of the aircraft he flew.

He invented the NIEUPORT, a fighter whose wide use in World War I contributed significantly to the ultimate supremacy of French and American air power during the hostilities.

Given this young man's unique role in aviation history, we decided to collect the family papers and recount his story.

Gérard et Bertrand Pommier.

Foreword

As the twentieth century came to an end, we witnessed a flurry of attempts to set new world records in flight. In particular, there was the formidable feat of going round the world in a balloon, the dream of so many aeronauts ever since Jules Verne first imagined it.

At the beginning of the century, however, flight was a matter of brief leaps off the ground, and the first turns executed by an aircraft were a major achievement. But progress was rapid: not long after those primitive speed and performance contests came the air raids and battles of the World War I! The enthusiasm for inventing and building ever more efficacious airplanes was spurred on by the public's infatuation for flying machines and backed by financial partners and patrons who were sought as far away as New York.

This book leads us to discover—or rediscover—Edouard NIEUPORT's career, and the brilliant solutions he so felicitously applied to cycling and the automobile before turning to the aeronautical aspiration he shared with so many pilots, inventors, and constructors of his day: the combining of mechanics and streamlining. We can only marvel at the durability of the achievements of this extraordinarily talented engineer (who died at thirty-six), of his brother Charles (killed less than two years later), and of that splendid company bearing their name, which at one time led the world in airplane production, continuing its activity until 1936.

Books about aviation history are often overly technical or else lacking in substance, or indeed romanticized. Moreover, the French tend to believe that the entire history is French, just as our neighbors across the Atlantic are likely to believe it is wholly American, especially if the sounds and pronunciations of the names suggest it.

In noting the records, prizes, and feats of arms that mark the history of world aviation, the reader will come across names of outstanding pilots, legendary squadrons, and celebrated builders of whom they have perhaps retained a vague memory. They will discover, along with our friends—veterans of the "Dawn Patrol"—that, as is often the case, the great French accomplishments are sometimes better known, or at least have left as many traces in foreign countries than as our own.

Gérard and Bertrand, the grandsons of Edouard NIEUPORT, are to be congratulated for having presented, using previously unpublished photographs and documents, a lively, objective, and straightforward portrayal of the generosity, clear-sightedness, scientific tenacity, courage, and trailblazing daring of their grandfather.

This admirable accomplishment was undertaken to give pleasure to all of us, but it is especially a loving tribute to their mother, who has been deeply moved by the interest this project has stimulated throughout the world.

The reader should understand that I have written this preface to a marvelous family history with deep emotion. Not only does it evoke the numerous aircraft flown by my father and uncle, but to some extent, it is thanks to Edouard NIEUPORT, and to them that I have the chance today to gratify my love of flying and to pass it on....

Jacques BONTE
Captain, AIR FRANCE

On n'a rien donné tant que l'on n'a pas tout donné
("As long as you have not given everything, you have given nothing.")

- Georges GUYNEMER*

*When his plane was shot down in 1917, Guynemer, at 23, was leader of the celebrated French "Swan Squadron" and their champion ace, having destroyed 54 enemy aircraft. His motto "*Faire face*" ("Face up to things") and his heroism have made him a legendary figure in French aviation. (Translator's note)

1

A Little Family History

According to legend, the most celebrated of the mythical men who attempted flight, Icarus, lost his life when he flew so high that the sun melted the wax with which his feathered wings had been attached. In human history, it was not until the Renaissance that a realistic approach was made to flight. Leonardo DA VINCI, believing that man could fly only by using the strength of his limbs, designed machines driven by arms and legs. Four centuries later, at the beginning of the Nineteenth Century, the imagination and visionary schemes concerning aviation had scarcely progressed beyond DA VINCI's conception.

It is precisely just beyond this point that we have been able to trace Edouard NIEUPORT's family, which distinguished itself in the various military conflicts that flared up in Europe for over one hundred fifty years, culminating in World War II.

Louis-Gabriel DENIEPORT, born in Dieppe on April 14, 1765, was the first person of note to emerge in a family that endured the tragedies of the French Revolution. Educated by the Oratorians, he left school at fourteen when his passion for the sea led him to sign on as a privateer on vessels sailing out of Dieppe. Hence, from his early youth, he was initiated into the mysteries of the wind's fickle play. But he could hardly have imagined that four generations later one of his descendants would launch himself into flight with a machine heavier than air.

Under the ancien régime, Louis-Gabriel advanced from apprentice to ordinary seaman to pilot's assistant. But he was to remain in subordinate posts.

In the wake of the Revolution, however, his promotion was rapid. After Toulon on the 27th of Messidor in the Year II (1791) he became an ensign. Three years later, on the 21st of Germinal in the Year V, he attained the rank of lieutenant. He took part in the lengthy Eastern Mediterranean campaign before being named commander in the same year.

He obtained his commander's "certificate" in the Year VI and led the *Léandes* into the Battle of Corfu, during which he was captured when his ship was encircled by Turkish and Russian vessels. But there was soon an exchange of prisoners and he returned to duty, pursuing a brilliant career. According to his superiors, he proved himself to be "a brave officer and noble republican."

After Napoleon seized power in 1799, DENIEPORT became the commander of the *Badine* and was sent to Martinique. The islands of the West Indies were the scene of frequent clashes with the British, France's major enemy.

Returning to Cadix on August 25, 1804, DENIEPORT took command of the *Achille*, a vessel armed with seventy-four cannon. On April 17, 1805, he set sail from Rochefort, once again for Martinique, joining Admiral MAGAN, who was commanding the *Algésiras*, to do battle with the British. After a devastating encounter the badly damaged *Achille,* with two hundred men on board, finally reached the Azores. All the bulkheads had been demolished to make room for the wounded, and by the time she dropped anchor there remained drinking water for only five more days.

Later the *Achille* joined Napoleon's Mediterranean based squadron, led by Admiral VILLENEUVE, which with Spanish vessels would meet the English fleet, commanded by Admiral NELSON, at the Battle of Trafalgar. This naval battle, one of the greatest in history, began on October 20, 1805, and was to be the last major combat involving sailing ships. It resulted in an irrevocable disaster for France and gave England undisputed control of the sea, hence protecting it from a possible invasion by French troops.

During the Battle of Trafalgar, the *Achille* lost her mizzenmast and was soon surrounded by three large enemy ships that bombarded her from three sides. One of the first volleys wounded Gabriel DENIEPORT in the thigh, and a subsequent one left him dead on the deck. The doomed ship was soon engulfed in flames and, after an enormous explosion, sank, carrying with her two other vessels that lay nearby.

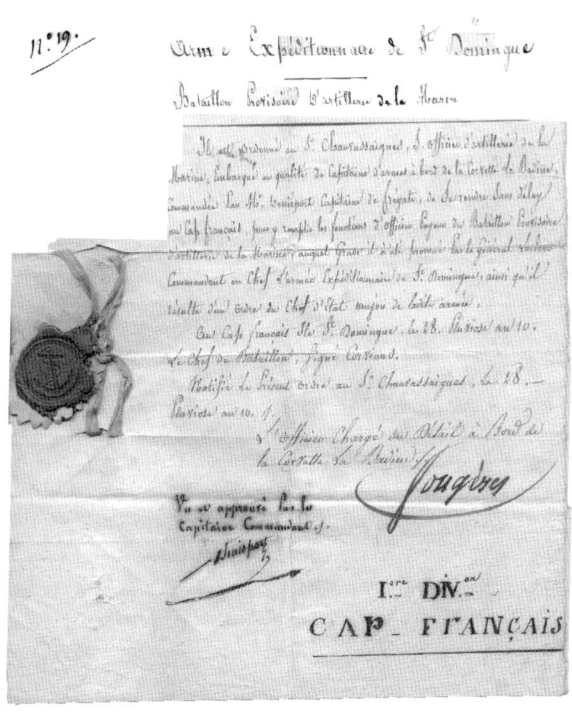

Photo of expeditionary order.

The *Achille* in the Naval Museum in Paris.

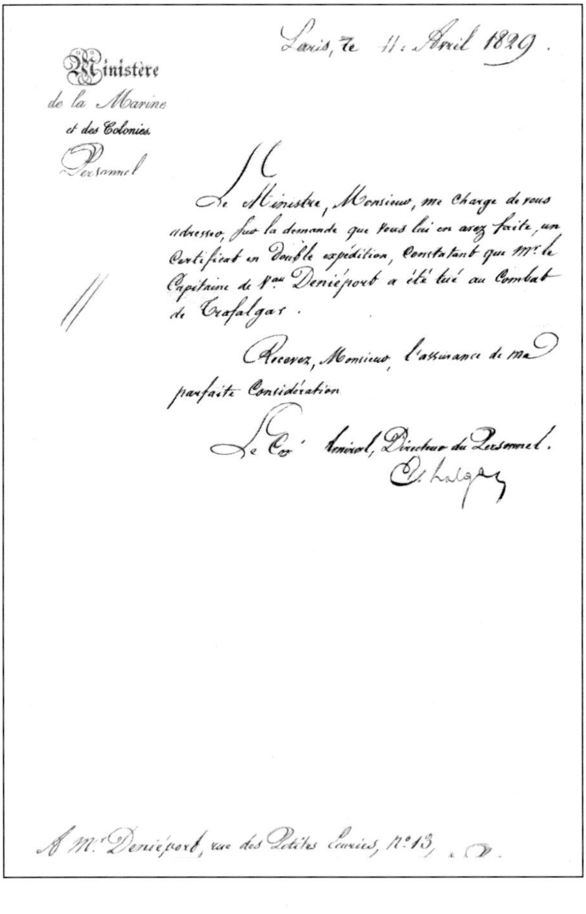

Paris, le 11 Avril 1829.

Ministère
de la Marine
et des Colonies.
Personnel

Le Ministre, Monsieur, me charge de vous adresser, sur la demande que vous lui en avez faite, un Certificat en double expédition, constatant que Mr. le Capitaine de Vau Deniéport a été tué au Combat de Trafalgar.

Recevez, Monsieur, l'assurance de ma parfaite considération.

Le Cre Amiral, Directeur du Personnel.

A Mr. Deniéport, rue des Petites Écuries, N°13, à P.

Document certifying that Gabriel Deniéport was killed in action at the Battle of Trafalgar.

In 1930, the city of Dieppe honored the memory of Gabriel DENIEPORT by naming one of its streets for him.

Gabriel DENIEPORT had a brother, Vincent-Jean, who became a merchant in Paris and a captain of the grenadiers (the 8th Batallion of the 3rd Legion) in the *garde nationale*.

In 1806, Vincent DENIEPORT had a son, Edouard, who grew up to practice law in Paris. In 1829, Edouard married Marie-Mélanie de Monge, with whom he had a son, Edmond, who was to follow a distinguished military career. Edmond was able to enter a military school after being aided by his mother, who wrote to a government minister, reminding him of the outstanding service record of her son's uncle, Gabriel, and the vicissitudes of his father:

> Monsieur Edouard has experienced numerous reverses of fortune supervened by a grave illness which for the past four years has necessitated considerable expenditure...
>
> She went on to specify the losses experienced by the family:
>
> ...Captain Deniéport, his paternal uncle, killed in combat at Trafalgar on October 21, 1805, on the Achille, which he commanded, and his maternal uncle, General Férrière, killed at Leipsick in 1813.

Apparently her arguments were effective, since the file contains the following comments:

> The father has a small interest in a steamship company, but owns nothing else. The DENIEPORT family having enjoyed a large fortune is now completely ruined. It deserves the greatest consideration.

When he entered military school Edmond made a voluntary commitment to remain in the army. He graduated 83rd in a class of 270, and on October 1, 1852, was commissioned a second lieutenant in the 42nd Regiment of the heavy infantry.

From June 1854 to the end of 1855, Edmond's regiment was engaged in the Crimean War and participated in the terrible seige of Sebastopol, during which he was wounded twice. He was soon afterwards promoted to the rank of lieutenant.

In 1859 he took part in the Italian Campaign and was made captain in 1861, shortly before being assigned to the 36th Infantry Regiment based in North Africa. He was to remain for a long period in Algeria, where his first son, Edouard, the future inventor, was born in Blida in 1875.

During the Franco-Prussian War (1870-71), Edmond fought in Eastern France with the 2nd Regiment, composed mainly of Algerian soldiers. First seeing action on July 20, 1870, he was wounded in his left thigh on August 6 in the Battle of Fraeschviller.

He was commissioned major and given a post in France in 1878. In 1879, having been promoted to lieutenant colonel, he joined the staff of the military school in Paris. Becoming a colonel in 1883, he took his well-earned retirement in 1890. His service record during these various military campaigns was recognized by his being named "Chevalier of the Legion of Honor" in 1859, *officier* in1871 and commander in 1887.

He received other decorations, among which were a medal from Queen VICTORIA for distinguished service during the Crimean War, and one awarded for his participation in the Italian Campaign.

Edmond DENIEPORT died in the military hospital of Val de Grâce on July 9, 1914, just before the outbreak of World War I. His wife, Caroline de MARTINET, lived on for twelve more years. She was the mother of three children whose destinies would be inscribed in the industrial history of France.

Edouard, born at Blida, Algeria, May 24, 1875, was an inventor and pioneer in aviation.

Charles, born at Lagny August 4, 1878, was just as fascinated by flight as his brother, and after Edouard's accidental death carried on with the adventure, until he, too, gave his life to it just over a year later.

Pauline, married Jean GUIMET, member of a prominent family of industrialists whose story is worth recounting briefly, since the DENIEPORTS and GUIMETS have remained closely linked.

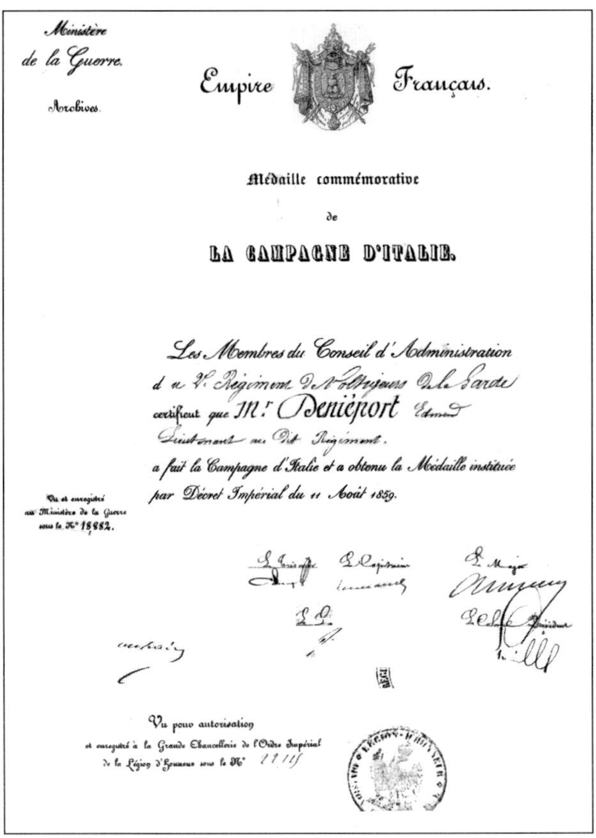
Ministère de la Guerre.
Archives.

Empire Français.

Médaille commémorative
de
LA CAMPAGNE D'ITALIE.

Les Membres du Conseil d'Administration
du 2e Régiment de Voltigeurs de la Garde
certifient que Mr Denieport Edmond
Lieutenant au dit Régiment,
a fait la Campagne d'Italie et a obtenu la Médaille instituée
par Décret Impérial du 11 Août 1859.

Vu et enregistré au Ministère de la Guerre sous le No 18882.

Vu pour autorisation
et enregistré à la Grande Chancellerie de l'Ordre Impérial de la Légion d'Honneur sous le No 2911

Commemorative Medal for the Italian Campaign.

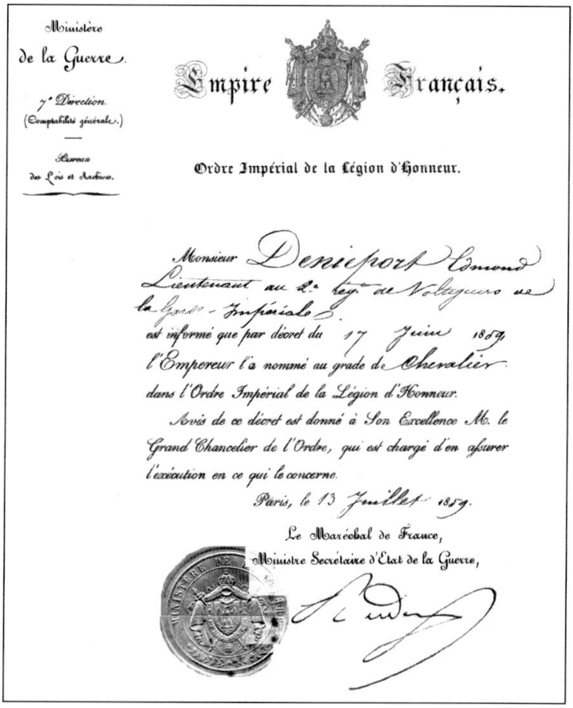

Ministère
de la Guerre.

7e Direction.
(Comptabilité générale.)

Bureau
des Lois et Archives.

Empire Français.

Ordre Impérial de la Légion d'Honneur.

Monsieur Deniéport Edmond
Lieutenant au 2e Regt de Voltigeurs de
la Garde Impériale
est informé que par décret du 17 Juin 1859,
l'Empereur l'a nommé au grade de Chevalier
dans l'Ordre Impérial de la Légion d'Honneur.

Avis de ce décret est donné à Son Excellence M. le Grand Chancelier de l'Ordre, qui est chargé d'en assurer l'exécution en ce qui le concerne.

Paris, le 13 Juillet 1859.

Le Maréchal de France,
Ministre Secrétaire d'Etat de la Guerre,

Document announcing Deniéport's being named "Chevalier of the Legion of Honor."

Edmond Deniéport.

Jean GUIMET's grandfather, Jean-Baptiste GUIMET, born July 20, 1795, was a Lyonnais chemist who married Zélie BIDAUT, daughter of a painter from the south of France, who had recently settled in the lively city on the Rhône. This union of the scientific and artistic was not only a source of happiness for Jean-Baptiste, but was to have an enormous influence on his future.

On November 22, 1826, the *Sociéte d'Encouragement pour l'Industrie Nationale* (The Society for the Encouragement of National Industry) announced a prize of 6,000 francs to be awarded for the production of a synthetic lapis lazuli which would combine all the qualities of the blue pigment that could then be obtained only by the extremely expensive process of extracting it from the mineral.

GUIMET was urged by his wife, who had inherited her father's artistic tastes, to direct his research towards finding this synthetic substance.

Known for his chemical expertise, Jean-Baptiste set to work, perfected his procedures, and produced industrially the famous ultramarine that had been so much sought after.

The process for fabricating the pigment initially intended for dying cloth was soon discovered by painters of the period. Ingres used this deep-blue purplish color to paint one of the rooms of the Louvre, and it came to be known as "Guimet blue."

Assured of success, Jean-Baptiste set up a factory near Lyon, which would subsequently bring fame and fortune to the GUIMET family.

2

The Need for a Personal Solution

The Man

Edouard DENIEPORT, who later became known as NIEUPORT, was born in 1875 in Blida, Algeria, where his father Edmond was commanding a garrison. He was married in Paris on April 24, 1903, to Jeanne Loubens. Two children were born of the union: a son, Edouard, in 1905 (he died in 1990), and a daughter, Pauline, on April 25, 1912, only a few months after her father's accidental death. Pauline continues to live quietly in a small village on the banks of the Loire.

Edouard was an unaffected, modest man. He was even regarded as being somewhat shy. But he was strong-willed and driven by a passion for aviation. Extremely hardworking, he shunned the spotlight.

On January 24, 1913, Edouard NIEUPORT's brother, Charles, who was a close collaborator in his work, was also killed while piloting his airplane.

He was also inspired by a keen sense of team spirit and fairness, as is illustrated by the following anecdote. On the day the accountant reported the first profits made by the original little company he had founded, Edouard immediately called his workers together, sharing with them the fruits of their common efforts.

Studies

Edouard DENIEPORT was a top student at the *Ecole supérieure d'électricité* (Electrical Engineering School), where he attended courses as an auditor. His academic success was so outstanding that it was predicted he would one day be first in his class at the prestigious Ecole Polytechnique in Paris. But his professors were astounded, and his father, Colonel DENIEPORT, indignant and distressed, when they learned that Edouard was abandoning his studies to devote himself to...cycling!

CYCL

Rude épreuve

EN 1894, NIEUPORT S'ETAIT ECROULE...

après avoir gagné le PRIX ZIMMERMANN, qui sera disputé à nouveau dimanche, au Vél' d'Hiv', sur 1 km. derrière entraîneurs

Le Prix Zimmermann, qui aura lieu dimanche, est une très vieille épreuve, qui remporta toujours un énorme succès.

C'est en 1894 que se déroula le premier Prix Zimmermann, au vélodrome de la Seine.

L'épreuve fut très dure, car elle se déroula derrière entraîneurs à triplette. Son vainqueur, Nieuport, qui devait devenir par la suite constructeur d'avions, fit un tel effort qu'il s'écroula après l'arrivée, victime d'une syncope cardiaque.

On dut l'emmener à l'hôpital.

Dimanche, au Vél' d'Hiv', la course se déroulera derrière Derny.

Et voici comment ont été composées les séries :

Première : Noblet, Rousset, Giri Nello.

Deuxième : Frosio, Verna, Hamadi.

Troisième : Dousset, Pujol, Vanni.

On voit tout de suite que si Noblet colle assez bien il pourra se qualifier assez facilement.

Mais Frosio aura beaucoup de mal à empêcher Verna de sprinter.

Quant à Dousset, il aura en Pujol un redoutable adversaire.

Espoirs de l'américaine

Le Vél' d'Hiv' a effectué, hier, la sélection de la course à l'américaine.

On note à ce sujet que plusieurs provinciaux feront le déplacement.

Sélectionnés : Blot-Garnault (Blois), Audenart-Lacroix (Beauvais), Rouget-Morphyre (Dijon), Cesbron-Maçon, Godeau - Lagorgette, Collett - Hary, Septier-Engelvin, Poulain-Deux, Giordani-Maelsait, Hollinger-Tillou, Grauss-Peyrrachia, Ballestra - Iris, Kuehien-Sapat, Schneider-Izorche, Brousse-Lespillez.

EDOUARD NIEUPORT

Édouard Nieuport, le génie de l'aviation disparu, que son frère Charles vient de suivre dans la tombe, fut un très remarquable sprinter.

EDOUARD NIEUPORT - Edouard NIEUPORT, the late aviation genius, whose brother Charles has just followed him to the grave, was a most remarkable sprinter.

DIFFICULT TRIAL IN 1894, NIEUPORT COLLAPSED...

After having won the ZIMMERMANN PRIZE, which will again be contested in a race of one kilometer behind tandems on Sunday at the Vel' d'Hiv.

The Zimmermann Prize Race, to be held on Sunday, is a very old competition that has always been a great success. The first contest, in 1894 at the Seine Velodrome, was very difficult because it took place behind trainers in threesomes. The winner, NIEUPORT, who was later to become a builder of airplanes, made such an effort that he collapsed after arriving, the victim of a blackout. He had to be hospitalized....

Cycling

The sport of cycling, in which he pushed himself to his physical limits, earned NIEUPORT several prizes in national competitions.

Although he lacked physical stamina, he was an excellent and highly successful racer. His greatest victory came in 1894 when he won the Zimmermann Prize at the Vélodrome de la Seine in Paris, a race that consisted of cycling a kilometer behind a tandum bicycle. In 1895, when he was twenty, he won ten handicap races, and he placed third in the French Championship in 1898.

His attention to aerodynamics is revealed in his choice of bicycles. Manufactured in London by Rudge Whitworth, they had very elongated frames, thus offering less resistance to forward movement.

His seemingly foolhardy passion for cycling was far from that of a schoolboy weary of the classroom and eager to play hooky in a big way. On the contrary, his roundabout method of research resulted from perfectly thought out plans, permitting him to study aerodynamic principles. Cycling was the best means he had found to experience the effects of air on his body. Nevertheless, his family continued to consider this strikingly unusual path to be a rather embarrassing oddity.

For this reason DENIEPORT—albeit only nineteen, but possessing a very determined character—adopted an assumed name, and from that time on was called NIEUPORT.

NIEUPORT understood the paramount importance of shape in aerodynamics. But how was he to instruct himself in this science when he had no money for a laboratory or workshop? There was only one way: the bicycle, which happened to be the first vehicle to allow for carrying out "life-size" tests on the mechanics of moving objects.

In 1897, Clément ADER had just presented his "airplane no. 300" to an Army commission at Camp Satory. It was a failure. But even its judges admitted that the airstrip had been unsuitable: it should not have been circular, but completely straight.

It was at this time that talk began of the correspondence between MOUILLARD and CHANUTE on their studies of the large gliding birds.

MAREY, a member of the Institute, also carried out remarkable studies on the flight of birds using "chronophotographs," which allowed him to analyze the movements of the birds' wings.

NIEUPORT, who had just turned twenty-one, was intensely interested by all this research, and followed especially closely the results of the glider flights made by the Pomerian engineer Otto LILLIENTHAL.

Mechanics

Parallel to his research in aerodynamics, Edouard NIEUPORT, who was an electrical engineer, became aware that most of the problems in the emerging automobile industry stemmed from the ignitions—the tricky gasoline burners and capricious tremblers. All these devices caused frequent breakdowns or accidents, often made worse by fires. Studying these problems, NIEUPORT invented high-voltage magnetos to replace these parts, which were far too unreliable.

In 1902, on the rue de Seine in Suresnes, near Paris, he set up a small factory for producing electrical devices for internal combustion engines.

La Nouvelle MAGNÉTO "NIEUPORT"

comparée aux meilleurs systèmes actuels, apparaît comme

NFINIMENT PLUS SIMPLE

Les deux grands tableaux représentent chacun l'ensemble des pièces qui, réunies et ajustées, constituent une magnéto pour moteur 4 cylindres, suivant les systèmes actuellement les plus répandus français et étrangers.

Le petit tableau représente l'ensemble des pièces, exécutées à la même échelle que les précédentes, qui constituent la **nouvelle Magnéto "Nieuport"**, à haute tension, pour 4 cylindres.

Il est à noter, de plus, que si le démontage des appareils avait été poussé plus complètement, de part et d'autre, et toutes les pièces représentées une par une, les avantages de simplicité de notre système se seraient trouvés encore accentués. La comparaison est donc absolument loyale.

La **Magnéto "Nieuport"** ne nécessite, dans la pratique, aucun réglage. Elle ne réclame d'autre soin que le graissage des deux seuls paliers à billes.

Elle permet une mise en marche extrêmement aisée et ne nécessite jamais de double allumage.

Elle permet d'adopter un point fixe d'allumage avec une avance extrêmement réduite, ce qui épargne le moteur et rend sa marche plus souple, tout en supprimant une opération dans la conduite de la voiture.

The new "Nieuport" magneto, when compared with the best systems presently available, appears infinitely simpler.

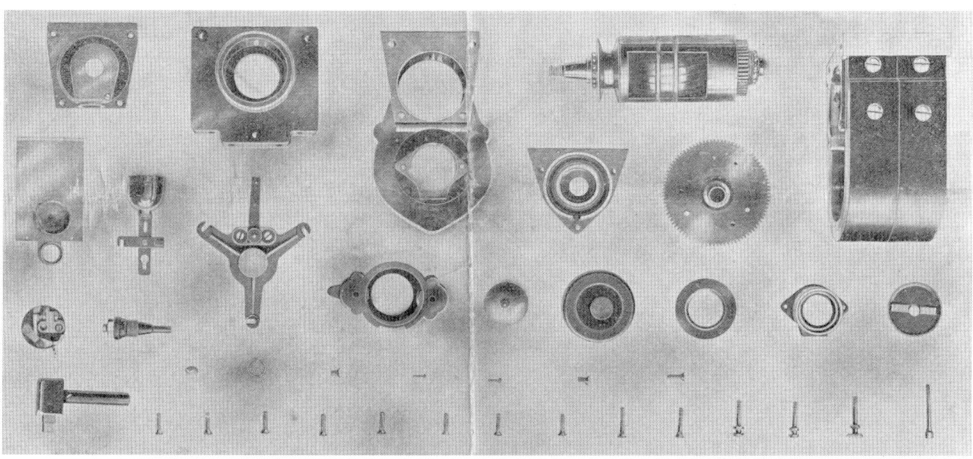

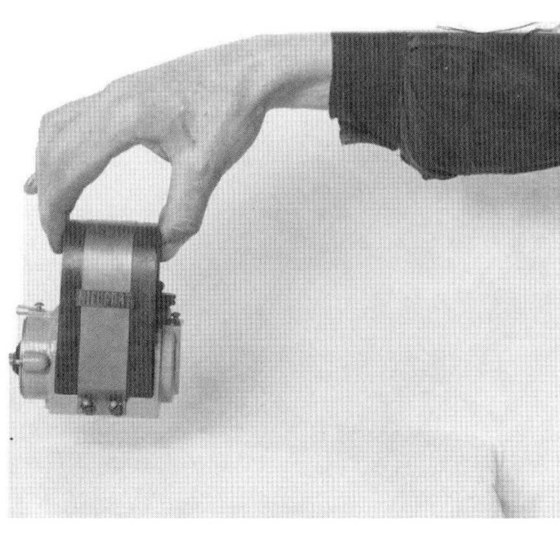

The new "NIEUPORT" magneto.

Under the brand name "NIEUPORT et Duplex," Edouard began to sell not only high-voltage magnetos, but electrical storage batteries and spark plugs. Thus, he solved the problem of igniting engines and became widely known as an expert in the field.

Text accompanying photographs: "The two large photographs show the parts that, when assembled and adjusted, compose a magneto for the 4-cylinder engine most widely used in motorized systems in France and abroad.

The smaller photograph, produced on the same scale as the preceding ones, shows the individual parts making up the new high-voltage "NIEUPORT" Magneto for 4 cylinders.

It should be pointed out that had the dismantling of these devices been more complete, and all the parts shown one by one, the simplicity of our system would be even more striking. The comparison is absolutely objective. The "NIEUPORT" Magneto needs no adjustment and requires no maintenance, other than the lubrication of the two ball bearings. It makes starting the engine extremely easy and never requires dual ignition.

It allows for a fixed point of ignition with an extremely reduced advance, which spares the engine and makes it run more smoothly, while at the same time eliminating an operation in the driving of the vehicle.

Il est très rare dans l'industrie, ou le progrès marche généralement pas à pas, de rencontrer une pareille différence de simplicité entre des appareils destinés au même but et remplissant exactement les mêmes fonctions. On peut donc affirmer que la

Nouvelle MAGNÉTO "NIEUPORT"
à haute tension

marque une **véritable époque dans l'allumage des moteurs** à explosion.

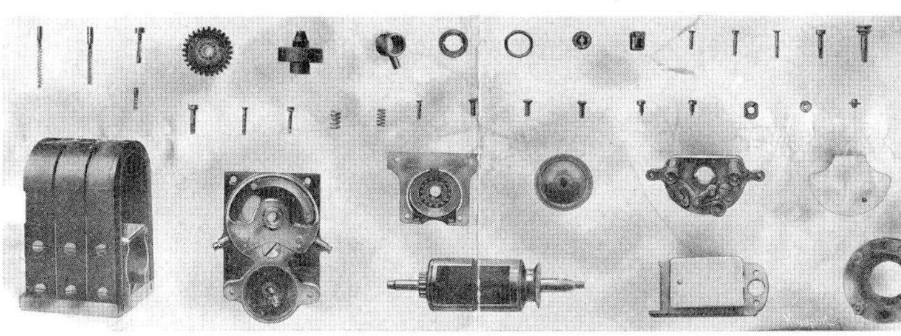

It is very rare in industry, where progress is generally made step by step, to find such a contrast in the degree of complexity existing in devices destined for the same use and filling exactly the same functions. It can thus be claimed that the NEW "NIEUPORT MAGNETO (High-voltage) marks a *real milestone in the ignition of combustion engines.*

The name "NIEUPORT" now takes it place alongside all the world records that have marked the enormous progress in locomotion.

ED. NIEUPORT
Administrateur Délégué
de la Société Ano^me des Appareils Electriques Nieuport

Suresnes
(Seine)

9, Rue de Seine.
et 28, Rue Ledru-Rollin
Tél. 85.

For example:

- It was the automobile Darracq, having an 8-cylinder engine equipped with a NIEUPORT magneto, that was the first in France to achieve 200 kilometers an hour.
- NIEUPORT ignition accessories were installed in the aircraft that allowed SANTOS-DUMONT and FARMAN to make their first flights.
- The BONNEMAISON hydroplanes, which reached the highest speeds on water, were also outfitted with NIEUPORT inventions.
- In 1907, Léon Lavasseur equipped his Antoinette engines with the NIEUPORT starters.
- On January 13, 1908, Farman completed the first kilometer in closed circuit in his Voisin biplane, which had an 8-cylinder Antoinette engine, with the direct fuel injection and ignition invented by NIEUPORT."

In 1906, despite the unquestioned success of his products and his contribution to the technical progress of locomotion, Edouard NIEUPORT needed financial help to ensure the continuation of his research. Looking around for partners who could provide the capital necessary for the sound development of his company, he was particularly interested in American and Italian firms, whose production was more economical than similar efforts in France.

So, in March 1909 he went to the United States to look into possibilities for registering patents there. It appears that his visit was not very fruitful, because even though he created a company, he did not expect very much from it. One of the rare existing letters that he wrote to his mother reflects his disappointment at not being able to establish himself on that side of the Atlantic. Little could he have dreamt that within a few years, the NIEUPORT fighters would bring glory to the "ESCADRILLE LAFAYETTE," and that even today, passionate enthusiasts like the DAWN PATROL fly replicas of the NIEUPORT planes in the four corners of America.

(Letter from the LAFAYETTE HOTEL)

Friday, January 22

Ma chère Maman,
I am well, and hope that all of you are also.

It is impossible to convey in a letter my first impressions of New York, especially since I have so little time. I shall say only that everything will seem very small when I get back to France and that I understand why people without strong ties in Europe no longer wish to live there once they have spent some time in the United States.

I was quite bored for the first three or four days, but I begin to adapt a little, even though I still cannot get used to being without any news from my family. Tomorrow it will be fifteen days since I boarded the boat and since then I have had no news from France, not even newspapers.

Regarding my company, things have taken a good turn, and there will certainly be a bright future for my devices if the firm is well launched. Nevertheless, I do not think I can leave before February 28.

With much love to you, Papa and Charles,

Edouard

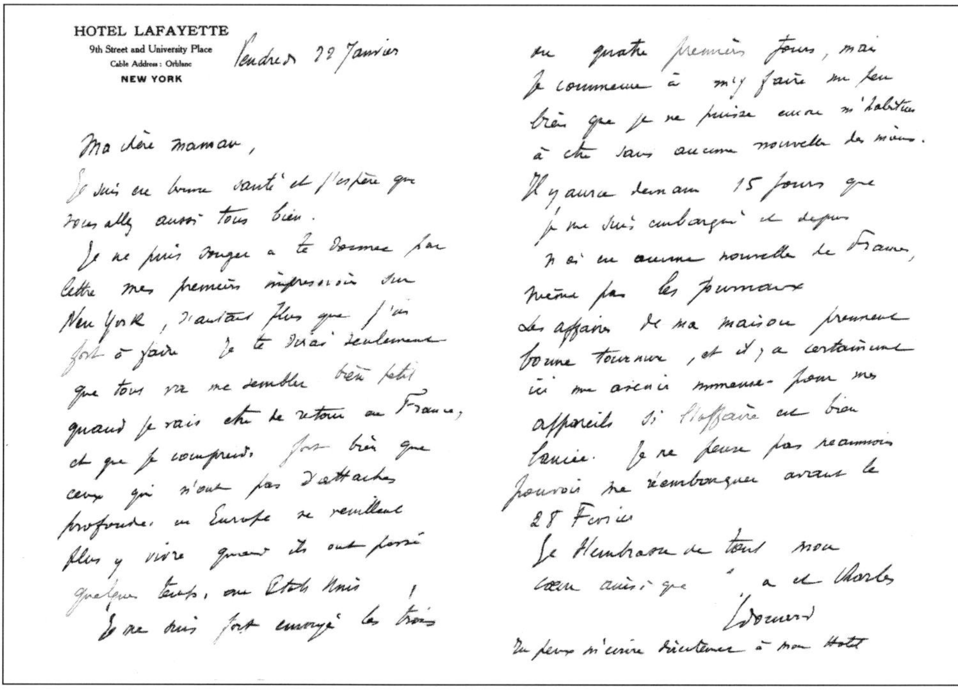

(Letter from the LAFAYETTE HOTEL)

New York
March 7, 1909

Ma chère Maman,

I have come back to New York and, consequently, have been much busier; but it won't be long before I can leave.

Unfortunately, I cannot hope to get away before the 18th, on the *Provence*, because beforehand there is only the *Bretagne*, which is not a good boat, or else foreign ships. In any case, I shall send a telegram to Suresnes and you will be notified. Certainly, by the time this letter reaches you I shall have already left or almost. I received your various letters and was very happy to learn that you are feeling better and that all the others are fine. I surely hope that everything will be going as well when I get back.

I do not know how you got it into your head that I intended to return to America. I assure that I have no desire to do so, quite the contrary, and I am convinced that the American NIEUPORT company, which I hope will soon be set up, will not be able to pay me enough to make me decide to return. I hope you will put your mind at rest on this subject.

See you soon, then, my dear *Maman*. I send you much love and please give my love to Papa, Charles and everybody else.

Edouard

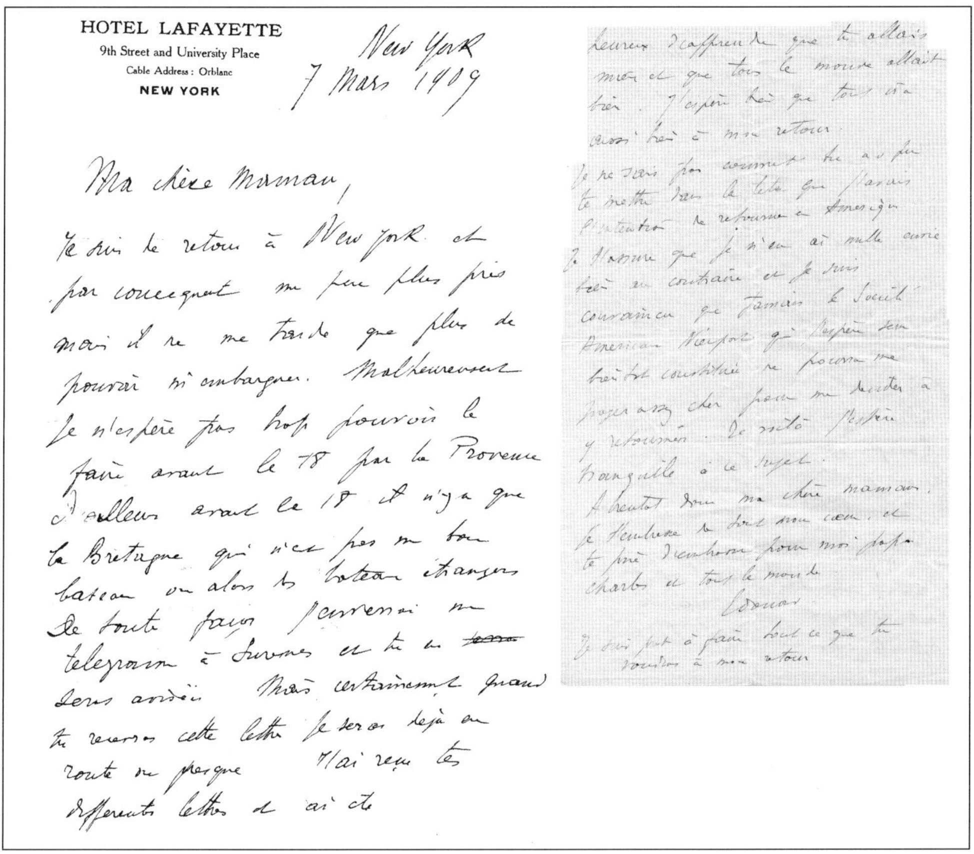

HOTEL LAFAYETTE
9th Street and University Place
Cable Address: Orblanc
NEW YORK

New York 7 Mars 1909

Ma chère Maman,

Je suis de retour à New York et par conséquent un peu plus près mais il ne me tarde que plus de pouvoir m'embarquer. Malheureusement je n'espère pas trop pouvoir le faire avant le 18 par la Provence d'ailleurs avant le 18 il n'y a que la Bretagne qui n'est pas un bon bateau ou alors les bateaux étrangers. De toute façon j'enverrai un télégramme à Suresnes et tu en seras avisée. Mais certainement quand tu recevras cette lettre je serai déjà en route ou presque. J'ai reçu tes différentes lettres et ai été heureux d'apprendre que tu allais mieux et que tout le monde allait bien. J'espère bien que tout ira aussi bien à mon retour.

Je ne sais pas comment tu as pu te mettre dans la tête que j'avais l'intention de retourner en Amérique. J'assure que je n'en ai nulle envie bien au contraire et je suis convaincu que jamais la Société Américaine Nieuport qui j'espère sera bientôt constituée ne pourra me payer assez cher pour me décider à y retourner. Je te prie d'être tranquille à ce sujet.

A bientôt donc ma chère maman, je t'embrasse de tout mon cœur, et te prie d'embrasser pour moi papa Charles et tout le monde.

Edouard

Je suis prêt à faire tout ce que tu voudras à mon retour.

Memorial lunch of survivors of the LAFAYETTE flying corps in March 1949 at the Lafayette Hotel in New York. These pilots did not know that Edouard NIEUPORT had stayed in this hotel in 1909 when he was looking into the possibilities of starting a business in the U.S. Edouard NIEUPORT could not have imagined that, later, the name of LAFAYETTE would be indirectly joined with his name.

PAGE 4. — 21-8-48. — N° 1.177.

LES BELLES FIGURES DE L'AVIATION

L'ŒUVRE MAGISTRALE DE NIEUPORT DANS L'ALLUMAGE DES MOTEURS

II. — Après la technique du sport cycliste, celle de l'automobile.

Avant d'imaginer lui-même son fameux 28-CV., dont il devait équiper ses premiers avions, Edouard Nieuport améliora puissamment la marche des autres moteurs en inventant des bobines, des bougies et surtout des magnétos, qui connurent, dans l'industrie et le sport automobiles, des succès vraiment retentissants.

NOUS avons laissé Edouard Nieuport, docile aux conseils de son médecin, et se résignant à abandonner les courses cyclistes (1).

Il leur demeura cependant fidèle, à sa manière, et comme spectateur assidu. Pouvait-il agir autrement? Pouvait-il abandonner les bons camarades de travail connus le long des routes et des pistes et que le peuple entourait de son admiration? Ceux que Nieuport retrouvait à l'étape, modestes, « couverts de sueur et dévorés d'idéal », se nommaient Charron, Renaux, Farman. Leurs propos contenaient l'avenir.

La bicyclette dans le tunnel

Il est assez curieux de constater combien la « petite reine » a donné de servants à la « grande reine » Aviation. Les Wright, les Farman, les Voisin ne commencèrent-ils pas leur mission sportive sur bicyclette. Et si l'on voulait chercher parmi nos maîtres modernes du vol acrobatique, on trouverait Marcel Doret qui, presque à la même époque, prenait part à des courses aux côtés des frères Pélissier, et Fernand Malinvaud qui l'année même où naissait Doret, remportait à l'âge de trois ans un championnat sur sa bicyclette d'enfant.

(1) Voir « Les Ailes », N° 1.176 du 14 août.

Mais en ce temps-là, seul, Nieuport songeait à l'aérodynamique du coureur et à la « traînée ». Il ne se doutait pas qu'en 1933, une bicyclette ferait une entrée sensationnelle dans le laboratoire installé rue Boileau par Gaston Eiffel et où officie aujourd'hui notre ami Marcel Chabonat. Le coureur cycliste Richard se plaça dans la soufflerie de la rue Boileau, sur son « vélo » suspendu aux tiges articulées des balances, pour peser la traînée et chercher ainsi l'attitude offrant la moindre résistance à l'avancement. On criait presque au génie, de voir ce coureur dans le vent du tunnel, mais personne ne rappela, à ce moment, les recherches de Nieuport quarante ans auparavant.

L'effort musculaire et le cœur

Nieuport donc, en « fidèle » des pistes s'enthousiasma lors des premiers duels du noir Major Taylor en Europe, et écrivit, sur sa rivalité avec Jacquelin, de fort jolis articles (sa sœur, Mme Guimet, ne nous disait-elle pas que tout ce qu'il faisait, il le faisait bien?) Là, Nieuport expliquait en termes lumineux la supériorité du félin Taylor sur son puissant adversaire, tout cela avec une parfaite objectivité.

A quelques mois d'intervalle, Nieuport, que sa syncope lors du Prix Zimmermann, avait rendu curieux des choses médicales, publiait dans *La Nature* des études fort remarquées et notamment des considérations très pertinentes sur les rapports entre le cœur et les efforts musculaires. On vint, paraît-il, souvent le consulter ensuite sur ce sujet. Tout cela montrait que Nieuport, excellent observateur, se doublait d'un excellent écrivain. Dans ce même temps, il publiait, au sujet de Santos-Dumont, des articles qui lui valurent la visite de celui-ci et sa meilleure amitié.

Dans la bibliothèque familiale

Edouard, silencieusement, travaillait. Le grand-père disait de lui, à la petite Pauline : « Ton frère est drôle! », parce que, dans la bibliothèque où beaucoup de beaux livres pouvaient tenter un adolescent, il ne lisait que ceux qui se rapportaient au vol des oiseaux et le reste du temps se consacrait aux sciences physiques et à l'électricité en particulier.

Mme de Nieport, voyant que son fils abandonnait le cyclisme militant et travaillait fort tard pour acquérir seul une instruction technique qui allait si bien servir son génie créateur, usa de ses relations pour obtenir en sa faveur une excellente situation dans une banque... Mais c'était méconnaître la secrète ardeur du jeune homme qui ne voulut point goûter à la discipline des comptabilités les plus nobles. Comment d'ailleurs sa charmante mère pouvait-elle exercer sur son destin quelque autorité, et l'influencer, elle, nature craintive que la vue des araignées mettait en grand effroi!

Article from newspaper *Ailes*, August 21, 1948, which recounts the life of the inventor, from cycling to the ignition of engines.

Nieuport et les moteurs

Tout naturellement, Edouard se sentit attiré vers les moteurs voués à la locomotion, et surtout par leur côté le plus mystérieux, par la source même de leur vie, l'allumage électrique, domaine encore mal exploré et peu familier aux praticiens.

Sans qu'il renonçât complètement à la bicyclette, l'auto le conquit, dès qu'elle parut. Il chevaucha d'abord le tricycle à pétrole pour goûter, de nouveau et plus fortement, les ivresses de cette vitesse à laquelle il devait vouer ses plus profonds enthousiasmes. M. A. Odier, qui venait de sortir de l'Ecole des Arts et Métiers d'Aix, en 1901, a raconté que les premières pannes de Nieuport sur son tricycle lui fournirent l'occasion de rechercher le perfectionnement nécessaire et de mettre au grand jour ses dons d'inventeur, car inventeur, il l'était par destination, se montrant toujours plus heureux de chercher que d'avoir trouvé. Il imagina donc l'accumulateur sec Davy, puis s'en désintéressa en faveur de nouvelles ambitions.

Débuts à Levallois

Dans le courant de 1902, il résolut, en effet, de se lancer dans la fabrication des bougies et de bobines pour l'allumage des moteurs à explosion, car à l'entendre, l'accumulateur inventé par lui présentait des défauts.

Il loua donc à Levallois-Perret, 13, rue des Frères-Herbert, un local. Local assez exigu d'ailleurs, car ses ressources personnelles ne lui permettaient pas de vastes entreprises.

M. Quentin qui, dès l'âge de dix-huit ans, entra au service de Nieuport et compte aujourd'hui dans cette Maison près d'un demi-siècle de fidèle présence, nous a raconté l'histoire de ces débuts. Edouard Nieuport possédait de modestes économies sur l'argent gagné dans les compétitions cyclistes. Cela n'allait pas bien loin. Sa famille lui vint en aide, sans hésiter et malgré qu'il ne suivit point la voie qu'elle désirait pour lui.

Comme le rappelait, au lendemain de sa mort, le Général Roques, à Verdun, « tous ceux qui vivaient auprès de lui, pleins de foi dans son avenir se montraient pénétrés de sa haute intelligence au point que leurs conversations reflétaient, malgré eux, l'état d'admiration de leur âme ». Son grand-père maternel, le comte de Martinet, descendant de ce fameux maréchal inventeur des ponts de bateaux (dont on trouve d'ailleurs le nom dans le « Siècle de Louis XIV » de Voltaire comme dans l' « Histoire de l'Armée française » du Général Weygand), possédait une petite fortune. Il soutint de ses deniers l'entreprise de son petit-fils. Celui-ci, dès l'apparition de ses bougies et de ses bobines, montra combien il méritait cette confiance, car elles firent sensation dans le monde industriel et la clientèle afflua : Clément, Darracq, Griffon, Alcyon, et d'autres...

Bougies et bobines Nieuport

Aussi bien, en 1904 et en 1905, les bougies et bobines Nieuport prenaient-elles leur part de lauriers dans les compétitions comme la Coupe du Motocycle-Club de France, le Circuit des Ardennes, le meeting de Château-Thierry, la Coupe des Voiturettes, où les machines équipées par lui enlevaient à tous coups la première place.

Les commandes devenant de plus en plus importantes et le local de Levallois manifestement trop petit, Edouard décida, vers le milieu de l'année 1905, d'agrandir ses ateliers.

Après avoir cherché un certain temps, il choisit 9, rue de Seine, à Suresnes (cette rue devint plus tard la rue Edouard-Nieuport) un local ayant servi à la vente de vins en gros. Après des transformations qui durèrent deux ou trois mois, notre inventeur, âgé de trente ans, possédait une petite usine.

Dans l'atelier de Suresnes

Nieuport émettait alors des idées nouvelles, et très heureuses, sur l'allumage des moteurs.

« Une des premières qualités de la bougie doit être sa simplicité, disait-il. Il faut donc se défier des bougies de forme bizarre et dont les électrodes sont compliquées. »

Il recommandait le platine, pour les pointes ou, à défaut, le nickel, et des pointes soudées, car, serties avec plus ou moins de perfection, elles risquaient de s'échauffer plus facilement et de produire l'auto-allumage. Il critiquait les pointes multiples et indiquait que l'étincelle ne saute jamais aussi facilement qu'entre des électrodes constituées uniquement par deux pointes aussi fines que possible.

Il appelait enfin l'attention sur l'extrême importance de l'étanchéité des bougies et la porcelaine comme isolant, malgré sa relative fragilité par rapport à la stéatite et au mica.

A cette époque, l'usage de la magnéto pour l'allumage des moteurs d'automobile se répandait de plus en plus. Cet autre problème devait également attirer Nieuport possesseur d'une petite Darracq, payée de ses deniers. Accroché au volant, penché vers la route, attentif à ses embûches, il y songeait.

Associé à son ami Depasse, il décida d'aborder la fabrication des magnétos, son principal client pour les bobines, la Maison Darracq en consommant un grand nombre. Il acquit l'outillage spécial et chercha d'autres appuis financiers. La renommée de ses bougies facilita les choses et, se séparant de Depasse, il créa une société où figurèrent des commanditaires notoires comme le directeur des autos Minerva, d'Anvers, et celui de la Fonderie des Ardennes.

La magnéto dans l'aquarium

Les premières magnétos fabriquées furent à basse tension parce que le client principal, Darracq, employait alors le système à rupture. Ces magnétos, entourées d'un carter en cuivre, absolument étanches, connurent rapidement le succès et on en vit un exemplaire au Salon de l'Automobile, en 1906, qui fonctionnait admirablement dans l'eau même d'un aquarium où évoluaient des poissons rouges. Trois mois après, sortait des ateliers de Suresnes, une magnéto à haute tension qui imposa à son tour.

Tout aussitôt, une voiture Darracq, 8 cyl., dotée d'une telle magnéto, battait à Salon le record du monde du kilomètre et le record de vitesse au meeting de Floride à raison de 197 km. 060 à l'heure. Meeting d'Ostende, meeting de Monaco, Coupe de Maisons-Laffitte, Tour de France, Course de Côte à Gaillon, autant de triomphes pour les magnétos Nieuport à bord de la 8-cylindres Darracq, d'un canot à moteur et de voitures ou motos de marques diverses.

Notre jeune constructeur avait, certes, en Allemagne un redoutable concurrent, les magnétos Bosch, disposant de moyens industriels considérables et cependant il gagna la bataille en France et en Belgique, ses équipements restant préférés à cause de leur simplicité. C'est là précisément, dans ce souci constant de faire « plus simple » (haute vertu, en mécanique), qu'apparaît ce besoin de la solution personnelle, témoignage de la puissante personnalité d'Edouard Nieuport.

Son mérite, par ailleurs apparaissait considérable. Alors que l'allumage demeurait l'opération qui laissait le plus à désirer dans le fonctionnement du moteur, il venait de résoudre avec éclat cette question délicate.

Un succès sans précédent

De toutes les industries se rapportant à l'Automobile, la construction et la mise au point des différents types de magnétos constituaient alors celles qui présentaient de beaucoup le plus de difficultés. Les nombreuses et puissantes Maisons Thomson-Houston, Bardon, Bréguet, la Société Industrielle des Téléphones, par exemple, qui paraissaient cependant bien qualifiées par leurs travaux antérieurs pour entreprendre la construction des magnétos d'allumage, et qui, malgré leurs efforts n'obtenaient pas de résultats satisfaisants, témoignaient de la réalité de ces difficultés.

(Suite en pa[illegible] 5.)

Problème ardu, en effet, que d'asservir les phénomènes électriques les plus complexes et de réaliser pour les rudes épreuves de l'automobile, un mécanisme réclamant une précision absolue et confié à des mains inexpertes.

D'un appareil auquel on attribuait neuf sur dix des pannes du moteur, deux années de labeur intelligent venaient de faire un appareil sûr, régulier, réclamant peu d'entretien. La maison Nieuport ne disait-elle pas aux chauffeurs toujours enclins à démonter la magnéto : « Si votre auto est munie d'un de nos appareils d'allumage, cherchez ailleurs la cause de l'arrêt du moteur. Vous gagnerez ainsi beaucoup de temps ! »

Les magnétos Nieuport, brevetées même en Allemagne se présentaient comme une création originale. Nieuport accoutumait, par nature, de sortir des sentiers battus et c'était toujours à lui que s'adressaient les industriels dans les cas difficiles.

Ses appareils triomphèrent des plus redoutables concurrences, celles des magnétos Bosch (dont on vit le stand au rez-de-chaussée du Grand Palais lors de l'Exposition Aéronautique de 1909) et des magnétos Lavalette.

Cela tenait à quatre vertus caractéristiques. Les masses polaires, encastrées dans un bâti fondu d'une seule pièce avec elles, présentaient un *entrefer réduit* et un rendement nettement supérieur. Dans les magnétos à haute tension, condensateur et rupteur tournaient avec l'induit et le circuit primaire n'offrait pas de solution de continuité. Les nouveaux modèles à étincelles directes, ne comportant aucun distributeur, se recommandaient par une *simplification extrême*, et un démontage remarquablement aisé. Enfin, avec un poids d'aimants deux fois moindre, ils donnaient des étincelles aussi chaudes que pouvaient les supporter rupteurs et bougies.

Un procès significatif

Leur simplicité valut même à leur auteur en 1908 un procès significatif.

La société Nieuport publiait un prospectus montrant à la même échelle, des photos de l'ensemble des pièces après démontage, pour la magnéto X, la magnéto Y, et la magnéto Nieuport.

La comparaison parut à ce point probante qu'un des concurrents attaqua Nieuport devant le Tribunal de Commerce. Celui-ci estima, dans son jugement du 10 mai 1908, que Nieuport avait parfaitement le droit de présenter côte à côte ses articles et ceux de la concurrence, et, reconnaissant pour parfaitement véridiques les trois clichés, débouta le concurrent et le condamna aux dépens.

Telle fut la première activité industrielle d'Edouard Nieuport. En lisant ses catalogues de 1907, riches d'observations et de conseils judicieux, on apprécie encore davantage la sûreté de ses connaissances et de son jugement.

Cet esprit, nettement en avance sur son époque, remportait là une première victoire.

D'autres, plus éclatantes encore, allaient suivre.

Edmond BLANC.

Outstanding Figures of Aviation
(translation of the previous article)

NIEUPORT'S BRILLIANT WORK ON THE IGNITION OF ENGINES

II. FOLLOWING HIS CONTRIBUTIONS TO THE CYCLING TECHNIQUE, HE TURNED TO THE AUTOMOBILE

Before dreaming up his famous 28-hp engine, with which he would equip his first airplanes, Edouard NIEUPORT greatly improved the operation of other engines by inventing ignition coils, spark plugs, and, above all, magnetos, which had a resounding success in the automobile industry and racing.

We left Edouard NIEUPORT heeding his doctor's advice and resigning himself to relinquishing bicycle racing (1).

He nevertheless remained faithful to the sport in his own way and became an assiduous spectator. How could he have done otherwise? Could he have abandoned the good pals he had met along the roads and bikeways and on whom the fans continued to bestow their admiration? Those unassuming cyclists, "covered with perspiration and burning with idealism," whom NIEUPORT joined at the stopover points, were called CHARRON, RENAUX, and FARMAN. Their conversations contained the future.

THE BICYCLE IN THE TUNNEL

It is rather curious to think just how much the "little queen," cycling, has served the "big queen," aviation. Did not the Wright Brothers, the FARMANS and VOISINS begin their sporting adventures on the bicycle? And if we look at our modern masters of acrobatic flight, we find Marcel DORET who, at almost the same period, was racing alongside the PELISSIER brothers, and Fernand MALINVAUD, who, the year DORET was born, won a championship on his child's bicycle at the age of three.

But at that time, only NIEUPORT was reflecting on the aerodynamics of the racer and his "drag." He could not have imagined that, in 1933, a bicycle would make a sensational entry in the laboratory set up on the rue Boileau by Gaston EIFFEL and now directed by our friend Marcel CHABONAT. There the racing cyclist RICHARD places himself in the wind tunnel, on his "vélo" suspended from steel wires joined to scales, to measure the drag and thus determine the position offering the least resistance to forward movement. Putting this racer in the wind tunnel has been acclaimed as a stroke of genius, but until now nobody has recalled NIEUPORT's research carried out forty years ago.

MUSCULAR EFFORT AND THE HEART

NIEUPORT, a racing "devotee," was swept away by enthusiasm from the moment he saw the black American, Major TAYLOR, compete in Europe, and he wrote some extremely good articles about TAYLOR's rivalry with JACQUELIN. (Didn't his sister, Madame GUIMET, tell us that everything he did he did well?) In them, NIEUPORT explained in crystal clear prose and with perfect objectivity the superiority of the feline TAYLOR over his powerfully built adversary. A few months later NIEUPORT, whose blackout after the race for the Zimmermann Prize had stimulated his curiosity about the medical effects of racing, published in *La Nature* some widely praised studies which included pertinent reflections on the relationship between the heart and muscular exertion. Apparently, he was subsequently often consulted on the subject. All that showed NIEUPORT was not only an excellent observer, but an excellent writer. At the same time he published articles about SANTOS-DUMONT, which resulted in a visit from the Brazilian aviation pioneer, just three years his senior, who was to become a close friend.

IN THE FAMILY LIBRARY

Edouard always worked silently. His grandfather, observing him, remarked to little Pauline, "Your brother is peculiar!", because in the library there were a great many good books that might have tempted the adolescent, but Edouard read only those related to the flight of birds, and the rest of his time he devoted to physical science, in particular to electricity.

When Madame DENIEPORT saw that her son had abandoned competitive cycling and was working very hard to give himself the technical education that was going to serve his creative genius so well, she contacted friends and found him a good job in a bank. But she had not reckoned with the secret ardor of the young man, who had not the slightest desire to sample the discipline of the noblest form of accounting. How then could his charming mother, a timid creature who was frightened by the sight of a spider, exercise some authority over his destiny and influence him?

NIEUPORT AND ENGINES

Quite naturally, Edouard was attracted by engines designed for locomotion, and especially by their most mysterious aspect, the very source of their life; electrical ignition, a field still scarcely explored and little known to practitioners.

Although he did not give up the bicycle completely, his imagination was captured by the automobile from the moment it appeared. First, he sat astride the kerosene tricycle to relish once again, and more intensely, the exhilaration of speed, a sensation to which he was to dedicate his deepest enthusiasms. Mr. A. ODIER, who in 1901 had just graduated from the School of *Arts et Métiers* in Aix, tells how NIEUPORT's first engine failures on his tricycle spurred him to seek improvements and revealed his talents as an inventor. Because, it must be stressed, NIEUPORT was a born inventor. After devising the Davy dry storage battery he lost interest in it, attracted by new problems to be solved.

BEGINNINGS AT LEVALLOIS

During 1902, NIEUPORT decided to manufacture spark plugs and coils for combustion engines because, according to him, the storage battery he had invented had defects.

He rented space in Levallois-Perret at 13, rue des Frères Herbert. It was rather cramped, since his limited personal resources precluded any larger undertaking.

Mr. QUENTIN, who began working for NIEUPORT when he was nineteen and has today given almost half a century of loyal service to the company, told us about these beginnings. Edouard NIEUPORT had some modest savings from the money won in cycling races, but it did not go very far. However, his family unhesitatingly came to his aid, even though he was not following the career they would have wanted for him.

As General ROQUES recalled just after NIEUPORT's death at Verdun, "All those who were his close associates, filled with faith in his future, were so impressed by his superior intelligence that their conversations reflected, in spite of themselves, their profound state of admiration." His maternal grandfather, the Count de MARTINET, a descendent of the famous marshal who invented the pontoon bridge (and whose name can be found in Voltaire's *Siècle de Louis XIV*, as well as in the *Histoire de l'Armée française* by General Weygand) had a small fortune, and gave generous support to his grandson's undertakings. And Edouard, with the appearance of the spark plugs and coils, proved just how worthy he was of that confidence, because these devices caused a sensation in the industrial world and the clientele—CLEMENT, DARRACQ, GRIFFON, ALCYON, and many others—flooded him with orders.

NIEUPORT SPARK PLUGS AND COILS

In 1904 and 1905, NIEUPORT spark plugs and coils took their share of laurels in races, such as the *Coupe du Motocycle -Club de France*, the *Circuit des Ardennes*, and the *Coupe des Voiturettes*, in which the vehicles equipped with them placed first every time.

With orders increasing and the premises in Levallois obviously too small, Edouard decided in mid-1905 to enlarge his workshops.

After having searched for a certain time he chose 9, rue de Seine in Suresnes (this street would later be named rue Edouard-NIEUPORT), a building formerly used by a wholesale wine firm. After alterations lasting two to three months, our inventor, then thirty years old, found himself the owner of a small factory.

IN THE SURESNES WORKSHOP

NIEUPORT began to come up with all sorts of new and very felicitous ideas for the ignition of engines .

"One of the primary qualities of the spark plug should be its simplicity," he said. "Beware of spark plugs with odd shapes and complicated electrodes."

He recommended platinum or, failing that, nickel, for the points. And the points should be soldered, because produced with more or less precision they risked becoming overheated and igniting spontaneously. He was critical of multiple points, and showed that the spark jumps far more easily from electrodes having only two points, which should be as fine as possible.

He called attention to the extreme importance of the watertightness in spark plugs and of using porcelain as an insulator, despite its relative fragility when compared to steatite and mica.

At this time, the use of magnetos for igniting automobile engines was spreading rapidly. Soon another problem was to attract the attention of NIEUPORT, who owned a little DARRACQ, paid for from his own pocket. Leaning over his steering wheel, scanning the road and avoiding the potholes, he began to reflect on the matter.

He and his friend DEPASSE decided to take up the manufacture of magnetos, and his principal client for coils, DARRACQ, used a great many. He bought special equipment and began to seek outside financial backing. The reputation of his spark plugs made matters easier and, eventually separating from DEPASSE, he created a company with such well-known silent partners as the directors of *Minerva Autos* in Anvers and of the *Fonderie des Ardennes*, respectively.

THE MAGNETO IN THE AQUARIUM

The first magnetos NIEUPORT produced were low-voltage, because his principal client, DARRACQ, was then using the circuit breaking system. These magnetos, surrounded by an absolutely watertight copper casing, were immediately successful, and at the 1906 *Salon de l'Automobile*, a perfectly functioning example was displayed in an aquarium where two goldfish were swimming about. Three months later a high-voltage magneto was produced at the Suresnes workshop, and it too soon made a name for itself. Straightaway, a Darracq 8 cylinder automobile, equipped with this magneto, beat the world record for kilometers in Salon and for speed, in Florida, reaching 197 km. 060 per hour. The Ostende and Monaco races, the *Coupe de Maisons-Laffitte*, the Tour de France, and the *Course de Côte* in Gaillon were all great victories for the NIEUPORT magnetos, with which not only the 8-cylinder Darracq, but other automobiles, motorcycles, and motorboats of diverse makes had also been outfitted.

The young constructor certainly had a formidable competitor in BOSCH, which disposed of important industrial means to produce its magneto, and yet he won the battle in France and Belgium, where his equipment was preferrred because of its simplicity. It is precisely the constant concern for making things "simpler" (a great virtue in mechanics) that reflects Edouard NIEUPORT's need for finding the personal solution, and demonstrates his unusually strong personality.

His talents, moreover, were considerable. Ignition had remained the most complicated problem in the functioning of the engine, and he had just solved this delicate question with brilliance.

AN UNPRECEDENTED SUCCESS

Of all the industries related to the automobile, the construction and perfection of different types of magnetos presented by far the most perplexing challenge. Witness to the reality of these difficulties is the fact that numerous powerful companies, such as Thomson-Houston, Bardon, Bréguet, and la *Société Industrielle des Téléphones*, who from their previous work would seem well qualified to construct ignition magnetos, never obtained satisfactory results despite repeated attempts.

It was indeed a thorny problem to master complex electrical phenomena and produce for rigorous automobile races a mechanism demanding absolute precision and yet entrusted to inexperienced hands.

Replacing a device to which nine out of ten engine failures were attributed, was one that was reliable, consistent, and required little maintenance. Did not the NIEUPORT Company say to drivers always inclined to dismantle the magneto when they had trouble: "If your auto is outfitted with one of our ignition devices, you can look elsewhere for the cause when your motor stalls. You will save yourself lots of time!"

The NIEUPORT magnetos, patented even in Germany, were presented as an original creation. NIEUPORT was accustomed by nature to leave the beaten path, and it was always on him that industrialists called when they had difficult cases.

His devices vanquished the most formidable rivals, including the magnetos from BOSCH (whose stand could be seen on the ground floor of the Grand Palais at the Aeronautical Exhibition in 1909) and from Lavalette.

This victory stemmed from four characteristic virtues. The polar extremeties, fitted into a frame cast from a single part with them, presented a reduced air-gap and a significantly greater efficiency. In the high-voltage magnetos, condenser and contact breaker turned with the armature and the primary circuit did not provide continuity. The new direct spark models, having no distributor, had the advantage of being extremely simple and remarkably easy to dismantle. Finally, even with a twofold reduction of the weight of the magnets, they produced sparks that were as hot as could be supported by the contact breakers and spark plugs.

SIGNIFICANT LEGAL PROCEEDINGS

The magneto's simplicity even brought their inventor a notable court decision in 1908. The NIEUPORT Company had published a brochure showing, on the same scale, photographs of the total number of parts, after dismantling, for Magneto X, Magneto Y, and the NIEUPORT Magneto.

The comparison had been so persuasive that his competitors brought NIEUPORT before the *Tribunal de Commerce*. In its decision of May 10, 1908, the court ruled that NIEUPORT had every right to show his own products side by side with those of his rivals. And it recognized the three photographs as perfectly veracious, dismissed the competitors' case, and ordered them to pay the court charges.

This incident is a reflection of the way it was with Edouard NIEUPORT's early industrial activity. In reading over his 1907 catalogues, full of observations and judicious advice, one appreciates even more the soundness of his knowledge and judgment.

This spirit, well in advance of the times, brought him in this case his first victory. Others, even more dazzling, were going to follow.

Edmond Blanc

3

Discovering the Principles of Aerodynamics

The subtlety in streamlining

EDOUARD NIEUPORT, PIONNIER DE LA FINESSE

par Gabriel VOISIN

Gabriel Voisin au travail

A 87 ans, je n'ai pas échappé aux lois redoutables de la vieillesse, et, si j'ai conservé une étonnante mémoire de mes jeunes années, il m'est impossible de faire appel au souvenir pour les événements de ma vie journalière.

Cependant, malgré tout mes efforts, il m'est interdit, dans un cas bien précis, de situer non seulement le jour, mais l'année où j'ai fait la connaissance d'Edouard Nieuport.

Tout me fait supposer que cet homme étonnant était au nombre de nos fidèles quand mon frère Charles Voisin « réceptionna » l'appareil de Delagrange le 15 mars 1907.

Le mot « réception » peut paraître déplacé pour un vol de soixante mètres mais, en 1906, au moment où Léon Delagrange, sculpteur parisien, nous commanda un Voisin muni d'un moteur Antoinette 50 chevaux, nous percevions à la commande un versement de 4.000 francs (1906) et le solde (8.000 francs) devait être versé à la livraison.

Or, cette livraison ne pouvait être que fictive. En effet, aucun de nos clients ne disposait d'un emplacement permettant l'abri de sa machine, même démontée.

L'appareil demeurait donc dans le hangar qui figurait nos ateliers. C'est mon frère qui prit l'initiative de la « réception », réception qui situait de manière précise le paiement de notre fourniture.

La lettre de commande de Delagrange contenait cette phrase : « La machine sera réceptionnée par un vol en ligne droite ».

La durée ou la distance de ce vol n'était pas indiquée.

Ce fut un peu plus tard, quand Henry Farman nous commanda, le 1er juin 1907, une machine Voisin semblable à celle de Delagrange, que les conditions de réception devinrent beaucoup plus difficiles. La lettre d'Henry Farman contenait, en effet, ces mots redoutables en 1907 :

Paris, le 1er juin 1907.

M. G. Voisin, 4, rue de la Ferme, à Billancourt.

Monsieur,

« D'après notre entretien, je vous commande un aéroplane muni d'un moteur Antoinette 50 chevaux dernier modèle.

« Cet appareil doit faire un kilomètre en ligne droite. Au cas contraire, M. Farman ne devra rien à M. Voisin. »

Pour bien comprendre la valeur de cette « réception » il faut savoir que seul Santos-Dumont, quittant le sol par ses propres moyens, avait couvert 220 mètres en ligne droite en 1906. Aucun avion au monde, quittant le sol par ses propres moyens, n'était capable de réussir un virage.

Ces réceptions étaient toujours difficiles. Je n'ai jamais été capable de faire un pilote convenable et, si vers 1932, au moment où mes voitures ont battu ou établi officiellement trente-trois records du monde, j'ai conduit l'une de mes voitures à Montlhéry au-dessus de deux cents kilomètres à l'heure, ce fut, non pas pour participer à cette furieuse compétition, mais pour vérifier certains phénomènes qui demeurent encore de nos jours mystérieux pour beaucoup de nos ingénieurs de l'automobile.

L'âge vraiment héroïque de l'Aviation qui semble avoir commencé au temps d'Icare s'est irrévocablement et officiellement terminé le 30 octobre 1908, par le premier voyage de ville à ville (Mourmelon-Reims) et la gloire de ce couronnement revient bien à Henry Farman qui pilotait ce jour-là son vieux Voisin du premier kilomètre officiel en circuit fermé exécuté le 13 janvier 1908 à Issy-les-Moulineaux.

Comme je l'ai dit, Edouard Nieuport faisait partie de nos fidèles dès 1907, mais ces fidèles avaient été inévitablement choisis dans une foule, car ils partageaient notre vie et nos espérances avec amitié.

Enfin, Edouard Nieuport était surtout lié avec mon frère, ceci parce que ces deux hommes partageaient une même passion pour les armes de jet.

Nieuport et Charles Voisin avaient fait accommoder la jambe droite de leurs pantalons d'une poche inhabituelle par sa profondeur, et, dans cette poche, mes deux compères transportaient un pistolet de tir Gastine-Renette d'une longueur absolument inusitée.

Ce pistolet utilisait la munition Flobert de six millimètres. Le petit projectile et l'arme étaient considérés comme « arme de salon », mais entre les mains de nos tireurs d'élite, cette arme inoffensive devenait un engin de chasse implacable, et l'adresse des deux tireurs était entretenue par un usage constant de l'arme dans des occasions impossibles.

Un pionnier de la grande époque, Sanchez-Besa qui, je crois m'en souvenir, devait être Chilien, fit un jour de 1908 son apparition dans nos ateliers. Sanchez-Besa était un homme charmant, et nos relations très étroites avaient un caractère très particulier.

Nous construisions pour notre ami des machines volantes assez différentes de notre modèle courant, et Sanchez-Besa présentait ces machines comme des productions personnelles.

Le jour où Sanchez-Besa rencontra Edouard Nieuport dans ce que nous appelions pompeusement nos usines, Charles Voisin et son ami Nieuport s'exerçaient à la cible contre le mur en planches d'un hangar.

Sanchez ignorait l'entraînement de mes deux compères, et, quand il vit la cible, les pistolets et les tireurs, il nous apprit en deux mots qu'il était champion de tir au Chili.

Edouard Nieuport proposa immédiatement un concours contre le mur du hangar.

Une croix à la craie devint le but de ce stand improvisé, et la compétition débuta séance tenante.

Notre ami chilien tirait avec une adresse consommée, et la cible tracée fut remplacée par une carte à jouer à la première manche.

L'as de cœur fut effrité en un instant et nos tireurs n'avaient pas encore défini leurs talents.

Edouard Nieuport prit alors l'as de cœur et glissa la carte entre deux planches. Le but était devenu un trait vertical de l'épaisseur d'une carte à jouer.

Charles et Edouard coupèrent le carton léger, mais Sanchez-Besa manqua le but d'un millimètre.

Notre ami ne se consola jamais de son échec.

Cette amitié d'armes, ajoutée à des projets de machines volantes, rendaient Nieuport et Charles Voisin inséparables, mais leur frénésie du projectile ne s'arrêtait malheureusement pas aux pistolets Flobert ; tous les moyens de projeter un « gris-gris » quelconque séduisaient mes tireurs.

Ils avaient constamment sur eux une cordelette de caoutchouc qu'ils attachaient au pouce et à l'index de la main gauche, puis, mettant à cheval sur le caoutchouc une épingle à cheveux, ou mieux encore un fragment de fil de plomb emprunté à des résistances électriques, ils étaient avec ce lance-pierre de forme particulière d'une adresse diabolique.

Vers 1908, les fumeurs de pipe avaient adopté volontiers de petites pipes en terre cuite inévitablement fragiles.

Edouard et Charles surveillaient étroitement ces fumeurs de pipes en terre, et, tirant à petite distance, brisaient la pipe aux dents de leurs victimes qui ne pouvaient évidemment pas deviner les causes de l'accident.

Mais l'arme la plus redoutable pour notre sécurité allait être une invention diabolique.

Dans la poche intérieure de leur vêtement, mon frère et Nieuport transportaient un tube de verre de petite dimension intérieure et d'une longueur de 20 à 25 centimètres.

Ce tube était une terrible sarbacane difficile à voir et qui tirait avec précision un petit plomb de chasse.

Larger photo p. 39

Edouard NIEUPORT, pioneer in streamlining.
By Gabriel VOISIN

At the age of 87 I have not escaped the formidable laws of aging, and even though I have retained an astonishing memory of my youth, it is impossible for me to recall recent events of my daily life. Nevertheless, in spite of all my efforts, I can recollect neither the day nor the year when I first met Edouard NIEUPORT.

Everyhing leads me to think that this amazing man was among the habitués who gathered when my brother Charles VOISIN made it possible for DELAGRANGE to "*réceptionner*," or "take delivery of" his plane on March 15, 1907.

The word "*réceptionner*" might seem out of place for a flight of only sixty meters, but in 1906, when Léon Delagrange, a Parisian sculpteur, ordered a "Voisin" equipped with a 50 horsepower Antoinette engine, we received a downpayment of 4,000 francs with the balance (8,000) to be paid on delivery.

But this delivery could only be hypothetical. Neither DELAGRANGE nor any of our other clients had a space large enough to shelter his plane, even when dismantled.

So the airplane remained for some time in the hangar that was a part of our workshops. It was my brother who finally took the initiative concerning the delivery, which meant precisely that we would at last be paid for our work.

DELAGRANGE's letter ordering the plane had contained this sentence: "The plane will be accepted after a flight in a direct course." The duration or distance of the flight was not specified.

A little later, on June 1, 1907, when Henry FARMAN ordered a Voisin plane similar to DELAGRANGE's, the conditions for acceptance became much more difficult. FARMAN's letter contained words which in 1907 were fearsome:

Edouard Nieuport conçut alors un deux cylindres opposés refroidi à l'air, en tous points semblable au moteur actuel de la 2 chevaux Citroën. Un essai avec une de nos hélices renseigna Nieuport. Il comprit instantanément qu'il fallait concevoir un avion pour son moteur.

Cet homme était le génie inventif personnifié. En quelques semaines il mit sur pied un petit monoplan dans lequel il conduisit avec adresse une chasse implacable aux résistances parasites.

A ses premiers essais, le Nieuport nous révéla ses vertus. Actionné par un moteur de 18 à 20 chevaux, cette merveilleuse machine approchait de 120 kilomètres à l'heure.

Le succès devait couronner cette magnifique construction. La maison Nieuport allait connaître une prospérité méritée.

Edouard Nieuport, mécanicien exceptionnel, avait su s'entourer. Son service technique comprenait des hommes de qualité, mais au moment où la maison Nieuport connaissait un succès justifié, les « règlements » allaient intervenir.

Une série d'essais statiques discutables allaient conduire mon ami à des augmentations de poids sensibles.

Enfin, les programmes de 1910 devenaient plus chargés. Nieuport abandonna son moteur dont la puissance était insuffisante et dut porter son choix sur le moteur Gnome.

Cet excellent moteur, œuvre d'un homme oublié, Laurent Seguin, était à sa naissance une merveille de cinquante chevaux aux environs de 1100 tours/minute (1).

L'ensemble était rotatif, et comportait, comme le moteur Antoinette, une injection directe de l'essence. Cette injection était conduite au centre du système par le vilebrequin lui-même ; le graissage onéreux mais très efficace accompagnait l'injection d'essence.

En résumé, le Gnome 50 chevaux était un moteur parfaitement adapté à nos machines de pionniers.

Mais le destin de tous les moteurs semble menacé d'un danger à peu près inévitable : l'augmentation de la puissance par des moyens souvent fragiles.

A partir de 1910, la pression militaire allait peser de tout son poids sur nos programmes.

Le 50 chevaux Gnome devint vite un 80 chevaux, puis un 100 chevaux 14 cylindres. Le concours militaire de Reims en octobre 1911 allait modifier profondément nos machines.

Il serait fastidieux de reproduire en détail le règlement de ce concours qui, s'il provoqua une activité exceptionnelle dans les maisons de constructions aéronautiques, ne devait pas atteindre le but visé.

Edouard Nieuport avait préparé un avion pour le concours militaire. Cet avion était muni d'un Gnome 100 chevaux. Le petit monoplan de mon ami était d'une finesse exceptionnelle.

Le 15 septembre 1911 Nieuport exécuta le voyage aérien de Mourmelon au centre militaire de Charny, près de Verdun.

Le 16 septembre, un mois avant le concours militaire, le général d'Asbignosc procédait à une revue des aviateurs, et Nieuport mit sa machine en marche pour une démonstration. J'avais assumé les fonctions de commissaire un peu plus tôt à l'un des poteaux du parcours vitesse de Mourmelon, et j'avais été littéralement terrifié par les imprudences de mon ami qui, dans ses virages, frôlait le fanion du côté nord absolument à la verticale.

Il renouvela ces manœuvres impressionnantes en présence du général, et, la démonstration terminée, il s'apprêtait à l'atterrissage lorsque sa machine s'écrasa sur le sol.

Edouard Nieuport était à ce moment précis à quelques mètres de terre, mais l'avion qui frôlait 150 km à l'heure avait un faible écart de vitesse. Nieuport était inanimé lorsqu'il fut secouru dans les débris de sa machine.

(1) V. l'article de Pierre Lallemant paru dans le nº 3 de « Pionniers » du 15 janvier 1965. (N.D.L.R.)

Paris,
June 1, 1907

Monsieur .G. VOISIN
4, rue de la Ferme
Billancourt

Monsieur,

"Following our conversation, I write to confirm my order for an airplane equipped with the latest 50-horsepower Antionnette engine.

This plane should complete a flight of one kilometer in a direct course. Failing this, M. Farman will owe nothing to M. VOISIN."

To understand the crucial nature of this "condition," you should know that by 1906 only SANTOS-DUMONT, lifting off by his own means, had managed to cover as much as 220 meters in a direct course. No airplane in the world, leaving the ground under its own power, was capable of making a turn.

These deliveries were always difficult; I could never have been a suitable pilot and, if around 1932, when my automobiles had officially beaten or set thirty-three world records, I drove one of them at Montlhéry, at more than two hundred kilometers per hour, it was not because I wanted to take part in that prodigious race, but because I wanted to verify certain phenomena which are still today a mystery for many automobile engineers.

The truly heroic "Age of Aviation," which seems to have begun with Icarus, was irrevocably and officially ended on October 30, 1908, by the first cross country flight (from Mourmelon to Reims), and the glory of this crowning achievement well belongs to Henry FARMAN, who that day piloted his prized VOISIN, which had achieved the first official kilometer in a circular flight on January 13, 1908, at Issy-les-Moulineaux.

As I said, Edouard NIEUPORT became one of our "habitués" around 1907, but this group had inevitably been selected from the crowd, since they shared our life and hopes and became our friends. Edouard NIEUPORT was especially close to my brother, because they had in common a passion for projectiles.

NIEUPORT and Charles VOISIN had an unsually deep pocket added to the right leg of their trousers, and in this pocket they carried a Gastine-Renette shooting pistol which was uncommonly long.

This pistol, which used six millimeter ammunition from Flobert, was considered a "parlor weapon," but in the hands of these sharpshooters, this inoffensive arm became implacable for hunting, and the marksmen's skill was maintained by the constant use of the arm on occasions that were not always opportune.

A pioneer of the Golden Age, Sanchez BESA—I seem to recall he was Chilian—appeared in our workshops one day in 1908. He was a charming man, and our close friendship had a very special character.

We were building airplanes for him that were quite different from our current model, and Sanchez BESA presented these craft as his personal productions.

The day that Sanchez BESA met Edouard NIEUPORT in what we pretentiously called our "factory," Charles VOISIN and his friend NIEUPORT were doing target practice against the wooden wall of a hangar.

Sanchez had not known about the training sessions of my two comrades and, when he saw the target, pistols, and marksmen, he informed us in no time short that he was the shooting champion of Chile. Edouard NIEUPORT immediately suggested a competition using the wall of the hangar.

A cross drawn with chalk became the target of this improvised shooting range, and the contest started without further ado.

Our Chilian friend fired with consummate skill, and the marked target was replaced by a playing card after the first round. The ace of hearts was pierced in an instant, and our marksmen had still not had a chance to display their talents.

Edouard NIEUPORT then took the card that had contained the ace of hearts and slipped it between two boards. The target thus became vertical, with the thickness of a playing card.

Both Charles and Edouard sliced through the thin cardboard, but Sanchez BESA missed the target by a millimeter. Our Chilian friend never got over his defeat.

This shared passion for arms, added to their schemes for creating flying machines, made NIEUPORT and Charles VOISIN inseparable, but unfortunately their enthusiasm for projectiles was not limited to the Flobert pistols; every means of projecting any sort of "*grigri*" whatsoever attracted these sharpshooters.

They always carried a rubber cord that they attached to the thumb and index finger of the left hand; then, placing a hairpin, or bettter still, a fragment of plumb line taken from the electrical resistance coils, astride the rubber, they developed a diabolical skill with this peculiarly formed catapult.

Around 1908 the pipe smokers at the workshop switched to the small pipes, which were inevitably fragile. Edouard and Charles kept a sharp eye on these smokers, and from a close range would shatter the pipes held between the teeth of their victims, who obviously had no idea of what had caused the accident. But the most redoutable weapon for our security was going to be an infernal invention.

In the inside pocket of their jackets, my brother and NIEUPORT carried a very narrow glass tube about 20 to 25 centimeters in length.

This tube served as a horrendous blowgun, which was difficult to detect and projected with astonishing precision a small lead hunting pellet. The blowguns of my Aborigines from the parade grounds at Issy were used especially in theaters.

At the precise moment when the tenor was quivering and kneeling before the heroine, his hands crossed on his heart, a little lead pellet would hit them, brusquely interrupting Romeo's light opera fervor. The prank was going to continue for quite a while before the blowguns achieved an exceptional success.

Passionately in love, the *chevalier des Grieux* was describing one day to a charmless Manon the cardiac torments by which he was going to perish, when my brother's projectile grazed the heroine's face. At the same instant, a similar twinge was felt by the knight in the upper left thigh. This remarkable hit had come from our friend NIEUPORT's blowgun.

The harmononious duet was then transformed into fulminations; des Grieux was rubbing his thigh and uttering curses, the music stopped, and the audience seated in the orchestra rose to its feet, thinking that a fire had broken out.

(PHOTO: It is not long before the term existed, a "*panne de château*," but a landing in 1912 of Guy de Montjou's NIEUPORT on the lawn at the Count de la Riboisière's property)

This mischief would have had no follow-up if a spectator in the gallery had not caught sight of the glass tubes. This odd fellow pointed to the authors of the offenses, and twenty minutes later we were being roughly introduced at the police station where full confessions were easily obtained. Two heavy fines condemned the blowguns, but the marksmanship in no way suffered from this cessation.

In the meantime, DELAGRANGE was lifting off by small bounds, and Henry FARMAN was approaching with giant strides the first official circular flight of one kilometer.

One day Edouard NIEUPORT asked us under what terms we would build him an aircraft similar to those that were winning fame every day. The craft was produced, but Edouard could not or did not wish to buy the Antoinette engine we had chosen.

Our friend was then earning his living from a small engineering factory located in Suresnes. It was the very model of ingenuity and efficient organization. Everything there was directed intelligently, and the company bustled with activity.

In 1908, following Henry FARMAN by a few weeks, my former associate, Louis BLERIOT, executed his first turns after having accomplished his first direct course flights. These results were obtained with ANZANI engines that had been made for large motorcycles.

Edouard NIEUPORT then devised a flat-2 air-cooled engine, similar in all respects to the present Citroèn "*2 chevaux*." A test with one of our propellers was very instructive for NIEUPORT. He immediately understood that he had to design an airplane for his engine.

This man was the personification of the inventive genius. Within a few weeks he put together a small monoplane in which he skillfully led a relentless chase against skin friction.

From its very first tests the NIEUPORT displayed its virtues. Driven by an 18 to 20-horsepower engine, the marvelous little plane approached 120 kilometers per hour. This magnificent construction was soon crowned with success, and the NIEUPORT Company experienced a well deserved prosperity.

Edouard NIEUPORT, an exceptional engineer, had known how to choose his associates. His technical service was made up of very able men, but just at the point when the company was enjoying a justified success, exterior regulations were going to intervene. A series of questionable static tests would lead my friend to appreciable increases in weight.

Finally, the schedule for 1910 became much more pressing. NIEUPORT then abandoned his engine because of its insufficient power and was forced to choose a Gnome.

This excellent engine, the work of a forgottten man, Laurent SEGUIN, was at its creation a 50-horsepower marvel with a speed of around 1,100 revolutions per minute (V. See the article by Pierre Lallemant in n° 3 of *Pionniers*; January 15, 1965. (N.D.L.R.)).

The whole mechanism was rotary and had a direct fuel injection just like the Antoinette engine. The injection was carried to the center of the system by the crankshaft itself; the costly but very effective lubricating accompanied the injection of gasoline. In short, the 50-horsepower Gnome was an engine perfectly adapted to our pioneering machines.

But the fate of all those early engines seemed threatened by an almost inevitable danger: the increase in power by means that were often flimsy. After 1910, the military began to exert enormous pressure on us.

The 50-horsepower Gnome quickly grew into an 80-horsepower, then to a 14 cylinder 100-horsepower. The military competition at Reims in October 1911 was going to modify our machines profoundly. It would be tedious to go into all the details of that competition which, even though it provoked an exceptional activity in the aeronautical construction companies, did not attain its goal.

Edouard NIEUPORT had prepared an airplane for the competition. Equipped with a 100-horsepower Gnome engine, my friend's little monoplane was superb. On September 15, 1911, he flew from Mourmelon to the military base at Charny, near Verdun.

On September 16, a month before the event, General d'ASBIGNOSC was conducting a review of the participating aviators, and NIEUPORT climbed into his machine for a demonstration. I had been marshal a short time before at a post on the Mourmelon speed course, and had been literally paralyzed with fear by the imprudence of my friend who, in his turns, skimmed the pennant on the north side absolutely vertically.

He repeated these impressive maneuvers for the General and, the demonstration over, he was preparing to land when his plane crashed.

Edouard NIEUPORT was at that precise moment only a few meters above the ground, but the airplane, moving at almost 150 kilometers per hour, had a momentary break in speed. NIEUPORT was lifeless when he was removed from the wreckage of his airplane.

My old and cherished friend, Dr. ESPANET, the celebrated pilot of our old Voisin from 1914-1918, gives the details of this drama in an article dedicated to the memory of one whom we loved. I think I have already said that Edouard NIEUPORT had known how to surround himself with loyal associates.

His company, plunged into despair by the absence of the genius, was nevertheless represented at the military contest in October 1911 by a NIEUPORT monoplane powered by a 100- horsepower Gnome.

In this trial the first place went to the NIEUPORT, piloted by WEYMANN, which reached 117 km/h. Second place went to the Bréguet piloted by MOINEAU, which achieved 95 km/h.*

After the First World War WEYMANN, the winner, was going to produce body works of a rare originality, which revealed to automobile manufacturers the advantages of lightness and the increased security resulting from improved centering.

At Issy-les-Moulineaux, where the NIEUPORT factory later occupied the west side of the parade grounds, a very high quality technical service accomplished miracles to defend a name that came nearer to being a coat of arms than a registered trademark.

But deprived of the Master, the company dedicated to speed disappeared between administrative hands, which were perhaps capable of doing big business but were little qualified to defend the most difficult of techniques.

On September 16, 1911, Edouard NIEUPORT had left us. On September 26, 1912, his friend Charles VOISIN joined him.

Both of them were under 30 (*sic*). If their shadows met in Nirvana, the gods must have granted them the right to play the joyful game of their youth: "parlor pistol shooting."

(*Below Right*: Humorous portrait of Edouard NIEUPORT, a "Modern Bird")

*The military competition of 1911, which brought together 42 entrants and 32 eligible competitors, resulted, after very severe eliminations, in the following placings after the final speed trial on November 26 on the course Reims-Amiens, Amiens-Reims, or 300 kilometers non-stop:

1. Charles T. Weymann (NIEUPORT), in 2 h 33, or 117 km/h
2. René Moineau (Bréguet), in 3 h 09, or 95 km/h
3. Maurice Prévost (Deperdussin), in 3 h 21, or 89.5 km/h
4. Henri Brégl (Bréguet), in 3 h 26, or 87.5 km/h
5. Jules Fischer (H. Farman), in 3 h 33, or 84.5 km/h
6. Frannk Barra (M. Farman), in 3 h 56, or 76 KM/h
7. Eugène Renaux (M. Farman), in 4 h 08, or 72 km/h
8. Joseph Frantz (Savary), in 4 h 27, or 67.2 km/h

Edouard NIEUPORT and his wife, participating in the making of the wings for his first airplane. Their son, Edouard, is seated on the floor.

The First Plane

During 1908 NIEUPORT contacted the VOISIN brothers, the best known aircraft manufacturers of the times, and ordered a biplane with which he learned to fly. The 8-cylinder Antoinette engine did not suit him, and he decided to study the problem and produce his own propeller.

Shortly afterwards, he set up the company "Aéro Locomotion" with his brother Charles and a friend, Lieutenant de CAUMONT, who contributed the financial backing he needed.

Lieutenant de CAUMONT, who had a personal fortune, was one of the first French military pilots. The commerical and financial aspects of the company were directed by Henri DEPASSE, who was an old cycling companion of Edouard NIEUPORT.

Very soon this new team set to work with a few colleagues, among whom were DESBORDES, RISPAL, GOBE, and a Swiss engineer, Franck SCHNEIDER.

1909 was the year of the first monoplane craft with the wing above the fuselage, which also had an exposed framework. This aircraft was equipped with a two cylinder 20 horsepower Darracq engine turning a two-bladed propeller.

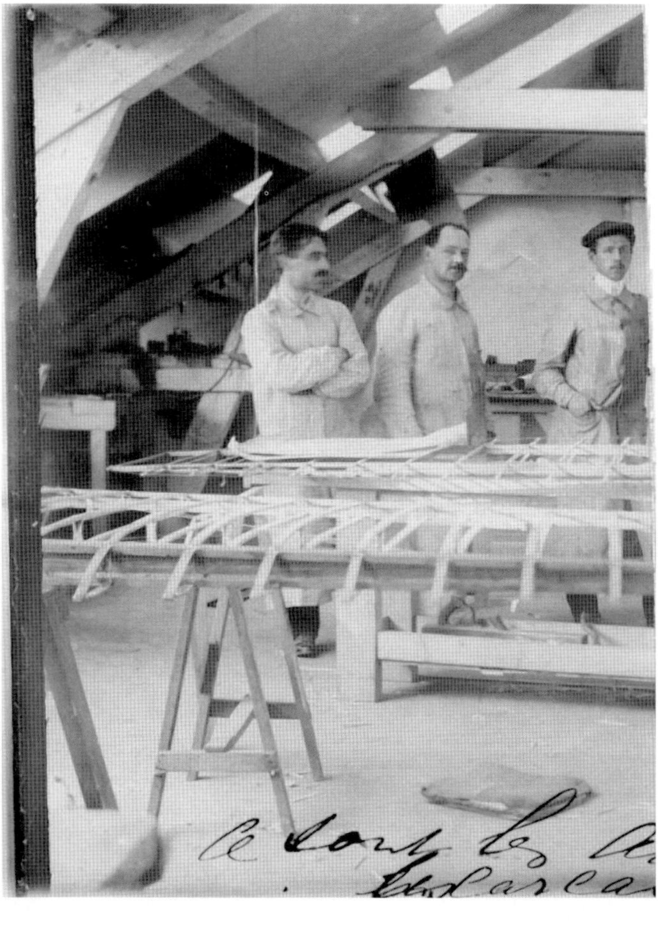

In producing his airplane, Edouard NIEUPORT took part in every aspect—down to the smallest details of its construction. Having designed the whole of the airfoil, he was determined to apply to his creation the same precision he had exercised in the preliminary research.

It must be said that at the time he had only slight means for analyzing aerodynamic phenomena. To compensate for this he often went to Brittany, where he sailed fishing boats along the coast, studying the effects of atmospheric pressure and depression on the sails.

Edouard NIEUPORT's first airplane, powered by a Darracq engine, was tested by its builder, who is pictured here in the cockpit at Issy-les-Moulineaux in December 1909.

The airplane took off for the first time from Issy-les-Moulineaux and performed sufficiently well to reinforce Edouard NIEUPORT's decision to choose the monoplane system, which until then had been so much disparaged.

The airfoil was 14 square meters, the wingspan 8 square meters, the width of the wings 2 meters, and the length of the aircraft 7 meters.

It was extremely light, weighing only 285 kilograms in full working order. The chassis was mounted on wheels and runners. The elevator and the rudder were single-winged. There was a unique control lever for both the elevator and rudder.

Unfortunately, this plane was destroyed during the catastrophic floods of 1910 when the Seine reached its highest level in over a hundred years and inundated a large part of Paris.

The first plane taking off.

The First Engine

However, the two cylinder engine designed by Edouard NIEUPORT and his team was completed shortly afterwards. This air cooled engine developed 28-horsepower at a nominal running speed of 1,200 revolutions. It consumed 16 liters of gasoline and 2 liters of castor oil per hour.

In December 1911 the engine would place first in the competition sponsored by the *Ligue nationale aérienne*, an important civilian group whose goal was to support aviation.

One of the first aviation engines produced by NIEUPORT.

NIEUPORT Airplanes Constructed by the *Société Générale d'Aéro-Locomotion* Open the way for Progress in Aviation.

The Second Plane: The 2N

In 1910 the *Société Générale d'Aréo-Locomotion* developed the second NIEUPORT plane, the "2," which underwent its first tests at the beginning of April 1910.

Edouard NIEUPORT obtained a patent for it from the *Aéro-club de France* on June 10, 1910, under the number 105.

The monoplane "type 2N" was 7.5 meters long with a wingspan of 8.4 meters and an airfoil of 14.9 square meters.

Empty, the plane weighed 220 kilograms. The wings were only slightly curved. The landing gear was fitted with a single runner, which itself was equipped with a transverse spring serving as an axle for the wheels.

The body of the fuselage was made entirely of canvas and enveloped the pilot, who was seated very much towards the front and could see what was happening on both sides.

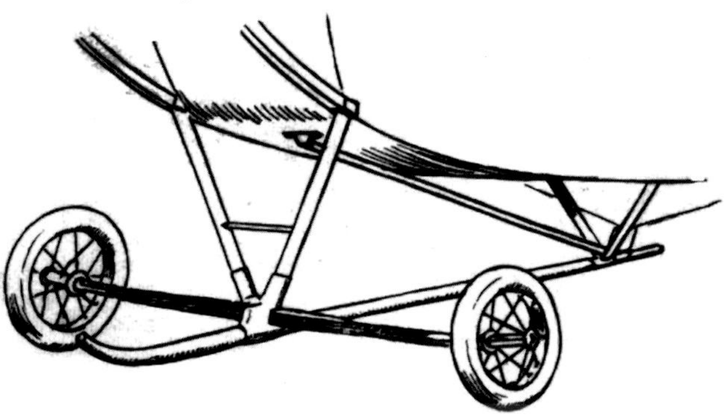

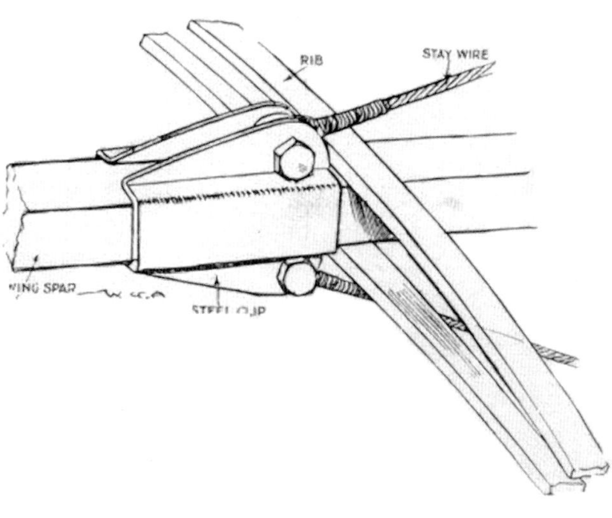

It is unquestionable that the mechanisms devised by NIEUPORT significantly reduced the great dangers of locomotion in heavier than air machines.

The monoplane was simple without its sturdiness having been diminished. The number of steel wires and tightening cables was reduced without affecting the solidity of the construction.

The warping of the wings was automatic, and the rudder and elevator were combined. Stability was ensured by an adjustable stabilizer at the rear.

The capital innovation of the NIEUPORT airplane was the automatic warping or bending of the wings. The distortion of one wing by a gust of wind automatically produced a corresponding distortion in the opposite wing and tended to stabilize the plane.

Automatic stability, considered by many aeronautical pioneers as an almost insoluable problem, was thus resolved in the simplest and safest way without adding any ex-

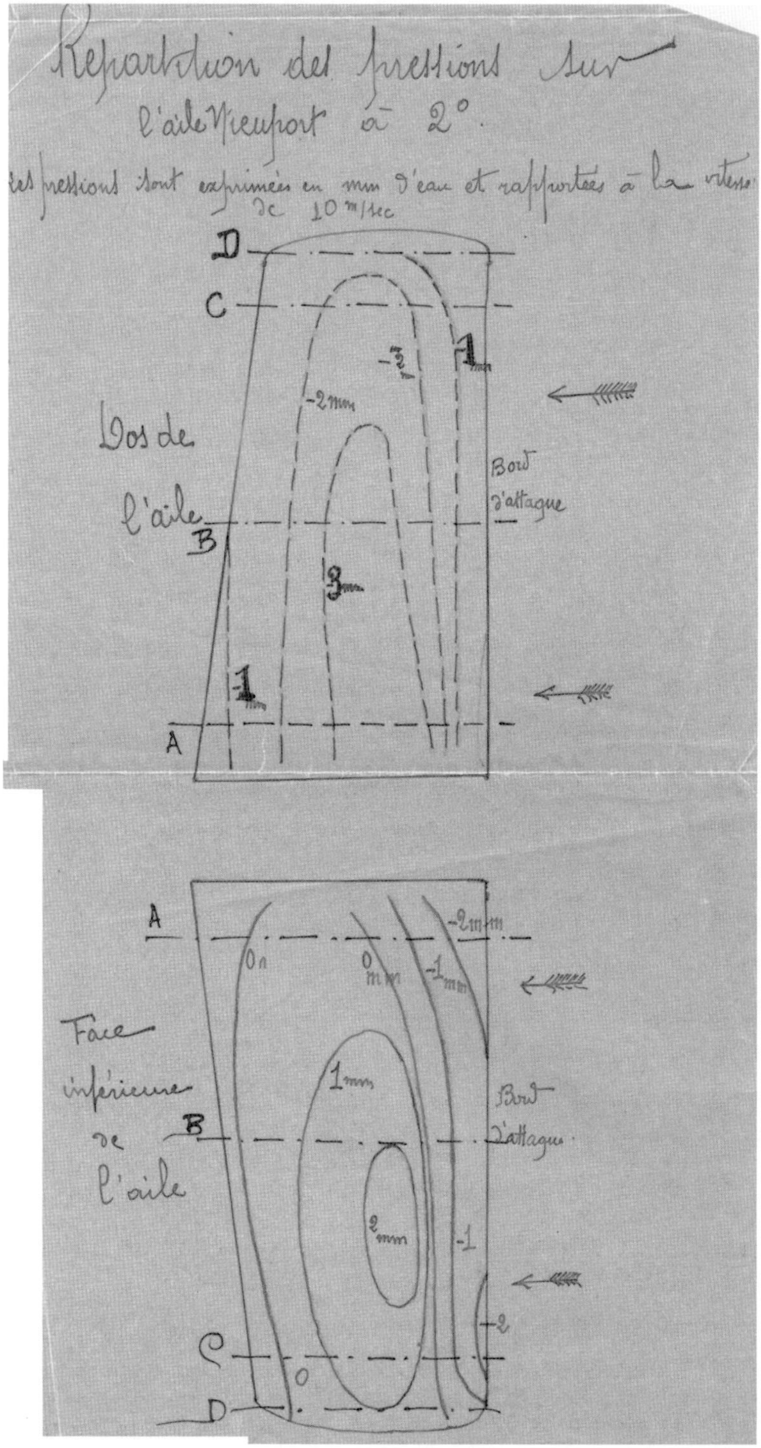

Drawing entitled "Distribution of Pressures on the NIEUPORT Wing at 2°"

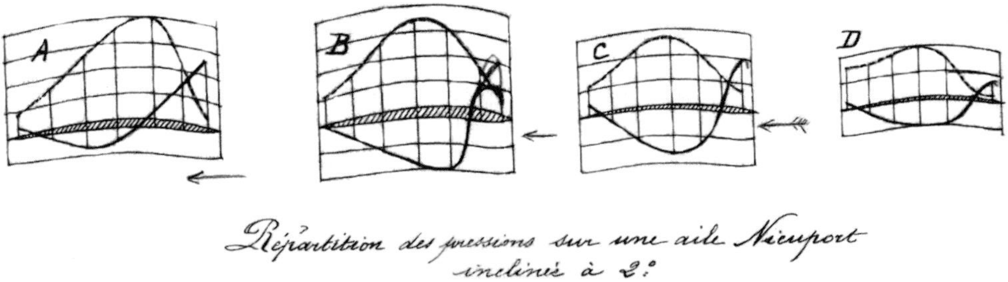

Distribution of pressures on a NIEUPORT wing tilted at 2°.

tra weight. It was the very stress that tended to make the plane wobble that simultaneously straightened it up. Thus, the principal cause of instability in airplanes of that period was eliminated.

The NIEUPORT airplane possessed another advantage of the utmost interest. It was equipped with only a flat-2, 28-horsepower engine, which had an output well below that of all the other planes then being produced; yet it raced with planes having engines that were three to four times more powerful.

In the spring of 1910 the "NIEUPORT 2N" took off for the first time from a field at Camp Châlons. During these tests it reached a speed of 120 kilometers per hour.

au Grand Air

LE MONOPLAN NIEUPORT

C'est l'appareil le plus simple et le mieux combiné pour un service utilitaire et pour les besoins de l'armée.

Le monoplan Nieuport.

Le Nieuport est le seul monoplan qui puisse décoller de terre avec un petit moteur de 18 chevaux et réaliser une vitesse moyenne de 84 kil. 400.

J'ai eu le plaisir d'accompagner lundi dernier un technicien de valeur dans sa visite au Grand Palais, et comme nous nous en revenions, nous échangeâmes avec lui quelques impressions. J'eus la curiosité de demander à mon interlocuteur : En somme, quel est, à votre avis, l'appareil dont la conception vous est apparue la meilleure ?

— Il y aurait, me dit-il, une réponse facile à faire, en fixant mon choix sur un des aéroplanes qui ont remporté les plus beaux succès dans les meetings et se sont partagé les prix les plus importants. Pour l'avenir qu'il me plait de voir à l'aéroplane, je ne puis accorder la préférence à un de ceux-là. Malgré tout l'intérêt que je leur porte et que je puis comparer à celui que j'ai pour une voiture de course, je préfère porter mon attention sur l'appareil qui me semble le plus pratique, le mieux établi et non pas le plus puissant. Je veux parler du Nieuport.

Le petit aéroplane de Nieuport que notre ami Depasse, nous a présepté est bien en effet, puisqu'il s'agit en l'occurence d'un oiseau mécanique, le plus mécanique qui soit. Son châssis d'atterrissage, entièrement métallique, est muni d'une suspension extrêmement simple

Nieuport.

Le parfait sportsman, le brillant aviateur auquel le sport est redevable de tant de découvertes.

Le Nieuport en vol.

Pour ses débuts, le Nieuport a fait sensation au meeting de Reims et il se prépare à nous enthousiasmer à nouveau.

et robuste, c'est un ressort de voiture avec deux roues et un patin.

Le Nieuport est le seul qui puisse décoller avec un moteur de 18 chevaux et réaliser une vitesse de 84 kilom. 400 avec ce joujou.

Ces chiffres qui surprennent, se comprennent fort bien quand on sait, tant le joli monoplan est bien établi, quelle est la facilité de son vol. Vingt fois au moins les pilotes du coquet appareil ont coupé l'allumage à cent mètres d'altitude et ont atterri entre 500 à 800 mètres.

Mais ce point fort intéressant a amené Nieuport, qui connait tous les dangers du vol plané, à étudier les résistances de son appareil. Il a totalement supprimé les commandes ou haubans en fil d'acier et les a remplacés par des câbles tressés en plusieurs torons auxquels il est impossible de se rompre d'un seul coup, comme le peut faire la corde à piano.

En somme, on voit que ce monoplan, dont on connait les qualités de démontage et de peu d'encombrement qui permettent de le transporter facilement en voiture, est avant tout et surtout un appareil utilitaire. Grâce à ce point de vue spécial, c'est un des aéroplanes les mieux compris pour les besoins de la stratégie moderne.

F.-A. W.

Translation of the article above.

The Nieuport monoplane is the simplest and the most adaptable to both practical and military needs.

(PHOTO: The NIEUPORT is the only Monoplane that can take off with a small engine of 18 horsepower and achieve an average speed of 84 km, 400.)

Last Monday I had the pleasure of accompanying a very talented aviation expert on a visit to the Grand Palais, and as we made our way home we exchanged several impressions. I was curious to know my companion's opinion as to which of the airplanes was the best conceived?

"It would be easy," he said, "to choose any one of the various planes that have been the most successful in the races and shared the most important prizes. However, for the future I would like to see for aviation," he continued, "I can give preference to only one. Despite the interest I have in all of them, comparable to my interest in racing cars, I would prefer to concentrate on the one that seems the most practical and best built, but certainly not the most powerful. I am referring to the NIEUPORT."

The little NIEUPORT that our friend DEPASSE presented works in fact because it is actually a mechanical bird, the most mechanical of them all. Its landing chassis, entirely in metal, is equipped with an extremely simple and sturdy suspension; it is, in fact, an automobile suspension spring with two wheels and a runner.

The NIEUPORT is the only plane that can take off with an 18 horsepower engine, and with this toy motor it can reach a speed of 84 kilometers, 400.

These surprising results are understandable when one knows how well the attractive monoplane is constructed, and how easy it is to fly. The pilots of this plane have at least twenty times turned off the ignition at 100 meters altitude and then landed within 500 to 800 meters.

But this highly interesting point led NIEUPORT, who knows all about the dangers of gliding, to study the resistance of his plane. He completely eliminated the controls or shrouds in steel wire and replaced them by cables twisted in several strands, which it is impossible to break with a single blow, as can be done to a piano string.

The 2N in front of NIEUPORT School in Mourmelon.

Edouard NIEUPORT oversees the preparations for take off of the 2N.

In a word, it is obvious that this monoplane, whose advantages of dismantlement and minimum bulk allow it to be transported by a motor car, is above all and especially a practical airplane. For this reason, it is one of the airplanes best adapted to the needs of modern strategy.

F.-A.W.

At this time, Edouard NIEUPORT, realizing that in order to sell and fly his airplanes he needed pilots, created a flight school at Mourmelon where WEYMANN, HELEN, GOBE, MAILLOT, and ESPANET were trained.

La Vie au Grand Air

L'AÉROPLANE LE PLUS RAPIDE

Le *Nieuport* fait de la vitesse.

C'est au camp de Châlons que le Nieuport *a fait ses essais qui ont merveilleusement réussi.* (Détail technique : monoplan Nieuport, construit par la Société Générale d'Aéro-Locomotion.)

De l'avis unanime, jamais aéroplane plus rapide et plus simple n'a encore été conçu. Dans les matches autour de la vaste plaine champenoise, Nieuport, sur ce monoplan-bolide, peut rendre une bonne distance aux autres appareils. Il les passe et les dépasse comme il veut. Tous ceux qui l'ont vu sont enthousiasmés et nous-mêmes, qui l'avons observé au camp de Châlons, nous ne pouvons décrire l'extraordinaire sensation de puissance et de rapidité qu'il donne.

Mais ce qui est vraiment prodigieux, c'est que Nieuport, qui a fait établir ce monoplan suivant ses propres données, obtint en un quart d'heure d'apprentissage la maîtrise de l'appareil, ce qui prouve surabondamment sa facilité de manœuvre et sa stabilité parfaite.

Le moteur n'est qu'un simple 20 chevaux, et encore, lorsque l'appareil vole avec cette vitesse foudroyante dont nous avons déjà parlé, il n'emploie même pas les trois quarts de la force. En le voyant filer élégamment dans l'air, on se demande si les 150 et 200 kilomètres à l'heure, espérés par les mathématiciens, ne vont pas être atteints à bref délai. Le monoplan Nieuport réalisera-t-il ce rêve? Nous le croyons fermement.

Donnons maintenant quelques renseignements techniques sur ce dernier venu qui, dès sa naissance, a su prendre la première place dans l'aviation, grâce à la valeur et à l'ingéniosité de son constructeur.

On est tout d'abord frappé de la simplicité extrême de l'appareil Nieuport qu'a construit la Société Générale d'Aéro-Locomotion. En fait, il est différent de tous les autres, jusque dans ses moindres détails. Son envergure est de 8 m. 50, sa longueur de 7 mètres, son poids de 220 kilos sans pilote, et il a 14 mètres carrés de surface. Les ailes ont très peu de courbure. Le chassis d'atterrissage est réduit à un patin unique, muni d'un ressort transversal qui sert en même temps d'axe aux roues. Le fuselage est fermé entièrement, et protège le pilote du froid et des projections d'huile. Le pilote, très à l'avant, peut voir perpendiculairement comme sur un biplan.

Autre innovation : le gauchissement est automatique et fonctionne admirablement. Même dans les remous, même par grand vent, il n'y a pas besoin d'y toucher. Le gouvernail de direction et de profondeur sont conjugués. Un plan fixe à l'arrière, réglable à volonté, donne à l'appareil une stabilité longitudinale parfaite. Point important : l'appareil se démonte et se remonte en dix minutes et cela tout simplement parce qu'il n'y a pas, comme dans les autres appareils, une multiplicité de tendeurs et de fils à régler et à accrocher.

Ajoutons un mot : si, pendant que ce monoplan vole, le moteur s'arrête brusquement, l'appareil plane et descend lentement pour atterrir comme un oiseau. Le pilote n'a pas besoin de faire la moindre manœuvre. Il ne peut donc pas être surpris par la panne. Cette dernière constatation est, comme on sait, des plus importantes. Pour que l'aéroplane devienne pratique, il faut qu'il offre le minimum de danger. Or, jusqu'à maintenant, le danger c'est que, si le moteur s'arrête brusquement, on pique souvent une tête, à moins d'avoir beaucoup de chance et beaucoup de présence d'esprit. Avec le monoplan Nieuport, on n'a plus cela à craindre. Si le moteur vous lâche, l'appareil plane sans se déséquilibrer et permet de choisir tranquillement l'endroit d'atterrissage.

Nous aurons d'ailleurs l'occasion, au meeting de Reims, d'admirer ce nouveau monoplan qui s'annonce comme un des principaux concurrents.

F.-A. Wheel

Le petit Nieuport admire son père.

« Quand mon père vole, nous disait le petit Nieuport, qui a quatre ans, il perce le ciel. C'est lui qui va le plus vite de tous. »

Reims, July 1910: Article from *La Vie au Grand Air* on Edouard NIEUPORT's airplane, containing a photograph of his son watching his father maneuver in the sky.

4

From Triumph to Triumph

The first races
On July 10, 1910, NIEUPORT entered three "N2" type planes, each with a different engine, in the second of the "*Grandes Semaines de Champagne*," held at the airfield in Bétheny near Reims. Piloting the plane with the 28 hp engine he had designed, NIEUPORT placed the two other planes, each equipped with a 25 hp two cylinder DARRACQ, in the hands of Maurice NOGUES and NIEL.

L'équipe Nieuport.
Ce sont de jeunes pilotes qui conduiront, pour ses débuts, le monoplan Nieuport, ce curieux petit appareil qui atteint des vitesses extraordinaires. — 1. Noguès. — 2. Nieuport. — 3. Niel.

The NIEUPORT Team: NIEUPORT, NOGUÈS, NIEL.

The main event of the day was the competition for the Michel EPHRUSSI Prize. For the first time, the competing planes were lined up side by side at the start of the race. This idea was so successful that the organizers of future "Air Meetings" would adopt it.

Endowed with a prize of 10,000 francs, the race consisted of a course obliging the aviators to turn at Mitry-les-Reims and then at Bazencourt before returning to the airport. The starting signal was given by EPHRUSSI himself. The fact that no accident or even minor incident occurred is the best proof of the immense progress that had been made by aviation within one year.

Nieuport en vol.

Sur son appareil, à moteur de 20 che- seulement, Nieuport s'est classé 3e du prix Michel Ephrussi.

Un des appareils les plus remarqués du meeting de Reims a été certainement le monoplan Nieuport, dont nous avons déjà eu l'occasion d'entretenir nos lecteurs. Ses départs faciles, ses atterrissages souples attirèrent l'attention de tous. Mais c'est surtout dans le prix Michel Ephrussi, course en ligne disputée au-dessus de la campagne, que le Nieuport se distingua. Il se classa troisième, couvrant les 22 kil. en 23 m. 22 s. 3/5. Mais il faut remarquer que le Nieuport est muni d'un moteur de 20 chevaux seulement, tandis que tous ses concurrents avaient

L'appareil chargé sur une voiture.

Une fois démonté, l'appareil peut se transporter sur une automobile. Il peut se remonter en une demi-heure. On conçoit l'avantage d'une telle disposition au point de vue militaire.

Un autre aspect de l'appareil Nieup

Malgré une faible puissance, le p appareil laisse derrière lui des conc rents munis de moteurs de 50 ch. et pl

des moteurs de 50 chevaux au moi Si, du temps des courses d'automo les, une voiture de 20 chevaux av battu une voiture de 50 ou 60 chevau on n'aurait pas eu assez d'éloges po le constructeur, on se serait émerve sur son rendement, et à juste tit Mais le sport de l'aéroplane n'est p encore assez classé pour que le publ soit amené à faire de pareilles const tations... Un jour viendra, et il e proche, où l'on établira des classific tions pour les aéroplanes, comme pou les voitures, et où la victoire d'u appareil sur des concurrents d'une c tégorie supérieure apparaîtra bie comme une preuve de sa réelle sup riorité. C'est ce qui est le cas pou l'appareil Nieuport dans le Prix Mich Ephrussi.

On a pu aussi remarquer la facilit avec laquelle l'appareil pouvait s démonter et se transporter. F. M.

Nieuport's plane shown in flight; NIEL's plane is on the car.

La Vie au Grand

LE PRIX MICHEL EPHRUSSI

Le départ en ligne.
Cette épreuve consistait en une course à travers la campagne, sur un circuit de 22 kilomètres, qui passait par Vitry-lès-Reims, Bazancourt Fresnes. Les départs étaient donnés par séries de trois coureurs partant simultanément.

From the newspaper *La Vie au Grand Air.*

The event was won by Alfred LEBLANC piloting a "BLERIOT" equipped with a GNOME engine. LEBLANC, a well known aviator, was the first pilot trained by Blériot, for whom he was to be an invaluable assistant when his instructor crossed the Channel. The results of this event were:

- First Place: LEBLANC 17' 14" 1/5
- Second Place: WAGNER 20' 57" 4/5
- Third Place: NIEUPORT 23' 22" 3/5

LATHAM and WEYMANN had dropped out of the race.

Edouard NIEUPORT in his NIEUPORT, gliding through the air

ance : 1 an, 6 francs ; 6 mois, 3 fr. 50
ranger : 1 an, 9 francs ; 6 mois, 5 francs

5, Rue Coëtlogon, 5 — PA

Svendsen qui vient de traverser le Sund

Le Monoplan Nieuport avant le départ

Portrait de Nieuport

L'Appareil en plein vol

From the newspaper *Aviation illustrée*: The Starting Line-up.

NIEUPORT's remarkable achievement deserves to be underscored. In his "N2" equipped with the 28 hp engine of his own design, he managed to compete with far more powerful motorizations and even beat some of them. It is certain that if there had been a placing for output, he would have won hands down. In any case, the performance of his plane had been most heartening and indicated to NIEUPORT the path to pursue.

Lieutenant Maillots, a NIEUPORT Pilot.

The NIEUPORT was easily transportable. Here it is shown arriving at Mourmelon.

The Air Locomotion Exhibition

This important exhibition, which exemplified the progress made in aeronautics, was held in Paris from October 15 to November 2, 1910. It was the occasion for Edouard NIEUPORT to display his aircraft. When the show ended, the NIEUPORT planes were much praised by the press. It was this kind of encouragement that incited NIEUPORT to continue his research.

The NIEUPORT stand.

The Loss of a Friend

1910 ended with a grievous disaster: Lieutenant de CAUMONT was killed while piloting the "N° 2" monoplane on December 10.

His death came as a great shock to Edouard NIEUPORT: he had lost not only a very dear friend, but a seemingly irreplacable collaborator.

De CAUMONT was the principal shareholder of the company and unquestionably the most outstanding pilot to emerge in the highly dangerous new world of aviation.

LE LIEUTENANT DE CAUMONT

L'année 1910 s'est terminée tristement. Après la fin affreuse de Cecil Grace, celle de Laffont et de Pola, nous avons enregistré la mort du lieutenant de Caumont. Cet officier de grande valeur s'était fait remarquer par des raids très brillants. Il se tua en essayant son appareil. A gauche, John Moisant, le recordman de Paris-Londres, et à droite Hoxey, le recordman du monde de la hauteur, qui sont morts en Amérique d'identique façon, étant projetés hors de leur siège, l'un d'un monoplan, l'autre d'un biplan.

De CAUMONT in front of his plane.

Le lieutenant de Caumont

dans un brusque atterrissage se brisait les deux jambes hier matin

A sept heures et demie du soir il était mort

Depuis huit jours, le lieutenant de Caumont s'entraînait en vue du prix Lazare Weiller de 25.000 francs, réservé aux aviateurs militaires. Pour cette épreuve de distance, le lieutenant de Caumont avait choisi comme parcours le trajet Saint-Cyr-Vendôme et retour.

Le monoplan avec lequel il devait faire sa tentative avait été amené avant-hier soir au hangar Nieuport, situé au sud de Saint-Cyr, qui est l'ancien hangar de Santos-Dumont.

L'appareil était neuf et n'avait pas encore été essayé, le lieutenant de Caumont ayant laissé à Buc le monoplan avec lequel il avait compté disputer la Coupe Deperdussin.

Deux heures avant qu'il ne prît le départ, hier, l'officier aviateur avait changé le moteur. Il devait, conformément au règlement, emmener un passager. C'était le lieutenant Caussin, du corps des aérostiers militaires.

Photo Matin.

Les opérations préliminaires du pesage des deux voyageurs avaient eu lieu d'abord à l'Institut aérodynamique de Saint-Cyr, puis chez un cultivateur, sous le contrôle du capitaine Etévé, du lieutenant d'infanterie Theucin, qui avaient examiné l'appareil. Le capitaine Duperron, du 11e régiment d'artillerie, assistait également à ces opérations.

Le lieutenant de Caumont, qui ne voulut pas s'engager dans ce voyage avant d'avoir essayé son appareil, fit un premier vol, à dix heures du matin, autour du champ de manœuvres de Saint-Cyr. Au bout de cinq minutes de vol, il revint atterrir à 60 mètres du hangar.

Il constata que le moteur ne fonctionnait pas bien, et il en fit modifier le graissage.

De plus, il fit observer à M. Nieuport que la commande du gouvernail de profondeur était extrêmement dure et qu'elle pouvait à peine être manœuvrée.

— C'est un appareil neuf, répondit M. Nieuport. Cela s'arrangera à l'usage.

Toutefois le lieutenant de Caumont tint à faire un second essai. Il pria son camarade Caussin d'attendre encore un peu avant de prendre place dans l'appareil et de filer ensuite sur Vendôme.

C'est au cours de cette seconde expérience que le malheureux aviateur fit une chute terrible qui lui coûta la vie.

Voici comment un témoin autorisé conte la chute.

— Le lieutenant de Caumont avait pris un excellent départ, face au vent qui soufflait assez fortement par bourrasques. En deux cercles, il atteignit la hauteur de 200 mètres environ. Il passait derrière un bouquet d'arbres et semblait voler sans à-coup, quand soudainement on entendit des ratés au moteur.

» Alors, comme il semblait faire un virage pour revenir vers nous, le monoplan s'inclina fortement de côté et en même temps glissa vers l'intérieur du virage.

» De Caumont sembla se redresser ; mais au même instant l'appareil piqua vers le sol comme une flèche et s'aplatit à terre, l'aile gauche effondrée et l'aile droite levée vers le ciel.

» La chute avait eu lieu vers dix heures et demie, en face de la redoute Bouvier et dans un champ qui fait partie de la ferme de la Crou, appartenant à M. Gast, ancien député de Seine-et-Oise.

» La première personne qui se porta au secours du lieutenant de Caumont fut M. Rabot, qui passait sur la grand'route qui borde le terrain. Il vit franchement l'aviateur se dégager de l'appareil et se traîner à l'aide des poignets, car il ne pouvait plus se servir de ses pauvres jambes, qui venaient d'être brisées.

» M. Rabot adressa quelques mots au lieutenant de Caumont, qui ne répondit pas et qui bientôt perdit connaissance.

En hâte, le capitaine Duperron et M. Toussaint, ingénieur de l'Institut aérodynamique, accoururent près du blessé. Aidés des autres officiers, ils le transportèrent près de la route.

Le médecin-major Bourcillon, de l'école d'artillerie, le docteur Langlois, médecin-major de deuxième classe, prodiguèrent les premiers soins au lieutenant de Caumont qui, examiné ensuite par le docteur Petit, médecin en chef de l'hôpital militaire de Versailles, fut transporté dans cet établissement avec tous les ménagements possibles, d'abord dans une voiture, puis sur un brancard, en raison des souffrances terribles du blessé.

Le lieutenant, qui avait repris toute sa connaissance, dit quelques mots pour remercier les médecins et ses camarades.

— J'ai du courage, dit-il faiblement.

Lorsque le général Roques, inspecteur permanent de l'aéronautique militaire, chargé par le ministre de la guerre de prendre des nouvelles de l'aviateur, vint voir le blessé, celui-ci eut la force de sourire, au moment où le général lui exprima des paroles réconfortantes et émues.

Cependant le lieutenant de Caumont était

From the newspaper *Le Matin*.

Phot. Branger.

Le génie enlève les débris de l'aéroplane du lieutenant de Caumont.

dans un état désespéré. Il avait de nombreuses fractures aux jambes et aux bras.

— Il est très mal, très mal, nous dit plus tard le lieutenant-colonel Bouttieaux, qui accompagnait le général Raques. La commotion a été si violente !

Vers cinq heures et demie, le colonel Hirschauer vint au chevet du blessé et il nous sembla voir des larmes sortir des yeux de l'officier supérieur.

Puis le général Roques revint. A 6 h. 45, le général Gallopin, commandant la place d'armes, vint à de Caumont qui, une fois encore, eut le courage de sourire. Il bravait le danger !

Mais, hélas ! s'affaiblissant de minute en minute, de Caumont entra dans le coma, et à sept heures et demie, il rendit le dernier soupir, pleuré de son frère et de son oncle, qui étaient accourus.

La mort inexorable venait de faucher la vie de ce jeune homme si brave, si doux, si sympathique.

Lieutenant du 8e régiment de dragons, Nompar de Caumont la Force, âgé de vingt-six ans, était venu à l'aviation, comme tant d'autres, par dilettantisme. Il s'était passionné pour cette science nouvelle qui lui permettait d'exercer son esprit aventureux.

Il fit ses débuts dans l'aviation à l'école Sommer, à Mouzon.

Il obtint son brevet de pilote il y a six mois, puis accompagna Sommer dans son raid Douzy-Verdun et retour. D'un caractère très affable, de Caumont gagnait toutes les sympathies. Il était aimé des ouvriers de l'école Sommer.

Comme officier aviateur, il prit part, au mois d'août dernier, au Circuit de l'Est du *Matin*. On se rappelle le magnifique voyage qu'il fit de Mourmelon à Nancy, en passant par Verdun. A Charleville, où il arriva de Douzy par l'air, il se fit applaudir.

Il avait été désigné pour prendre part aux grandes manœuvres d'automne. Il y vint par l'air. Chargé de porter un pli du quartier général de Beauvais à Rouen, il accomplit sa mission sans incident, et il revint quelques jours après sur le ter[rain] des manœuvres avant de regagner Mourmelon.

Depuis deux mois, il avait abandonné le biplan pour le monoplan, et il se préparait à conquérir de nouveaux lauriers. Il était attaché à la direction de Vincennes, sous les ordres du lieutenant-colonel Estienne.

L'impression à Mourmelon

MOURMELON-LE-GRAND, 30 décembre. — *De l'envoyé spécial du « Matin »* (par téléphone). — Dois-je vous dire que la nouvelle de l'accident survenu à de Caumont a causé ici une vive émotion.

Certes les civils sont navrés. Les officiers sont plus profondément troublés : c'est un membre de la « grande famille » qui est atteint. Camerman, atterré, se prend la tête dans les mains, d'un geste désolé. Féquant ne dit mot, mais il n'en est pas moins troublé. Mailfert jette et rejette ses gants par terre comme pour tuer le génie malfaisant qui a tenté d'arrêter l'essor de l'aviation militaire.

Devaux, Letheux, Raimbert se sont levés et écoutent anxieusement les détails que je leur transmets.

Comme tant d'autres, ils pleurent la mort d'un camarade estimé.

Dans le *Matin* du 31 décembre, où a paru le compte rendu de l'affreux accident survenu au lieutenant de Caumont, on a rapporté certains propos qui pourraient prêter à confusion, car on pourrait croire qu'il a pu y avoir de ma part une négligence, et que celle-ci serait une des causes indirectes de l'accident.

Cette supposition ne peut être admise, étant donnée l'affection que je portais à ce pauvre ami, dont la mort a été pour moi un des plus cruels chagrins que j'ai ressenti.

Ce n'est pas dans un défaut de fonctionnement du moteur, qu'on doit rechercher les causes de l'accident.

En ce qui concerne les commandes, le lieutenant de Caumont m'a fait observer, en effet, dès le premier essai (qui n'avait duré que quelques secondes et sur un kilomètre environ) qu'il avait dû exercer sur le levier de commande un effort très grand pour se maintenir horizontalement tant que le moteur était en marche, et que cet effort, était sensiblement plus grand que sur l'appareil dont il avait l'habitude de se servir précédemment.

Il ne voulait pas dire par là que la commande était dure par elle-même, ce qui n'est pas du tout la même chose.

Je lui ai alors fait observer que l'appareil étant étudié et réglé pour porter un passager et une très grande quantité de combustible, il était probable qu'il serait mieux équilibré avec cette lourde charge, et que l'effort à exercer pour la conduite redeviendrait normal, comme cela avait lieu d'ailleurs avec un appareil d'un modèle identique sur lequel il avait fait récemment des expériences très remarquées.

On sait que les efforts nécessaires pour conduire un appareil dans les conditions imparfaites où se trouvait celui-ci ne proviennent pas de frottement ou de résistance dus à une construction défectueuse des organes de commande, mais à la pression de l'air sur les surfaces mêmes du gouvernail. Il n'y avait donc aucune chance pour que « cela s'arrange à l'usage », comme on me l'a fait dire.

Pour mieux faire saisir le phénomène qui a pu se produire, je dois le comparer à celui qui a lieu dans un bateau à voiles, qui est plus ou moins facile à conduire, et qui est dit trop ardent ou trop mou, suivant que la voilure est disposée de telle ou telle façon, par rapport aux surfaces de dérive.

A la suite de cette observation du lieutenant de Caumont, j'ai tâché de savoir de lui s'il croyait, d'après l'essai qu'il venait de faire, pouvoir conduire l'appareil avec son chargement normal pendant le temps que pouvait durer l'épreuve du prix Lazare-Weiller. J'ai ajouté que dans le cas contraire, il serait nécessaire de modifier l'incidence du plan fixe, afin de soulager convenablement la commande ; mais que dans ce cas, cette modification nécessitant une ou deux heures, il serait trop tard pour tenter le jour même le prix Lazare-Weiller, et que l'épreuve devrait être remise au lendemain.

Le lieutenant de Caumont a jugé bon alors de faire un nouvel essai, mais contrairement à la recommandation que je lui avais faite quelques instants auparavant de ne pas s'élever à plus de trois ou quatre mètres du sol tant qu'il n'aurait pas l'appareil complètement en main et ainsi que l'indique d'ailleurs la plus élémentaire prudence, il est monté de suite à 150 ou 200 mètres.

» J'ajouterai que le terrible accident qui est survenu par la suite et que je déplore plus que tout autre, ne peut être imputé ni au vent qui était nul, ni au moteur, que le lieutenant de Caumont a peut-être eu le tort, au contraire, de ne pas arrêter à temps.

Il ne peut pas davantage être attribué à la rupture d'une pièce, même dans les commandes. L'examen postérieur de l'appareil n'a en effet révélé aucune rupture des pièces de commande. Si cela se fût produit, j'aurais été le premier à le dire, car un accident dont on peut déterminer les causes exactes est facile à éviter pour l'avenir.

Le malheureux événement me paraît donc nettement dû aux causes que j'indique ci-dessus, causes absolument indépendantes de la construction et de l'équilibrage de l'appareil.

E. NIEUPORT.

Le Matin.

Edouard NIEUPORT, perplexed by the circumstances of the accident, set about investigating the causes and subsequently gave an explanation in the newspaper *Le Matin.*

The New "4G" Monoplane

Following the first definitive results of the "N2," 1911 saw the birth of a new airplane, the two-seater "4G."

The "4G" was still a monoplane, having a median wing with a span of 11.6 meters and an airfoil of 20 m^2. The fuselage and airfoil were built from spruce and steel tubes (braces) entirely covered with canvas.

The plane weighed 350 kg in flying order, and was equipped with a rotary air-cooled 7 cylinder Gnome engine which could reach 50 hp. So as to diminish the resistance to air, the engine was entirely cowled.

The initial tests of the plane having been conclusive, NIEUPORT was eager to try and beat the existing speed records.

The 4G.

Getting the 4G ready for flight, spring 1911.

Revving up the engine before take-off; Edouard NIEUPORT in the cockpit.

On March 6, 1911, Edouard NIEUPORT, carrying a passenger named Paul Leprince, took off from Mourmelon with the desire to set a world speed record for a distance of more than 100 kilometers.

According to the timer, the "4G" reached 101 kilometers, 250 meters per hour. This shattered all the previous records, which had been set by planes with engines exceeding 100 hp and flying without a passenger.

NIEUPORT, informed of his speed at each round, continued his flight until his engine stopped because he had run out of gasoline. He thus covered 150 kilometers in 1 hour, 28 minutes, 37 and 4/5 seconds, and hence achieved 101.5 kilometers per hour.

If one considers that this airplane had made only two short test flights and that the pilot was still not completely familiar with the adjustment of a new engine and therefore could not exploit it for maximum benefit, the performance is remarkable. In fact, given that the plane was obliged to turn around pylons to carry out its course, observers estimated that the true speed was 110 kilometers per hour.

The 4G, piloted by Edouard NIEUPORT, flies round a pylon.

On the same day NIEUPORT also flew without a passenger , hoping to set another speed record. For the occasion, his airplane was fittted out with a two-cylinder, 30 hp NIEUPORT engine with the NIEUPORT Magneto and spark plugs. He covered 80 kilometers in 44 minutes, 52 seconds, reaching an average speed of 109 kilometers per hour. Thus he came within a hair's breadth of the world speed record set by LEBLANC at Belmont Park shortly before. Only nightfall prevented him from continuing his attempt.

AÉRONAUTIQUE

Nieuport bat de nouveaux Records

Effectuant sur son monoplan avec deux passagers
110 kilomètres en 1 h. 4 m. 58 s. 1/5

Dans son vol avec passagers, il atteint, avec son moteur Gnôme 50 HP, une vitesse de 102 kil. 855 à l'heure. — Dans un autre essai, seul, sur son monoplan, moteur Nieuport, magnéto Nieuport et bougie Nieuport, il couvre 80 kil. en 44 m. 52 s. 2/5, atteignant une vitesse de 109 kil. à l'heure, et approchant sensiblement les records du monde de Leblanc, établis à Belmont-Park.

« Nieuport obtiendrait une vitesse plus considérable, que ceci ne surprendrait que ceux qui ne connaissent pas Nieuport ».

Jécrivais ceci il y a trois jours : or, depuis hier, Nieuport est recordman du monde avec deux passagers.

Avec trois personnes à bord

A Mourmelon, Nieuport entrait hier en piste, avec deux voyageurs : Leprince et Chavagnac ; l'appareil s'enlevait avec une vitesse formidable, emportant dans un tourbillon les trois passagers, pour ne s'arrêter qu'après avoir accompli une heure de vol et couvert 110 kilomètres.

Voici les temps par tour, chronométrés par l'aimable M. Gaudichard :

10 kil. en 6 m.; 20 kil. en 11 m. 59 s. 2/5 ; 30 kil. en 17 m. 52 s. 3/5; 40 kil. en 22 m. 44 s. 2/5; 50 kil. en 29 m. 39 s. 2/5; 60 kil. en 35 m. 34 s. 2/5; 70 kil. en 41 m. 25 s. 1/5 ; 80 kil. en 47 m. 2 s. 2/5 ; 90 kil. en 53 m. 15 s. 2/5 ; 100 kil. en 59 m. ; 110 kil. en 1 h. 4 m. 58 s. 1/5.

Le recordman de la vitesse avec deux passagers, Bréguet, mettait lundi dernier, pour effectuer les 50 kilomètres, 38 m. 37 s. 2/5 ; le temps de Nieuport est de 20 m. 30 s. 2/5. Et Nieuport a parcouru les 100 kilomètres en 59 m. 8 s., tandis que Bréguet avait mis 1 h. 15 m. 17 s. 2/5.

C'est donc à une moyenne de 101 kil. 466 à l'heure que Nieuport s'attribue le record du monde de vitesse avec trois personnes à bord de son monoplan, que le Gnôme de 50 HP lui tirait. A un moment donné, le sympathique constructeur atteignait la vitesse de 102 kil. 855 à l'heure.

Nieuport vole seul

Albo notanda lapillo ! Oui, Nieuport peut marquer d'une pierre blanche sa journée d'hier.

A peine a-t-il descendu ses deux passagers, qu'il se dispose à s'attaquer à un autre record.

Ici entre en scène, ou mieux en piste, un seul passager, le vaillant constructeur, pilotant son monoplan et l'emmenant presque à l'assaut de tous les records du monde, avec tout le bagage de son génial cerveau : dans cette randonnée unique dans l'histoire des locomotions. Indépendamment du record des temps, qu'il a presque atteints, Nieuport s'est attribué un record qui ne lui sera pas de sitôt ravi.

En effet, c'est sa bougie Nieuport, c'est sa magnéto Nieuport, c'est son moteur 30 HP Nieuport, c'est son monoplan, autrement dit c'est tout lui-même, son cerveau, son énergie, ses études, ses labeurs qui répondent à son appel et le secondent vaillamment, sans une défaillance, sans un incident, sans un accroc et concourent à un résultat magnifique.

Donnons le détail des temps comparativement aux records qui appartiennent toujours à Leblanc :

	Temps de Nieuport			Temps de Leblanc		
	M.	S.		M.	S.	
10 kil..............	5	35	3	5	30	92/100
20 kil..............	11	14		11	4	78/100
30 kil..............	16	52	3	16	38	31/100
40 kil..............	23	22	1	22	12	58/100
50 kil..............	28	13	4	27	48	70/100
60 kil..............	33	51	2	33	22	80/100
70 kil..............	39	21	4	38	55	80/100
80 kil..............	44	52	2	44	29	50/100

Et seule, la nuit a mis Nieuport dans l'obligation d'atterrir. Il résulte des temps qui précèdent que Nieuport a atteint à un moment donné le 109 kilomètres à l'heure.

⁂

Cette journée consacre les efforts persévérants d'un travailleur tenace : c'est la juste récompense de longues recherches d'ordres divers, de conception variées, sorties du cerveau de Nieuport et par lui réumies dans un seul mot : le succès !

G. Le Grand.

NIEUPORT Sets New Records, March 10, 1911.

Records d'aéroplane

Nieuport vole à plus de cent à l'heure avec un passager

Chaque jour amène un exploit nouveau :n aviation. Avant-hier c'était le record du 'oyage au-dessus de la mer. Hier c'étaient à a fois les records officiels de vitesse et de listance des vols avec un et avec deux passagers, et le record officiel de distance.

La performance relative au vol avec un bassager fut accomplie au camp de Châons, par l'aviateur Nieuport, qui pilotait ın monoplan de sa construction, et qui ıvait emmené avec lui M. Paul Leprince, ın de ses élèves-pilotes.

Jusqu'au cinquantième kilomètre, il ne put battre le temps de Busson, du 13 février dernier. Celui-ci avait mis 30 minutes 33 secondes 2/5 ; Nieuport était en retard de 20 secondes. Mais à partir de cette distance, il améliora ses temps et franchit les 100 kilomètres en 59 minutes 16 secondes, soit à la vitesse de 101 kilomètres 200 à l'heure. Busson avait mis 1 heure 1 minute 32 secondes pour effectuer la même distance.

Enfin Nieuport a établi le record de vitesse des 150 kilomètres par 1 heure 28 minutes 39 secondes 2/5 (moyenne de l'heure : 101 kilomètres 500).

Bréguet vole à 80 kilomètres à l'heure avec deux passagers

DOUAI, 6 mars. — *Dépêche particulière du « Matin ».* — Louis Bréguet, ayant comme passagers le lieutenant Peralda et M. Boland, s'est élevé aujourd'hui à 4 heures 1 minute 11 secondes, de l'aérodrome de la Brayelle, dans l'intention de battre les records établis par Mamet le 9 juillet 1910.

Il y réussit pleinement, puisque avec la charge réglementaire de 75 kilos par passager, soit 225 kilos, il vola les 50 kilomètres en 38 minutes 37 secondes 2/5, alors que le record était de 52 minutes 56 secondes 1/5.

Alors que Mamet et ses deux compagnons avaient couvert 92 kilomètres 750, en tenant l'air pendant 1 heure 38 minutes 40 secondes, Bréguet ne revint à terre qu'après avoir parcouru 100 kilomètres en 1 heure 15 minutes 17 secondes 2/5.

RNAL

Le "Nieuport" Roi de la Vitesse

La superbe performance réalisée avant-hier à Mourmelon par Nieuport, tout à la fois constructeur et aviateur, mérite plus qu'une simple mention. Les résultats obtenus sont en effet splendides.

Le monoplan Nieuport, muni seulement d'un moteur de 50 chevaux, chronométré par M. Gaudichard, chronométreur officiel de l'Aéro Club de France, vient de battre les records du monde pour aéroplane ayant deux personnes à bord (le pilote et un voyageur).

Les temps officiels sont les suivants : 100 kilomètres en 59 m. 16 s. Dans l'heure : 101 kilomètres 250 m.

Les 150 kilomètres en 1 heure 28 m. 37 s. 4/5.

Plus grande vitesse atteinte : 103 kilomètres 211 mètres.

Comme on le voit, le rendement du monoplan Nieuport est plus du double que celui des autres appareils. On se souvient, en effet, que le précédent record établi l'avait été avec un moteur de 100 chevaux.

Chose curieuse, le record établi il y a 48 heures par Nieuport aurait pu tout aussi bien l'être il y a un an, l'appareil étant celui que nous vîmes au meeting de Reims.

A Reims, en effet, un Nieuport, muni d'un simple moteur de 20 chevaux, avait atteint la vitesse de 84 kilomètres 400 m. à l'heure.

Les splendides résultats obtenus par le monoplan Nieuport — peu connu du grand public — n'ont pas étonné les connaisseurs et le monde de l'aviation.

Nieuport, déjà inventeur, constructeur de la magnéto qui porte son nom, est un chercheur, un travailleur opiniâtre.

Il se prépare, d'ailleurs, à de nouvelles prouesses. — ARGEO.

M. DESPLAS, DÉPUTÉ DE PARIS,

Les monoplans qui battent les records de vitesse

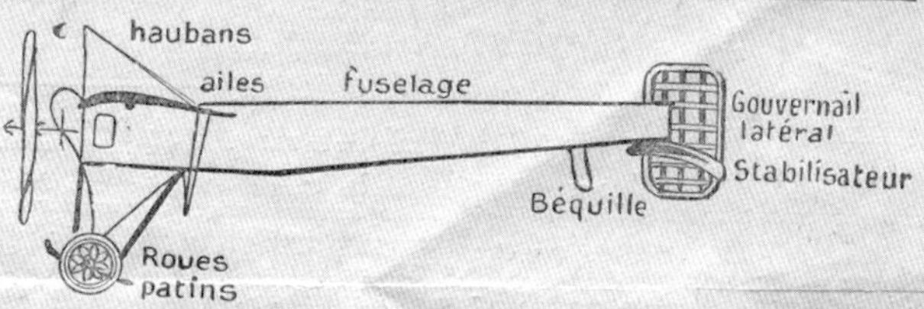

En haut, l'appareil de Nieuport battant les records du monde avec un passager, à Bouy, et faisant du 105 à l'heure. .. En bas, le profil schématique du Blériot avec lequel Alfred Leblanc a fait du 125 à l'heure.

Louis Blériot explique les particularités de l'appareil de Leblanc, qui a fait du 125 à l'heure.

Alfred Leblanc, qui prend part en ce moment aux éliminatoires de la Coupe Gordon-Bennett, a réussi, avant-hier, à battre tous les records de vitesse existants. Alors que Nieuport, détenteur de l'ancien record, avait volé les 100 kilomètres en 50 m. 36 s., le 11 mai dernier, le triomphateur du Circuit de l'Est n'a mis que 48 m. 56 s. 1/5. Sa plus forte vitesse fut de 125 kilomètres à l'heure, et il termina les 150 kilomètres en 1 h. 13 m. 35 s.

Nous avons demandé à M. Louis Blériot, le constructeur de l'appareil, de bien vouloir nous donner des renseignements sur cet engin qui vient de faire accomplir un aussi grand progrès dans l'industrie de l'aviation.

— Ce monoplan, nous a-t-il déclaré, est le type 23 de la série. De même que tous ceux qui l'ont précédé depuis le type 20, il a l'empennage en queue de pigeon. Le fuselage, renflé à l'avant, est très pointu à l'arrière. Il donne à l'aéroplane la forme idéale de moindre résistance à l'avancement. Il est entoilé et, grâce à ce dispositif, l'air ne peut y entrer. Partant, la vitesse est augmentée. Les ailes vernies permettent de glisser dans l'espace. Elles sont très diminuées en profondeur. C'est leur courbure nouvelle qui a le plus d'importance pour la vitesse obtenue et espérée. Je vous demande la permission de ne pas vous en dire plus long sur ce point, jusqu'à la Coupe Gordon-Bennett.

Alfred Leblanc, qui avait réussi, aux premiers essais à Pau, à faire du 108 à l'heure, puis du 118, enfin du 125, espère pouvoir dépasser ces moyennes. Il en a même la conviction, car il y a un notable excès de force.

La difficulté réside dans le départ pour les mécaniciens, dans l'atterrissage pour le pilote. Les quatre hommes qui tiennent l'appareil sont obligés de se coucher à plat ventre et, au moment où ils lâchent les roues et la béquille arrière, ils sont cependant traînés à terre sur une distance de dix mètres. Quant à l'atterrissage, il se fait à 100 kilomètres à l'heure, et si l'aviateur coupe complètement l'allumage, il est littéralement happé par le sol. La conduite de semblable engin, on le voit, ne saurait être confiée qu'à un virtuose de l'air.

Quant au moteur, c'est un Gnôme de 100 chevaux qui, comme tous ses semblables, est constitué par deux 50 chevaux accolés. Il a 14 cylin-

Edouard Nieuport fait le récit de son record de 105 à l'heure avec passager, établi malgré la pluie et le vent.

Le constructeur aviateur Edouard Nieuport, qui vient de battre, à Mourmelon, les records du monde de vitesse avec passager, de 5 à 150 kilomètres, records qu'il détenait déjà depuis le 9 mars dernier, a bien voulu donner aux lecteurs d'*Excelsior* quelques détails sur son vol.

— Nous nous sommes envolés, mon passager M. Trausch et moi, de l'aérodrome de Bouy, dont la piste réglementaire de 5 kilomètres, bordée de quatre pylônes, permet les plus grandes vitesses. M. Gaudichard remplissait les délicates fonctions de chronométreur, et quatre commissaires veillaient à ce que tout fût régulier.

» Nous montions un appareil de série, muni d'un moteur Gnôme de 70 chevaux, que M. Trausch, fervent de la locomotion aérienne, venait d'acheter. C'était donc un essai de réception qui s'est traduit par un vol record.

Mon passager pesant 71 kilos et moi 65, on nous avait adjoint 4 kilos supplémentaires. Nous volions, depuis environ trente minutes, à une vitesse de 105 kilomètres à l'heure, quand le vent s'éleva. La pluie vint nous cingler le visage; bientôt nous fûmes fortement ballottés, et dans les virages déportés à l'extérieur.

» Sans la préoccupation que me causait la conduite de l'appareil dans ces conditions pénibles, je crois bien que j'aurais eu le mal de mer. M. Trausch, Américain flegmatique, ne disait mot, mais il était un peu pâle. On nous annonça, par des banderoles de calicot, que les records étaient battus et, la bourrasque ayant cessé, notre voyage se poursuivit sans incident, jusqu'au moment où les 150 kilomètres étant atteints, on nous fit signe de descendre.

» A ce moment, à l'autre bout de la piste, apparut un Nieuport qui, après un tour bouclé à grande vitesse, vint se poser doucement devant son hangar. C'était Weymann qui, parti à 5 h. 50 de Villacoublay, venait, tout souriant, à 7 h. 27, dîner à Bouy, accomplissant en 1 h. 37 m., soit à près de 120 kilomètres à l'heure (record), la distance classique Paris-Mourmelon, et ce, malgré un fort vent debout. »

Ajoutons que le constructeur aviateur Nieuport tentera prochainement, avec son 70 chevaux, de battre les records de vitesse sans passager que Leblanc lui a ravis au moment où

"Monoplanes That Are Setting New Speed Records."

Cent kilomètres en 50 minutes

L'aviateur Nieuport a fait hier du 118 à l'heure

L'exploit de l'aviateur Nieuport, volant hier à Mourmelon, en circuit fermé, 100 kilomètres en 50 minutes 36 secondes, soit à la vitesse de 118 kilomètres 577 à l'heure, constitue un double progrès.

D'abord, l'aviateur a battu son propre record qui était avant-hier de 116 kil. 500 à l'heure, ensuite la puissance motrice du monoplan qu'il pilote n'est que de 28 chevaux. On sait que généralement les records de vitesse sont établis avec des appareils munis de moteurs de 50, 70 et même 100 chevaux.

Voici quelques détails sur le vol de l'aviateur.

NIEUPORT

MOURMELON, 11 mai. — *Du correspondant* *rticulier du « Matin »* (par téléphone). — r la piste de l'aérodrome de Bouy, Nieurt, sur son monoplan, a volé ce matin 100 omètres en 50 minutes 36 secondes, avec temps suivants de 10 en 10 kilomètres : 10 kilomètres, 5' 7" ; 20 kil. 10' 9" 2/5 ; kil. 15' 11" 2/5 ; 40 kil. 20' 22" ; 50 kil. 14" 2/5 ; 60 kil. 30' 18" 1/5 ; 70 kil. 35' 1/5 ; 80 kil. 40' 20" 4/5 ; 90 kil. 46' 26" 3/5 ; kil. 50' 36".

Le meilleur temps sur 10 kilomètres a été 5 m. 1 sec. 3/5, ce qui donne une vitesse 119 kil. 688 à l'heure.

L'exploit a été contrôlé par MM. Gaudiard, chronométreur officiel ; Henry Kaper, commissaire sportif ; lieutenants Féant et Debriey, docteur Espanet, Trausch Lazard.

During the same period NIEUPORT, accompanied by an American passenger—a Mr. Trausch, who had come to buy a plane—broke his previous record by logging 105 kilometers per hour with a 70-hp Gnome engine.

On May 11, 1911, again in Mourmelon, NIEUPORT set a new record with his "N 2" model, equipped with a bicylinder engine he had designed, by completing a course at the never before attained speed of 119.68 kilometers per hour. And with that feat, Edouard NIEUPORT acquired international fame, all the more so since his airplane required only a very light motorization of 28 hp, whereas the competing planes had engines ranging from 50/70 to 100 hp.

Forever seeking to improve his aircraft, NIEUPORT was constantly breaking his old records. Still flying the "N 2," he reached a speed of 130.057 kilometers per hour on June 16, 1911, and 133.136 kilometers on June 21.

"A Hundred Kilometers in 50 Minutes."

L'aviateur Nieuport fait du 119 kil. 680 mètres.

A Mourmelon, le 11 mai. Nieuport a battu jusqu'aux 100 kilomètres ses propres records.

Le moteur de 28 HP avec lequel Nieuport a établi le record du monde de vitesse.

LES RECORDS D'AVIATION TOMBENT

NIEUPORT S'ADJUGE LES RECORDS SEUL ET A TROIS

Nieuport vient d'accomplir prouesses sur prouesses, à Mourmelon. Le 6 mars, il s'adjugeait les records à deux des 100 kil. en 58 m. 10 s. et 150 kil. en 1 h. 28 m. 37. s. 4/5. Le 9 mars, avec deux passagers, couvrait 110 kil. en 1 h. 4 m. 58 s. 1/5 (100 kil. en 59 m.). Enfin, seul, il battait les records jusqu'à 10 kil. Ce monoplan, moteur (dans son vol seul), bougie et magnéto sont l'œuvre de Nieuport lui-même.

NIEUPORT breaks records alone and with two passengers.

At Mourmelon on May 11, 1911.

One of the rare technical documents (following translation below) found in the cartons stored at the *Société dAéro-locomotion* concerns the adjustment of the "4G" airplanes which took part in the meetings in Reims, March/June 1911.

ADJUSTMENT OF NIEUPORT AIRPLANES

An airplane adjusted normally should meet the following conditions:

1. The respective angles of the engine, tubular spars, and stabilizer should conform to those given below.
2. The diagonals of each right section should be equal.
3. The tubular spars should be parallel to each other.
4. The fuselage axis should be perpendicular to the spars.
5. The part of the tail on which the stabilizer rests must be perfectly aligned with the spars.

FIRST CONDITION

Respective angles of the engine, spars, and stabilizer. Using the stabilizer as the baseline, the line of the axis of the spars should form a 30° angle with it. The engine axis should be parallel to the stabilizer. If these conditions are not met, either tighten or loosen the wires on the tail or those on the forward frame to bring these parts into the correct position.

SECOND CONDITION

Measure exactly the diagonals d and d' with a gauge and tighten the wires to equalize these lengths; repeat the operation for all the vertical sections of the fuselage.

THIRD CONDITION

Make certain that the tubular spars are aligned. For that, insert into each spar a long ruler extending beyond each side of the fuselage and align the two rulers by tightening the wires so that their edges, resting on the braces, and struts are aligned. Verify that the distance between the tubular spars is equal to that of the wing spars.

FOURTH CONDITION

Stretch across the fuselage, from left to right, a cord tangential to the ends of the tubular spars. At the tail, measure the distances a and a', which should be the same. If a difference is noted, bring the tail back to the correct position by tightening the wires.

FIFTH CONDITION

This condition can be verified by placing three rulers across the fuselage, the first on the sternpost at the point where the rear frame is attached to the stabilizer, the second near to the horizontal strut that attaches the stabilizer to the front, and the third to the tubular spars. These three rulers should be perfectly aligned. If necessary, tighten the wires.

The fuselage, having been adjusted, as well as the runner should be aligned with plane's axis. If the contrary is true, it is because there has been a distortion of the frames or the strut.

The spring should be at right angles to the axis of the fuselage. This can be verified by taking the distance of these two extremities by projecting on the ground any point of the longitudinal axis of the airplane.

ASSEMBLY OF THE STABILIZER

Place the stabilizer on the bolts intended to receive it. The fuselage, having been adjusted, is naturally parallel to the level at which the wings are attached to it. Put the struts, whose length has been determined by the first assembly, in place.

ADJUSTMENT OF THE RUDDER AND ELEVATOR

Move the control lever to the midway point in both directions. The rudder should be aligned with the axis of the aircraft. The elevator should be tilted slightly backward for take off. The last two adjustments can be made easily by using tightening wires mounted on the control cables.

ADJUSTMENT OF THE WINGS

Fix the wings and support them with overhead cables. Put the cables underneath in place.

(DRAWING)

The forward cables should be adjusted first. Place on the forward spar a 20 cm wedge on the next to the last rib of each wing. Stretch a cord from one side to the other. Measure the distances h and adjust the length of the wing cables so as to obtain for h the following lengths:

type 6,000	type 4,000	type 3,000
33 cm	32 cm	30 cm

The height should be measured between the cord and the rib that touches the fuselage.

Adjustment of rear cables. The forward cables having been adjusted, wind around each wing 2 cords, encircling the second and next to last rib. In this way the underlying cords supporting each of these two ribs can be determined. With the warping control horizontal at the midway point and the warping lever vertical, the two cords should be parallel.

This result is sometimes difficult to obtain when, for some reason or other, a wing has been subjected to an important distortion. In that case, the distortion must be corrected by suspending from the wing for several hours a weight sufficient for bringing it back to its proper position.

REGLAGE DES APPAREILS NIEUPORT

-:-:-:-:-:-:-:-:-:-:-

Un appareil réglé normalement doit répondre aux conditions suivantes :

1°;- Les angles respectifs du moteur des tubes d'ailes , du plan fixe doivent être conformés à ceux donnés ci-après :

2°.- Les diagonales de chaque section droite doivent être égales .

3°.- Les tubes d'ailes doivent être parallèles entre eux .

4°.- L'axe du fuselage doit être perpendiculaire aux tubes d'ailes .

5°.- La partie de la queue sur laquelle repose le plan fixe doit être parfaitement dégauchie avec le plan des tubes d'ailes .

PREMIERE CONDITION

ANGLES RESPECTIFS DU MOTEUR , DES TUBES D'AILES , DU PLAN FIXE .- L plan fixe étant compté comme ligne de base . La ligne des axes des poutres doit faire un angle + de 30' avec lui . L'axe moteur doit être parallèle au plan fixe . Si ces conditions ne sont pas réalisées , agir , soit sur les tendeurs de la queue , soit sur le tendeur du cadre AV pour ramener les organes à la bonne position

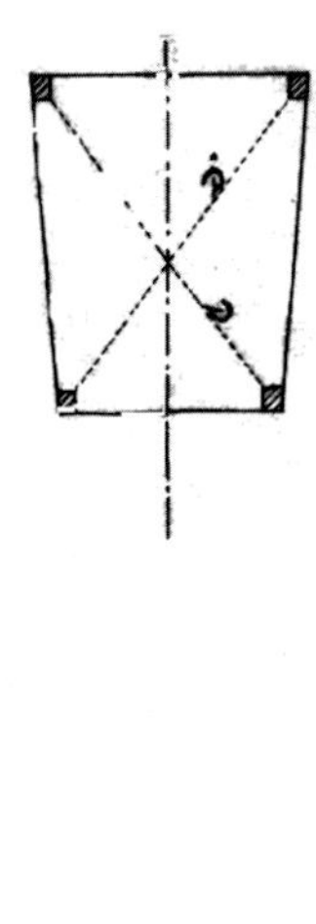

DEUXIEME CONDITION

Mesurer exactement les diagonales d et d' avec une jauge et agir sur les tendeurs pour égaliser ces longueurs ; ceci pour toutes les sections verticales du fuselage .

TROISIEME CONDITION

S'assurer que les tubes d'ailes sont dans le même plan . Pour cela , passer dans chaque tube une longue règle débordant de chaque côté du fuselage et dégauchir les deux règles entre elles en agissant sur les tendeurs de telle sorte que leurs bords d'appui sur les tubes soit dans un même plan . Vérifier l'entre-axe des tubes qui doit être égal à celui des poutres d'ailes .

- 2 -

QUATRIEME CONDITION

Faire passer à gauche et à droite du fuselage un cordeau tangent aux extrèmités des tubes d'ailes . Mesurer à la queue les distances a et a' qui doivent être égales . Si une diffèrence est constatée , ramener la queue en bonne position en agissant sur les tendeurs .

CINQUIEME CONDITION

Cette condition se vérifie au moyen de trois règles placées transversalement au fuselage , la première sur le montant terminus à l'endroit de la fixation AR du plan fixe . la 2ème près de la traverse de fixation du plan fixe à l'avant , la 3ème dans un tube d'ailes . Ces trois règles doivent se dégauchir parfaitement . Agir sur les tendeurs pour obtenir ce résultat .

Le fuselage étant ainsi réglé , le patin doit être dans le même plan que l'axe de l'appareil , dans le cas contraire , c'est qu'il y a eu déformation des cadres ou des V .

RESSORT .- doit être perpendiculaire à l'axe du fuselage , le vérifier en prenant la distance de ces deux extrèmités à la projection sur le sold'un point quelconquede l'axe longitudinal de l'appareil .

MONTAGE DE L'EMPENNAGE

Placer le plan fixe sur les goujons destinés à le recevoir , le fuselage étant réglé , se trouvera naturellement parallèle à l'emmanchement des ailes . Mettre en place les jambes de force dont la longueur a été déterminée au premier montage .

REGLAGE DES COMMANDES DE DIRECTION ET
DE PROFONDEUR

Placer le levier de commande à mi-course dans les deux sens . Le Gouvernail de Direction doit être dans le même plan que l'axe de l'appareil .

Le gouvernail de profondeur doit être légèrement à la montée .

Ces deux derniers règlages se font facilement au moyen des tendeurs montés sur les câbles de commande

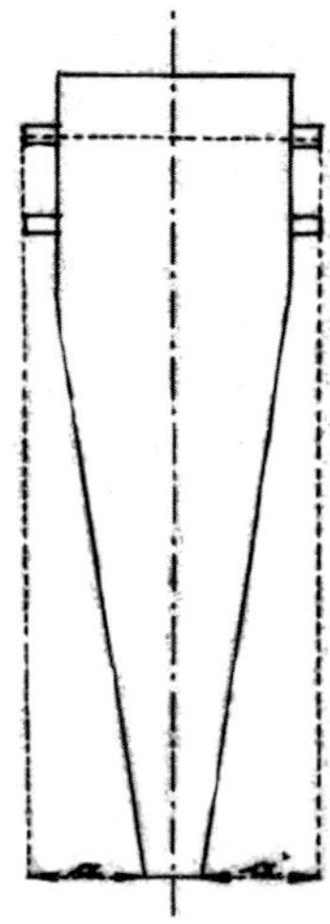

- 5 -

REGLAGE DES AILES

Monter les ailes , les soutenir par les cables supèrieurs . Mettre en place les câbles infèrieurs .

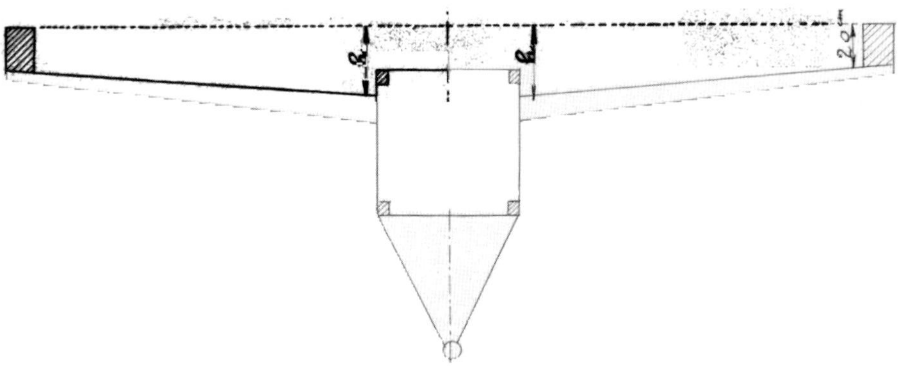

Les câbles AV doivent être règlés les premiers
Placer sur la poutre AV une cale de 20 cm. sur l'avant dernière nervure de chaque aile . Tendre un cordeau d'un coté à l'autre . Mesurer les distances h et règler la longueur des câbles d'ailes de façon à obtenir pour h les valeurs suivantes :

type 6.000	type 4.000	type .000
33 cm	32 cm	30 cm

La hauteur h doit être mesurée entre le cordeau et la nervure qui touche le fuselage .
REGLAGE DES CABLES AR .- Les câbles avant étant règlés , passer autour de chaque aile 2 cordeaux faisant le tour de la 3ème et de l'avant dernière nervure .

On détermine ainsi les cordes sous tendant chacune de ces deux nervures .
La commande de gauchissement étant horizontale à mi course et le levier de gauchissement verticalé , les deux cordes doivent être parallèles .

Ce résultat est parfois difficile à obtenir quand pour une raison quelconque une aile a subi une déformation importante . Il faut alors reprendre la déformation en suspendant pendant plusieurs heuresa une ferrure d'attache de l'aile un poids suffisant pour faire revenir l'aile en bonne position .

Le Monoplan Nieuport

De l'avis unanime, jamais aéroplane plus rapide et plus simple n'a encore été conçu. Dans les matches, Nieuport, sur ce monoplan-bolide, peut rendre une bonne distance aux autres appareils. Il les passe et les dépasse comme il veut. Tous ceux qui l'ont vu sont enthousiasmés et nous-mêmes, qui l'avons observé au camp de Châlons, nous ne pouvons décrire l'extraordinaire sensation de puissance et de rapidité qu'il donne.

Mais ce qui est vraiment prodigieux, c'est que Nieuport, qui a fait établir ce monoplan suivant ses propres données, obtint en un quart d'heure d'apprentissage la maîtrise de l'appareil, ce qui prouve surabondamment sa facilité de manœuvre et sa stabilité parfaite.

Le moteur n'est qu'un simple 20 chevaux, et encore, lorsque l'appareil vole avec cette vitesse foudroyante dont nous avons déjà parlé, il n'emploie même pas les trois quarts de la force. En le voyant filer élégamment dans l'air, on se demande si les 150 et 200 kilomètres à l'heure, espérés par les mathématiciens, ne vont pas être atteints à bref délai. Le monoplan Nieuport réalisera-t-il ce rêve ? Nous le croyons fermement.

Donnons maintenant quelques renseignements techniques sur ce dernier venu qui, dès sa naissance, a su prendre la première place dans l'aviation, grâce à la valeur et à l'ingéniosité de son constructeur.

On est tout d'abord frappé de la simplicité extrême de l'appareil Nieuport qu'a construit la Société Générale d'Aéro-Locomotion. En fait, il est différent de tous les autres, jusque dans ses moindres détails. Son envergure est de 8 m. 50, sa longueur de 7 mètres, son poids de 220 kilos sans pilote, et il a 14 mètres carrés de surface. Les ailes ont très peu de courbure. Le châssis d'atterrissage est réduit à un patin unique, muni d'un ressort transversal qui sert en même temps d'axe aux roues. Le fuselage est fermé entièrement, et protège le pilote du froid et des projections d'huile. Le pilote, très à l'avant, peut voir perpendiculairement comme sur un biplan.

Autre innovation : le gauchissement est automatique et fonctionne admirablement. Même dans les remous, même par grand vent, il n'y a pas besoin d'y toucher. Les gouvernails de direction et de profondeur sont conjugués. Un plan fixe à l'arrière, réglable à volonté, donne à l'appareil une stabilité longitudinale parfaite. Point important : l'appareil se démonte et se remonte en dix minutes et cela tout simplement parce qu'il n'y a pas, comme dans les autres appareils, une multiplicité de tendeurs et de fils à régler et à accrocher.

Ajoutons un mot : si, pendant que ce monoplan vole, le moteur s'arrête brusquement, l'appareil plane et descend lentement pour atterrir comme un oiseau. Le pilote n'a pas besoin de faire la moindre manœuvre. Il ne peut donc pas être surpris par la panne. Cette dernière constatation est, comme on sait, des plus importantes. Pour que l'aéroplane devienne pratique, il faut qu'il offre le minimum de danger. Or, jusqu'à maintenant, le danger c'est que, si le moteur s'arrête brusquement, on pique souvent une tête, à moins d'avoir beaucoup de chance et beaucoup de présence d'esprit. Avec le monoplan Nieuport, on n'a plus cela à craindre. Si le moteur vous lâche, l'appareil plane sans se déséquilibrer et permet de choisir tranquillement l'endroit d'atterrissage.

F.-A. Wheel.

The Great Pilots of the NIEUPORT School.

In 1911 there arrived at the NIEUPORT School in Mourmelon several pilots of outstanding ability who were subsequently to become important participants in the Suresnes firm.

The first to show up was Charles T. WEYMANN, an American born August 2, 1889, in Port au Prince, Haiti. He obtained his pilot's license on June 10, 1910, at Camp Châlons.

From May 21 to May 25, 1911, he joined the long-distance flight from Paris to Madrid, piloting a "G 4" monoplane with a 50 hp Gnome engine. He undertook this adventure with a young man named CHEVALIER, who was not as well- known but just as talented.

A few weeks later, WEYMANN took part in the marathon airplane race, Paris-Rome-Turin. This event, which was of supreme interest for the sporting world, brought together the thirty best civilian and military pilots of the day. Among the civilians were three from the NIEUPORT School: WEYMANN, NIEMELA, and LEPRINCE, who all flew NIEUPORT "G 4" monoplanes.

The same plane had been chosen by three military pilots: Lieutenants MIALLOLS and FIQUANT and Captain DELAGE.

A prominent patron of aviation, Monsieur DEUTSCH de la MEURTHE, provided the race with a cup, which was an impressive object d'art worth 2,000 francs. It would be awarded to the first pilot to reach Nice.

DEUTSCH de la MEURTHE also happened to be a great admirer of NIEUPORT's work and would later contriibute to the development of the NIEUPORT factories.

VEDRINES with a MORANE SAULNIER won this race, but it would seem likely that the NIEUPORT planes made a most creditable showing, because they won 2nd, 3rd, and 4th places.

The Gordon-Bennett Cup Race.

On July 1, 1911, WEYMANN won the Gordon-Bennett Cup at Eastchurch, England, piloting a NIEUPORT "4 G" equipped with a 100 hp Gnome engine. He covered the 150 kilometer course in 1 hour 11 minutes and 39 seconds, achieving an average of 127 kilometers per hour. Edouard NIEUPORT placed third in one of his monoplanes driven by a 70 hp rotary Gnome engine.

The American flag being waved at the finish line of the Gordon-Bennett Cup Race, since Weymann was an American.

Around this time Edouard NIEUPORT met a pilot called HELEN and recruited him for his school in Mourmelon. He considered this young man to have the makings of an aviator for the future, capable of doing sensational things.

Fearlessly daring and fervent by nature, HELEN was a supremely skilled engineer, completely dedicated to aviation. He set to work with a determination, tenacity, and loyalty that very quickly brought him a success which was as merited as it was extraordinary.

Near the end of August 1911, HELEN earned his pilot's license and, wasting no time, on August 26 he informed the *Aéro-Club de France* that he intended to compete in the Michelin Cup race.

The itinerary started at the crossroads located to the right of the Champagne Airport and included a turn at Somme-sur-Vesle before returning to the point of departure. The circuit measured 102 kilometers, 400 meters, as the crow flies.

HELEN's plane was housed in the NIEUPORT Company hangars in Mourmelon. At the first light of dawn, he took off for the Champagne Airport in Bétheny. This flight allowed him to survey a part of the course he would be covering during the day.

He landed at five in the morning and was welcomed by Monsieur FOURNIER, the steward for the *Aéro-Club de France*, who looked over his plane. After one final check, now called "*visite de prévol,*" or "preflight inspection," HELEN notified the few people present that he was ready to go; he seated himself at the controls of his aircraft, and the officials responsible for verifying the flight took their places.

At five minutes 48 seconds past five, HELEN crossed the starting point formed by the road from Reims to Bétheny and headed towards Somme-sur-Vesle.

HELEN taking off with a passenger and a wheel?

Hélen and the NIEUPORT Monoplane.

Monsieur GAUDICHARD, the official timekeeper for the *Aéro-Club de France*, who had made a special trip from Paris, began to note the hour each time Hélen flew over.

At 6:15 HELEN completed his first round. At 7:19, the second, at 8:21 the third, and at 9:53 the fourth.

Arrival at the Michelin race.

He flew regularly until the eleventh and final round that he completed at 6 hours, 53 minutes and 7 seconds in the evening, accomplishing an official flight of 1,126.4 kilometers in 13 hours, 47 minutes and 19 seconds. With this performance he broke the previous record set by Vedrines, who had covered 811 kilometers.

On September 8, 1911, at Etampes, HELEN surpassed his record by flying for 14 hours and 7 minutes and covering a distance of 1,252 kilometers.

UNE RÉVÉLATION. — L'AVIATEUR HÉLEN S'ATTRIBUE LA COUPE MICHELIN (1)

Le 26 août, le jeune aviateur Hélen, un inconnu, se mettait en piste pour tenter de batire le record de Védrines (811 kilomètres) pour la Coupe Michelin. Il commençait à 5 heures du matin sur le parcours Bétheny à Somme-Vesle et retour, soit 102 kilom. 400. Malgré le vent, il réussissait à merveille dans sa tentative et s'arrêtait au crépuscule, ayant accompli la distance fantastique de 1.126 kilom. 400 en 13 heures 47 minutes 19 secondes et n'ayant fait que trois escales. Le lendemain il gagnait, par la voie des airs, Paris, où il va consacrer sa célébrité récente, mais hardiment acquise. Détail technique : Hélice intégrale Chauvière.

5

The Fate of a Passion

The Death of the Pioneer

Dr. ESPANET, a pilot for NIEUPORT and a faithful companion, recounts the death of his friend, who was only 36 years old.

In 1911, Edouard NIEUPORT was mobilized as a reserve engineer in the squadron made up of his airplanes and led by the naval lieutenant Delage. Military maneuvers were being held from September 10-18 in the Ardennes.

On September 9 when NIEUPORT arrived at Mourmelon from Issy, with a wind of 24 m/sec, piloting the monoplane he had built and equipped with a 50 hp Gnôme engine, he found an order to fly to Verdun, where Colonel ESTIENNE would be waiting. Unfamiliar with the area, he installed an ash board in front of the pilot's seat so that he could place a map there.

And on September 10, he set out for Verdun. Colonel ESTIENNE, surrounded by a few officers whom he hoped to attract to aviation, was waiting on the airfield. In spite of the bad weather, the Colonel was certain that NIEUPORT would appear.

However, his officers were expressing polite sketicism, convinced that no aircraft would take off in such violent gusts of wind. While they were discussing the matter, to their amazement they heard the sound of an engine and then noticed a black speck growing larger in the sky: it was the little NIEUPORT, and after an impeccable lap, it landed as if on a bed of rose petals.

And that is no rhetorical image, I saw it myself. Colonel ESTIENNE was jubilant, terribly excited by NIEUPORT's performance. And wanting to have his enthusiasm shared by the others, wanting to highlight the talents of his special *sapeur*, he insisted, "That perfect landing, despite the dreadful atmospheric condi-

En 1911, Edouard Nieuport est mobilisé comme sapeur dans une escadrille de ses appareils commandée par le lieutenant de vaisseau Delage. Or, du 10 au 18 septembre, se déroulent les manœuvres des Ardennes. A ce titre, Nieuport, arrivé à Mourmelon le 9 par un vent de 24 m/sec venant d'Issy aux commandes d'un monoplan de sa construction muni d'un moteur Gnôme de 50 CV, reçoit l'ordre de se rendre à Verdun où l'attend le Colonel Estienne. Ne connaissant pas le secteur, il fait installer, devant son siège de pilote, une planchette de frêne où il pourra fixer la carte de la région pour lui inconnue et, le 10, il se met en route pour Verdun. Cependant, le Colonel Estienne entouré de quelques officiers qu'il entend gagner à l'aviation attendent, sur le terrain de Verdun, l'appareil qui a reçu l'ordre de rejoindre. Aux affirmations du colonel, certain de l'arrivée de Nieuport, les officiers opposent un scepticisme poli, persuadés qu'ils sont que par le vent qui souffle par rafales, aucun appareil ne peut prendre l'air. Ils en étaient à discuter de la question lorsque, à leur stupéfaction, ils entendent un bruit de moteur, aperçoivent un point noir qui grossit dans le ciel : c'est le petit Nieuport qui arrive et après un tour de piste impeccable se pose comme sur des fleurs : ceci n'est pas une image de rhétorique, je l'ai vu moi-même. Le Colonel Estienne jubile, enthousiasmé par la performance de Nieuport et, désireux de faire partager son enthousiasme à son entourage comme de mettre en valeur son sapeur de choix, il affirme : « Ce que vous croyez un coup de chance, cet atterrissage impeccable malgré les détestables conditions atmosphériques, eh bien, Nieuport avec cet appareil peut le refaire devant vous, et, impulsivement, il demande au pilote de redécoller et de refaire une démonstration.

Bien que fatigué, celui-ci, sans hésitation, remonte à bord, redécolle et monte à 800 mètres. A cette hauteur, nous l'entendons distinctement couper son moteur. Il commence alors une admirable descente en spirale une à droite, une à gauche. Arrivé à la hauteur des bessonneaux, une rafale de vent le fait passer juste au ras de l'un d'entre eux, ensuite, son appareil, brutalement rabattu vers le sol, pique et atterrit en pylône. Nous sommes stupéfaits, et nous précipitons. L'on aide Nieuport à sortir de son monoplan. Très

tions, that you consider luck can be made again by NIEUPORT." And, impulsively, he asked the pilot to repeat the demonstration.

Although he was tired, NIEUPORT returned to the cockpit without hesitation, took off, and climbed to 800 meters. At this altitude, we could distinctly hear him cutting off his engine. He then began an admirable spiral descent, one to the left, one to the right. Having reached the level of the trees, a gust of wind caused him to pass just above one of them.

Then, his plane suddenly pulled towards the ground, went into a dive, and landed vertically. We were dumbfounded and rushed to the scene, and NIEUPORT was helped out.

Very pale, he started explaining what had happened: wanting to make a descent with a stalled propeller, he had cut off the power. But, forgetting that he had a Gnome engine, he had failed to stop the flow of gasoline which, since there was no carburetion device, went directly into the crankshaft of the rotary engine, flooding it as he came down. Thus, he could not restart the engine for the landing.

While he was telling us all this, his expression suddenly changed dramatically: "I am bleeding in my stomach," he said. And, in fact, when he had hit the pâle, il nous explique ce qui lui est arrivé : désireux de faire une descente hélice calée, il avait coupé le contact, mais, oubliant qu'il avait un moteur Gnôme, il avait omis de couper l'essence qui, sans aucun dispositif de carburation, coulait directement dans le Vilebrequin fixe du moteur rotatif, de sorte que, pendant sa descente, son moteur s'est noyé, l'essence continuant d'arriver. Il s'ensuit que lorsqu'il a voulu relancer son moteur lors de l'atterrissage, le moteur n'a pas repris. Pendant qu'il nous donnait ces explications, son visage se décomposait : « Je saigne dans mon ventre », nous dit-il. Et de fait, lors de sa mise en pylône, le choc brutal qui le jeta vers l'avant (il n'était pas attaché) lui fit éclater le foie contre la petite planchette qu'il avait fait installer pour sa carte. Lorsque l'on se rendit compte de la gravité de son état, l'on téléphona au Docteur Doyen, le plus grand chirurgien de l'époque, qui vint immédiatement de Paris à Verdun dans une voiture rapide. Lorsqu'il arriva au chevet de Nieuport, celui-ci ne parlait plus et mourut un quart d'heure après l'arrivée du chirurgien.

Ainsi, par un malheureux concours de circonstances, l'aviation perdait un de ses plus remarquables pionniers, et cela précisément au moment où le mécène le plus éclairé et le plus généreux de l'époque, Deutsch de la Meurthe, ayant apprécié ses exceptionnelles qualités, l'avait déjà dégagé de tout souci financier et décidé la construction de l'usine d'Issy-les-Moulineaux.

Malgré cet incontestable malheur, la maison Nieuport allait continuer : un mois après l'accident tragique, Weymann, pilote de la maison, remporta au concours militaire de Reims une victoire éclatante avec un Nieuport augmenté de dimensions, en atteignant la vitesse de 116 km/h 976 contre 95,10 au second.

Et pourtant, Weymann a bien failli ne pas concourir. Il était arrivé par la route sur le lieu du concours très peu de temps avant son ouverture. A sa demande de participer il lui fut répondu par les commissaires qu'il était trop tard pour s'inscrire. « Et si je vole dans 20 minutes ? » propose Weymann. « Dans ce cas nous sommes d'accord », rétorquent les commissaires, persuadés de l'impossibilité de réaliser une telle performance... Et 20 minutes après, Weymann étant prêt, fut admis à concourir. On connaît la suite !

Une conclusion à ces quelques souvenirs. Elle n'est pas de moi mais de Louis Breguet qui, évoquant avec moi la mémoire d'Édouard Nieuport, lors d'un entretien à l'Aéro-Club de France, termina notre entretien par cette affirmation : « Edouard Nieuport, c'était notre maître à tous ».

ground, the brutal shock had thrown him forward (he was not attached) against the little board installed for his map, and ruptured his liver.

When the seriousness of his injury became obvious, Dr. DOYEN, the most eminent surgeon of the day, was telephoned. He came as quickly as he could by car from Paris. But by the time he arrived, NIEUPORT could no longer speak, and he died a quarter of an hour later.

Thus, by an unfortunate combination of circumstances, aviation lost one of its most remarkable pioneers, and this happened precisely at the moment when the most enlightened and generous patron of the period, DEUTSCH de la MEURTHE, having recognized NIEUPORT's exceptional qualities, had just rid him of all financial burdens and decided to build a factory at Issy-les-Moulineux.

In spite of this incontestable calamity, the NIEUPORT Company was going to continue: a month after the tragic accident WEYMANN, a company pilot, achieved a dazzling victory at the military competition in Reims with a larger NIEUPORT, reaching a speed of 116 km/h, 976 against 95.10 achieved by the second place winner.

And yet, WEYMANN had almost missed the race. He had arrived at the starting point by car shortly before the event was to begin. At his request to participate, the marshals had replied that it was too late. "And if I am prepared to fly in 20 minutes?" WEYMANN proposed. "In that case, we agree," they answered, convinced that he could never be ready in time... But 20 minutes later, WEYMANN was admitted. And we know what followed!

As a conclusion to this brief souvenir I quote Louis BREGUET, with whom I was one day recalling Edouard NIEUPORT at the *Aero-Club de France*. BREGUET ended our conversation by insisting: "Edouard NIEUPORT was the master of us all."

ESPANET

LES OBSÈQUES DE NIEUPORT

LE SUPRÊME HOMMAGE AU HÉROS (Plaques Jougla.)

Le mardi 19 septembre ont été célébrées les obsèques du regretté Nieuport. La Légion d'Honneur n'ayant pu lui être officiellement décernée, les honneurs militaires ne lui furent pas rendus. Mais il y avait mieux et l'église de Suresnes était trop petite pour contenir la foule profondément émue où on remarquait toutes les notabilités de l'aviation civile et militaire. — 1. Le général Faurie, représentant le ministre de la guerre, prononce son discours. — 2. Le départ pour la dernière demeure.

The funeral of Edouard NIEUPORT, from *Illustration and Vie au Grand Air*, September 23, 1911.

DISCOURS PRONONCE PAR M. QUINTON

Président de la LIGUE NATIONALE AERIENNE

aux obsèques de l'Ingénieur NIEUPORT

-:-

Messieurs,

L'évènement qui nous réunit ici, devant cette tombe si douloureusement, si injustement ouverte, est un des plus cruels qui puissent être. Depuis la fin tragique du Capitaine FERBER, aucun coup plus sensible n'avait été porté à l'aviation.

Nous avions eu à déplorer, depuis trois ans, la mort d'hommes intrépides dont les exploits furent tels qu'ils resteront légendaires, mais cela est peu de chose que des hommes courageux qui succombent dans un pays producteur d'héroïsme. La mort d'un NIEUPORT, la mort d'un FERBER sont plus graves. Avec eux, des intelligences créatrices disparaissent; et la nature, féconde en courages, l'étant moins en esprits, ce sont là des pertes que rien ne répare et dont l'humanité se trouve appauvrie.

Ce que fut l'oeuvre de NIEUPORT, vous le savez. Vous savez que, mécanicien, physicien, constructeur, il put être l'inventeur de toutes les parties animant ou constituant sa machine. Souvenons-nous surtout que, dès 1909, il réalisait l'engin le plus pénétrant, le plus fin coursier des airs, et, qu'hier encore, il triomphait en vitesse sur un appareil présentant une surface double de ses concurrents.

La mort d'un homme comme NIEUPORT est une véritable perte nationale. Dans une science aussi jeune, qui peut savoir ce que nous réservait un esprit aussi heureux?

Et je ne parlerai point longuement de l'homme, car les paroles sont trop vaines. Vous savez tous ce qu'il fut. Cela c'est une chose douloureuse de penser que tant de distinction, de naturel et de modestie ne sont plus aujourd'hui qu'un souvenir. Aucun de nous n'oubliera cette figure si douce où l'intelligence et l'énergie tranquille le disputaient à la bienveillance et à la bonté.

Au nom de la LIGUE NATIONALE AERIENNE, je prie sa femme, sa mère, son père, tous les siens, d'agréer l'hommage de nos plus douloureux sentiments. Nul plus que nous ne comprend la perte qu'ils viennent de faire dans cette âme d'élit dont la France entière porte le deuil avec eux.

-:-:-:-:-:-:-:- -:- :-

19 Septembre 1911

Funeral Oration given by M. Quinton, president of the *Ligue Nationale Aérienne*.

LIGUE NATIONALE AÉRIENNE

27, RUE DE ROME, PARIS-VIIIe

COMITÉ DIRECTEUR :

Président : RENÉ QUINTON.
Vice-Présidents : ARCHDEACON; DEUTSCH DE LA MEURTHE PAINLEVÉ, de l'Académie des Sciences; Ct Paul RENARD, ancien Directeur du Parc d'Aérostation militaire de Châlais Meudon.
Secrétaire général : L.-N DE CÉLIGNY.
Trésorier : Gaston FRANCHELLI.

Membres : APPELL, de l'Académie des Sciences; ARMENGAUD jeune; d'ARSONVAL, de l'Académie des Sciences; BALLIF, Président du Touring-Club de France; MAURICE BARRÈS, de l'Académie Française; S. A. I. Prince ROLAND BONAPARTE, de l'Académie des Sciences; LOUIS BREGUET, Président de la Section de Douai de la Ligue Nationale Aérienne; Duc de BROGLIE; CARPENTIER, de l'Académie des Sciences; LOUIS DAUSSET, Ancien Président du Conseil Municipal de Paris; MARCEL DEPREZ, de l'Académie des Sciences; DESLANDRES, de l'Académie des Sciences; Marquis DE DION, Député; PAUL DOUMER, Ancien Président de la Chambre des Députés; D'ESTOURNELLES DE CONSTANT, Sénateur de la Sarthe; GABRIEL HANOTAUX, de l'Académie Française; HENRY-COÜANNIER; PAUL HERVIEU, de l'Académie Française; KLEINE, Directeur de l'Ecole Nle des Ponts et Chaussées; ETIENNE LAMY, de l'Académie Française; LÉAUTÉ, de l'Académie des Sciences; E.-A. MARTEL, Ancien Président de la Société de Géographie; MAZURE, Secrétaire du Conseil d'Administration de la Cie des Chemins de Fer P.-L.-M.; ALFRED MAYEN, Ancien Président de l'Union syndicale des Compagnies d'Assurances; ANDRÉ MICHELIN; EDMOND PERRIER, de l'Académie des Sciences; RAYMOND POINCARÉ, ancien Ministre; ANDRÉ RISLER; GUSTAVE RIVES, membre du Conseil d'Administration de l'Automobile-Club de France.

78, RUE CHARLES-LAFFITTE
NEUILLY

Je n'ai pas l'honneur de connaitre tes parents. Je te prie cependant de leur transmettre l'expression de mon respect.
G.D.

Voreppe, Isère
22 Septembre

Mon cher Charles

J'ai voulu attendre que soit passé pour toi et ta famille le flot des condoléances et que ton lourd chagrin se soit, s'il est possible, quelque peu apaisé, pour te dire de quelle grande peine j'ai été envahi à la nouvelle de la mort de mon pauvre ami Edouard ! Dès la nouvelle de son accident apprise ici d'un journal local je lui ai télégraphié à l'hopital de Verdun. Sans doute est-ce toi qui auras pris connaissance de la dépèche. Puis j'apprenais le lendemain matin qu'il était comparativement hors de danger... La surprise pour moi a été d'autant plus rude.

Je plains sa digne et charmante femme ! Tu te souviens peut-être que le pauvre ami m'emmena un jour, il y a six ou sept ans de cela, dans une belle Darracq 4-cylindres là-bas dans ce petit pays du Loir-et-Cher. Et te souviens-tu encore de notre inauguration de cette grande propriété un peu sauvage, les vélos, les motos, les chiens, ma chambre plutôt rudimentaire au premier étage, et "l'ingénieur" Schmidt et Félix Henri ! Dans ce grand calme, ce début d'organisation, Edouard pensait et agissait, silencieux, en bas de cycliste, levé à 4 heures du matin... Tout cela est loin mais lumineusement revenu dans ma pensée à cette minute. Nous nous revoyions souvent dans la suite. Je me suis marié. Il vint quelquefois à la maison. Et un jour qu'il partait par la route au Camp d'Auvours, voir Wright, il voulut m'emmener pour lui servir d'interprète. Son aéroplane est parti de ce voyage.

Ce qu'il voulait il le voulait puissamment. Son esprit de vision, son intelligence, sa façon rapide de concevoir et, au total, sa solide érudition en faisaient un homme remarquable.

Pauvre cher Edouard, toujours un peu triste !

A ton loisir, mon cher Charles, fais-moi donc le plaisir de m'envoyer de tes nouvelles ici. Moi, je lutte toujours, avec assez de courage, mais je ne me fais plus d'illusions...Je suis marqué comme les moutons d'abattoir.

De tout coeur à toi,

Georges Dupuy

Letter to Charles from an old friend of Edouard.

The Cross of the Legion of Honor

Monsieur MESSIMY, who was Minister of War, had decided to submit immediately to the *Président de la République* a decree conferring the Cross of the Legion of Honor on Edouard NIEUPORT, who had been mobilized as a military engineer in the squadron formed by his own planes. When he had heard about the accident, without knowing that it was fatal, Monsieur MESSIMY had left at once for Verdun. It was at the hospital that he learned of the pilot's death, and without delay he pinned the Cross of the Legion of Honor on the sheet covering Edouard NIEUPORT's body. He then sent a telegram to the President of the Republic:

Having learned of the military aviator NIEUPORT's accident, and having signed yesterday at ten o'clock in the evening the decree to be submited to you with the utmost urgency by an aide-de-camp, this morning I myself carried the decoration to the military hospital at Verdun where this reserve engineer had been taken. I learned on arriving that he was dead. I felt I was doing the right thing, and even responding to my own instincts, by placing the Cross of the Legion of Honor on the victim's chest in the presence of his comrades and family, and by determining that the honors due to the legionnaire would be conferred.

A controversy led by General FLORENTIN, *grand chancelier* of the Legion of Honor, promptly ensued. In fact, until that time no Cross of the Legion of Honor had ever been bestowed posthumously. General FLORENTIN, standing on ceremony, refused to countersign the decree.

The world of aviation, as well as the press, shocked by this incomprehensible refusal, vigorously protested and urged that the rules of this institution reserved for the nation's heroes be immediately changed. In face of widespread indignation, the *grande chancellerie* ceded and, exceptionally, allowed this particular decoration to be awarded posthumously.

L'arrivée à Paris

Le cercueil contenant le corps de Nieuport est arrivé à la gare de l'Est par le rapide de 1 h. 42.

Etaient présents sur le quai à l'arrivée du train : Mme Nieuport, veuve de l'aviateur; son beau-père; son frère; M. Delanney, préfet de la Seine; un officier représentant le ministre de la Guerre; M. Etienne, député, ancien ministre; plusieurs membres de l'Aéro Club de France; les pilotes de la maison Nieuport; l'aviateur Hélen; de nombreuses personnalités sportives, etc.

Une foule émue se découvrait sur le passage de la famille en larmes.

Le cercueil, extrait du fourgon, a été placé sur une voiture des pompes funèbres, et dirigé sur les établissements Nieuport, à Suresnes.

Les obsèques ont lieu ce matin, à 11 heures. On se réunira à la maison mortuaire, 9, rue de Seine, à Suresnes.

Left: Description of the arrival of Nieuport's coffin.

Following: Newspaper articles concerning General FLORENTIN's refusal to award the Cross of the Legion of Honor.

LE GÉNÉRAL FLORENTIN

Grand-Chancelier de la Légion d'Honneur

REFUSE LA CROIX DE NIEUPORT

VERDUN, 17 septembre. (*Par dépêche.*) — En rentrant ce soir, à cinq heures, des magnifiques manœuvres du 6e corps d'armée, j'apprends par un télégramme personnel de Paris que M. le général Florentin, grand-chancelier de la Légion d'honneur, refuse de contresigner le décret conférant la croix de chevalier de la Légion d'honneur à l'aviateur Nieuport.

Je veux exprimer tout de suite dans le *Journal* l'indignation qui éclatera demain matin, dès que cette invraisemblable nouvelle sera connue du public.

En effet, les raisons invoquées par M. le général Florentin pour justifier son opposition ne peuvent être fondées que sur un seul fait : Nieuport avait cessé de vivre au moment où M. Messimy a épinglé sur sa poitrine l'étoile des braves, et une interprétation récente des règlements de l'Ordre interdit les décorations posthumes. Même en admettant le bien-fondé de cette interprétation, l'application qui en est faite à l'héroïque victime du camp de Charny repose sur une grave erreur matérielle.

Nieuport était vivant lorsque le ministre de la guerre a présenté et lorsque le Président de la République a signé le décret prescrivant son inscription sur les contrôles de l'Ordre. En effet, il est tombé vendredi. Prévenu aussitôt de l'accident et de sa gravité, M. Messimy, qui s'apprêtait précisément à partir pour la Meuse, a fait préparer d'urgence le décret de nomination et l'a fait porter le jour même par un de ses officiers d'ordonnance à Rambouillet, où M. Fallières s'est empressé de le signer séance tenante.

Il y a mieux. Samedi matin, à six heures, lorsque M. Messimy arrivait à Verdun, son premier soin fut de s'informer du blessé et on lui donna l'assurance que son état s'était plutôt amélioré pendant la nuit. Le ministre en exprima toute sa satisfaction et ajouta :

— Puisqu'il en est ainsi, allons à la manœuvre. En descendant de cheval je me rendrai à l'hôpital militaire et je remettrai moi-même au sapeur Nieuport la croix de chevalier de la Légion d'honneur que lui décerne le gouvernement de la République.

En réalité, le malheureux Nieuport a expiré à 9 h. 5 du matin, pendant que le ministre, sur la route de Damvillers, se rendait compte du degré de préparation et d'entraînement de nos corps frontières.

Voilà uniquement pourquoi M. le général Florentin estime qu'il n'est pas décorable et refuse d'apposer son visa sur le décret déjà signé par le ministre et par le Président de la République.

Si M. le grand-chancelier avait assisté aux funérailles de Nieuport comme je l'ai fait moi-même ce matin, en compagnie du général Roques, de presque tous les aviateurs civils et militaires encore présents dans les casernes et les forts de notre grand camp retranché; s'il avait pu entendre les sanglots qui secouaient toute cette foule, à commencer par les

LE GÉNÉRAL FLORENTIN

petits soldats du piquet d'honneur, pendant le discours que le général Roques, les yeux embués de larmes et le cœur serré d'angoisse, ne parvenait pas à achever, il comprendrait peut-être comment sa décision va être accueillie par l'armée, par la région de l'Est et par le pays tout entier.

Ainsi donc, si ce soldat, tué en service commandé après avoir comme constructeur doté sa patrie d'un instrument de guerre que les connaisseurs disent merveilleux, a reçu les honneurs institués par Napoléon comme la suprême récompense du mérite militaire et civil, ce fut par erreur. Vraiment, pendant que M. le grand-chancelier est en veine de formalisme, il ne lui reste plus qu'à faire ouvrir le cercueil pour en retirer l'insigne que porte illégalement, d'après lui, le corps rompu de l'infortuné et glorieux Nieuport !

Tandis que j'écris ces lignes, les manœuvres de l'air continuent. Trois autres aviateurs militaires viennent de passer à toute vitesse sur leurs biplans de course, au-dessus des arbres. J'aime mieux ne pas essayer d'imaginer l'indignation qu'ils éprouveront demain, quand ils sauront.

Après tout, peu importe. La mort héroïque de Nieuport a été suffisamment glorifiée. Sa famille en deuil a été suffisamment réconfortée par la foule qui a salué ce matin son cercueil. Le ministre de la guerre et le Président de la République avaient fidèlement traduit en la circonstance le sentiment unanime de la nation. Le geste du général Florentin, empêchant la réalisation de leur dessein, n'aura d'autre effet que de froisser sans raison le cœur de tous les Français.

CHARLES HUMBERT,
Sénateur.

L'INCIDENT MESSIMY-FLORENTIN

Nieuport n'est pas décoré

Encore que la croix figurât hier sur le cercueil de Nieuport, l'aviateur défunt n'est pas décoré. Il ne le sera pas. On nous l'a dit à la grande chancellerie.

— Les règlements sont formels. On peut le regretter. Mais tant qu'ils n'auront pas été modifiés, le rôle du grand chancelier sera simple : les faire appliquer. Or le conseil de l'ordre ne peut approuver une décoration que si le bénéficiaire est encore vivant au moment de la signature par le président de la République. Nous avons été saisis de la proposition, cela est indiscutable, lorsque Nieuport n'était déjà plus. Nous en sommes au désespoir, car c'était plus qu'un intrépide aviateur : c'était un véritable homme de science et un grand inventeur.

Aux obsèques pourtant, la croix reposait sur la couronne et le général Faurie attestait qu'elle avait été bien gagnée

Nous avons aussi demandé à M. Messimy ce qu'il allait advenir de cet incident. Le ministre de la guerre nous a répondu :

— L'incident est clos. Le général Florentin invoque des règlements. Soit ! Les textes sont, en effet, pour lui... Mais si j'avais, moi aussi, suivi les textes, j'aurais dû demander, avant de donner ma signature, celle du général Roques : et la procédure aurait pris quatre jours !

» Donc, aujourd'hui, admettons que le règlement l'ait emporté. Mais nous nous retrouverons ! »

Ainsi parla M. Messimy, qui semblait fort mécontent.

La Croix de Nieuport

SERA ACCORDÉE

Les motifs du retard. — Ce que l'on dit à la grande chancellerie

On sait qu'après le terrible accident dont fut victime le sapeur-aviateur Nieuport, M. Messimy, ministre de la Guerre, s'était rendu au chevet du mourant et avait épinglé sur sa poitrine la croix de la Légion d'honneur.

Tous les amis du célèbre aviateur et tout le monde de l'aviation étaient unanimes à reconnaître que ce dernier hommage était mérité par celui qui fut à la fois un habile constructeur et un audacieux pilote d'aéroplanes.

Or, le bruit s'est répandu que M. Florentin, grand chancelier de la Légion d'honneur avait refusé de contresigner le décret conférant la croix de la Légion d'honneur au sapeur Nieuport.

A la grande Chancellerie, où nous nous sommes rendu ce matin, on nous a répondu :

— Aucune décision n'a encore été prise au sujet de la croix de l'aviateur Nieuport. Le grand chancelier est en ce moment en villégiature dans le Jura, c'est ce qui explique le retard apporté dans la décision du conseil. Vous pouvez affirmer que le décret n'a pas été signé par le président de la République avant d'être communiqué à la Chancellerie. Si le fait s'était produit, nous n'aurions pu que confirmer la décision du chef de l'Etat. Il existe bien un règlement ne permettant pas de conférer l'ordre de la Légion d'hnoneur à des morts, mais, sans aucun doute, ce règlement sera contourné et le décret sera signé.

Tout le monde est convaincu que le conseil de l'Ordre, obéissant aux mêmes sentiments que le ministre de la guerre, prendra une décision en faveur du héros qui mourut au champ d'honneur.

When the legislative assembly reconvened in 1911 the deputies, conscious of the deficiency in the rules, immediately enacted a law legalizing all posthumous awards of military decorations.

Just before his death, after long years of struggle and persistent effort, Edouard NIEUPORT had, it seemed, attained his goal. The outstanding engineer, having abandoned the electrical engineering aspects of the automobile in which he had become an expert, had succeeded in producing airplanes that were beginning to be just as much appreciated by civilian aviation as by the military. Encouraged by his first triumphs and having found substantial financial backing, he was hoping to obtain, at last, the consecration of his efforts by participating in the military competitions then being organized by the Army. He had been urged to leave the piloting to others, but he was an extremely skilled aviator who was also an extraordinarily clever technician. He knew his airplanes down to their least details. To him it was inconceivable not to pilot those craft himself, so as to gain maximum advantages from their qualities. The risks to which he was exposed seemed negligible when compared to the necessity of experiencing himself the results of the research that occupied his mind both night and day. By an accident which, when all is said and done, was quite banal, destiny saw to it that the dream of the passionate engineer came to a dead halt, violently shattered on an airfield near Verdun.

L'aviateur Nieuport était un savant et un héros

Le général Roques l'a justement dit hier à Verdun, près du cercueil de l'aviateur, cependant qu'un dirigeable évoluait au-dessus du cortège.

(De notre correspondant particulier, par dépêche)

Verdun, 17 septembre. — Les obsèques de Nieuport sont terminées, et je ne puis vous en retracer l'émouvante grandeur.

Le cortège s'est formé devant l'hôpital. Le char funèbre était encadré de soldats du 162e de ligne. Les couronnes étaient portées par des délégations de toutes les troupes de la place.

Immédiatement après marchaient les deux frères de la victime, dont l'énergie ne parvenait pas à dominer la douleur.

Puis le général Roques, M. Humbert, sénateur; les autorités civiles; plus de trois cents officiers en tenue, les aviateurs militaires; enfin les délégations des différentes armes de la place, formant un total de près de 4.000 hommes environ.

Sur le parcours du cortège, la foule rassemblée salue avec émotion le cercueil du héros qu'elle acclamait, vivant, hier encore. On n'entend que le pas lent et cadencé des chevaux. Les musiques militaires étant retenues aux manœuvres, c'est sans l'accompagnement habituel des marches funèbres que se fit le douloureux voyage. Mais le silence rendait plus manifeste encore le deuil de tous ces chefs, de tous ces soldats, de tous ces citadins inclinés devant la même fatalité.

A la gare, le général Roques prononça un discours dont nous extrayons le passage suivant :

Entre les trop nombreux aviateurs que la mort nous dérobe, nous ne saurions faire de différence. Ils meurent avec le même courage, leur dévouement est le même, notre cœur souffre de la même douleur.

Pourtant, lorsque celui qui disparait est, en même temps que l'aviateur le plus habile et le plus déterminé, un ingénieur consommé, qui a donné d'étonnantes preuves de science et qui a consacré avec un succès tous les jours plus éclatant ses admirables facultés à l'étude de l'aviation, pourtant alors, nous ne pouvons nous empêcher de mesurer toute l'étendue de la perte.

Ce sentiment que quelque chose de fort, qu'un germe de progrès a disparu, nous l'avons éprouvé lors de la mort du capitaine Tarron; il nous étreint, aujourd'hui que vient de disparaître Nieuport, dont les travaux ont établi la réputation mondiale.

Je connaissais Nieuport, mais je le connus mieux, je le compris, le jour où les difficultés de la lutte, les coups de la fortune adverse conduisirent un cœur de mère dans mon bureau.

Il avait enfin surmonté tous les obstacles, il réussissait. Un homme supérieurement intelligent et bon, que les choses de l'air passionnent, l'avait compris, lui aussi, et l'avait mis en situation de poursuivre la réalisation de ses admirables conceptions.

Jusqu'au dernier moment, la mort, qui l'a si cruellement frappé, a respecté son beau cerveau ; et ce n'est pas sans une poignante émotion que j'ai entendu Nieuport, près de mourir, me demander des nouvelles du camarade Latham, qu'il croyait en route par ce vent qui l'avait abattu. Ce savant, ce héros est venu mourir dans cette place forte de Verdun, dans ce boulevard de la patrie, dont la population, comme les aviateurs à l'égard de la mort, envisage avec gravité, mais sans le redouter, le jour du suprême sacrifice.

La mémoire de Nieuport restera gravée dans le cœur de tous les Français, parmi le souvenir de ceux qu'a chantés le poète : « Ceux qui, pieusement, meurent pour la patrie. »

Pendant qu'un dernier adieu était dit devant le cercueil, par le directeur des services de l'aéronautique militaire, un dirigeable, *Le-Temps*, vint planer au-dessus de nous.

Newspater article: The Aviator NIEUPORT was a Scientist and a Hero

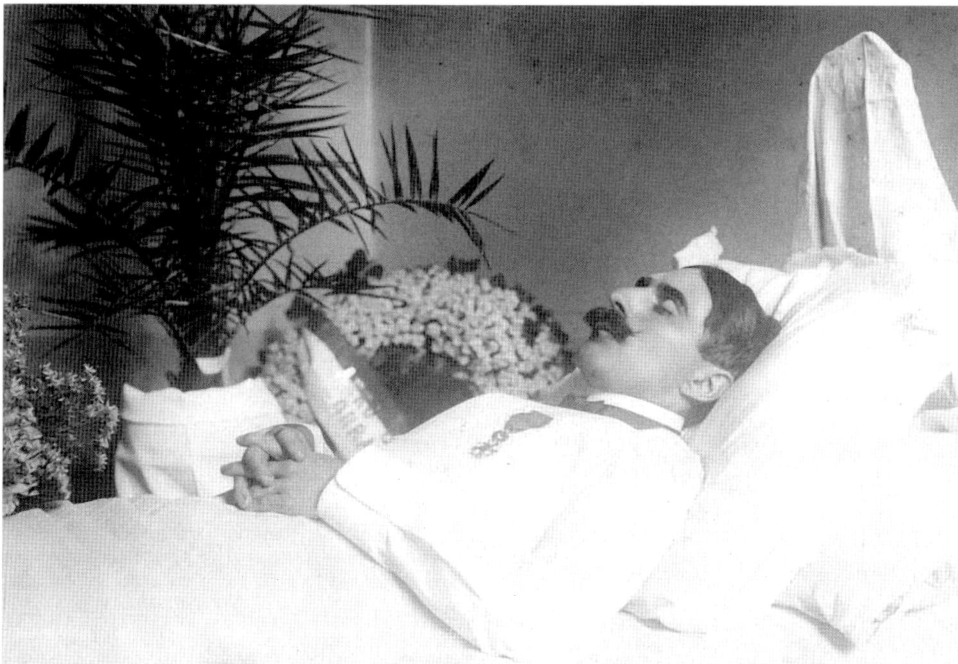

Edouard NIEUPORT on his deathbed in Verdun.

Charles Continues His Brother's Work

His brutal disappearance plunged the little factory on the rue de Seine into deep mourning, but the energy of Edouard NIEUPORT's associates never slackened, because their path had been marked out and they all knew that, in spite of their grief, the passionate adventure was far from over. They, too, possessed the enthusiasm and vitality for projecting themselves into the future.

According to the people around him, Charles NIEUPORT's deep admiration for his brother bordered on worship. Above all, he wanted the name NIEUPORT to remain associated with the important work his sibling had undertaken. Dynamic and determined, he himself climbed into an airplane immediately after Edouard's death. He did not have the talents required for becoming an outstanding pilot, yet he understood that thanks to willpower he could still accomplish wonders. Never com-

Hôtel Hirschen-Post
Inhaber:
FRIEDRICH HIRTLER
Telephon Nr. 20.
Telegramm-Adresse: POST-HOTEL.

Endingen a. K., 5 Octobre 1911

Mon cher Charles,

J'ai été vivement impressionné en lisant les journaux qui relataient votre arrivée à Issy avec Hélen. Je comprends que vous vouliez que votre nom ne soit pas oublié mais maintenant que c'est fait c'est suffisant. Bien que vous puissiez me dire que je me mele de ce qui ne me regarde pas, je croirais manquer à mon devoir en ne vous disant pas ce que je pense.

Il vous faut renoncer completement à monter en aéroplane pour le moment vous avez mieux à faire. Occupez vous de la maison mais <u>ne montez pas</u>. Vous vous devez à vos parents très éprouvés aussi bien comme appui moral que comme appui matériel.

si cela était nécessaire par la suite. Enfin
vos fonctions nouvelles de tuteur du petit vous
obligent aussi à certains devoirs dont le
premier est de ne pas venir à manquer à ce
petit auprès de qui vous devez remplacer
le cher papa qui n'est plus —

Si toutes ces raisons qui ne sont d'ailleurs
que des devoirs ne suffisent pas à vous
convaincre, il ne me reste plus qu'à vous
supplier à mon nom personnel et aussi bien
à celui de vos parents de leur épargner
les émotions terribles que vous leur donneriez,
en renonçant définitivement à monter.

Je vous embrasse bien affectueusement.

Jean Guimet

Letter from Jean GUIMET, after the death of Edouard's death, implores Charles not to fly.

Chère Maman,

Enfin je trouve un moment pour vous écrire. Je n'ai pas voulu le faire avant, pendant que j'étais aux manœuvres car j'espérais que vous l'ignoriez ce que je faisais et ne voulais pas être une cause de craintes pour vous à cette époque cet affreux anniversaire.

Tout s'est bien passé. Je crois avoir bien fait mon devoir.

Je regrette de ne pas avoir été avec vous à la douloureuse cérémonie mais je crois avoir fait la plus belle manifestation que je pouvais faire

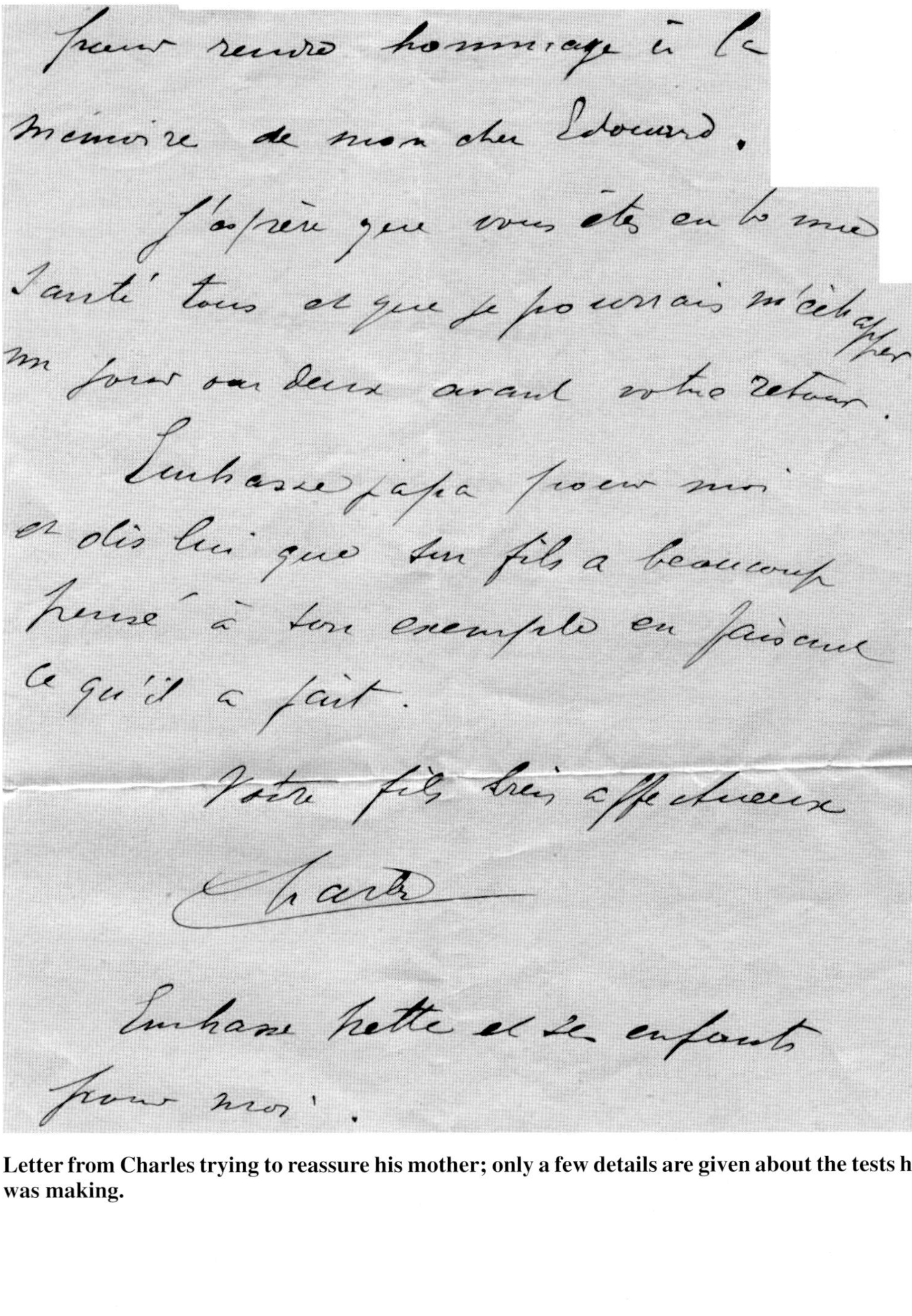

pour rendre hommage à la
mémoire de mon cher Edouard.

J'espère que vous êtes en bonne
santé tous et que je pourrais m'échapper
un jour ou deux avant votre retour.

Embrasse papa pour moi
et dis lui que ton fils a beaucoup
pensé à ton exemple en faisant
ce qu'il a fait.

Votre fils très affectueux

Charles

Embrasse Nette et ses enfants
pour moi.

Letter from Charles trying to reassure his mother; only a few details are given about the tests he was making.

Charles NIEUPORT in the cockpit of a 4G shortly after he obtained his pilot's license.

pletely at ease in the air, he overcame an instinctive fear against which there is generally no remedy. He received his civilian pilot's license on January 22, 1912, under Number 742. He subsequently participated brilliantly in various military maneuvers. Very much appreciated and aided by his associates, he vigorously ensured the company's continued development.

Those closest to him tried in vain to dissuade Charles from flying, but he paid no attention. So as not to upset his parents, he did not tell them about his flying activities until after they had taken place. The letters he received from members of his family reflect their apprehension, but the advice and entreaties had no effect.

Charles NIEUPORT took over the management of the firm, backed financially by the most important patron of aviation, Henry DEUTSCH de la MEURTHE, who bought up all of Edouard NIEUPORT's patents and created the limited company *Etablissements NIEUPORT.*

Léon BAZAINE was appointed commercial director, and Gustave DE LA FRESNAY became head of the techni-

Gustave DELAGE at the beginning of his military career.

cal department. While retaining Edouard NIEUPORT's original designs, the engineer DELAGE was able to provide the necessary impetus for creating all the future NIEUPORT airplanes.

A new factory was built at Issy-les-Moulineaux, and a Flight School was set up in Villacoublay. Very rapidly the factory acquired an industrial dimension, as it started to produce the ten planes ordered by the Army after Weymann's victory at the military competition in Reims, details of which will follow.

The NIEUPORT aircraft interested not only the French government, but foreign ones, as well. Several planes were sold to Russia, Sweden, Italy, and Great Britain. Some time afterwards, the "8 G" would be built as a "licensed product" in Italy by the Machi company.

Posthumous Triumph

The military competition in Reims was the major aviation event of 1911. It was organized by General ROQUES, inspector of military aeronautics, who was responsible for equipping the recent invention with engines adapted to the army's requirements. At the time, the role envisaged for the airplane was to carry out reconnaissance missions for observing enemy troop movements. These planes were to be two-seaters and easy to transport and operate. They had to be capable of taking off and landing on unprepared fields, and the observer aboard needed perfect visibility. Finally, of course, the plane, including its motorization, had to be 100% French.

As far as the performances demanded in the competition, the program was extremely comprehensive. The planes had to be able to complete, nonstop, a 300 kilometer circuit at more than 60 kilometers per hour with 300 kilograms of live load. The winner would be rewarded by the purchase of his plane for 10,000 francs and a subsequent order of ten identical planes, each costing 40,000 francs.

Forty-three airplane constructors entered the eliminatory events presenting a total of 140 planes. Charles NIEUPORT came with the "4 G" NIEUPORT monoplane equipped

Assembly of a 4G at the Reims competition.

with a rotary 100 hp engine, which would be piloted by WEYMANN. The plane could embark two passengers seated side by side behind the pilot. Its tare was 485 kg and its airfoil 22 m^2.

Two years earlier, the Champagne airfield had been the scene of the first and most important aeronautical event ever organized, and had offered to astonished crowds the unforgettable spectacle of the original "bird-men."

On October 1, 1911, the first day of the eliminatory trials, the French Army had brought together every example of the aircraft and engines that the robust genius of the country's constructors had conceived during the previous two years.

In fact, this first military competition would mark an important milestone in the aviation industry: after the eliminatory trials there remained thirty airplanes of different designs.

The planes were housed in hangars built to the south of the magnificent airfield, located just outside Reims in Bétheny. The military terrain was a vast 700 hectares (1,729 acres), and the pilots could overshoot the state's property without any risk. To the right of the entrance, charming little buildings housing various services of the Army Post Office, Telegraph, and Press had been arranged in a semicircle. They surrounded a large garden, in the middle of which an iron pylon had been erected for French Radio.

The Selection Committee was headed by General ROQUES, and was composed of a large number of engineers and military aviators who carried out the inspection of the aircraft.

Each constructor met the commission members—led in their peregrinations by General ROQUES—at the door of his hangar, and provided them with information regarding his planes.

The entire month of October was devoted to official trials, which took place in more or less difficult conditions, assessing take-off, landing, climbing time, and speed.

The NIEUPORT plane was thus competing with twenty-nine others, including some redoutable adversaries.

From the first day the NIEUPORT "4 G" stood out from its rivals. At the beginning of the eliminatory trials, WEYMANN was the only pilot to complete in one day the two landing trials separated by the transport of his plane by a truck.

Taking off from Reims for Montcasnet at ten o'clock, he returned with his dismantled plane, reassembled it, and again took off from Reims at four o'clock. Following this impressive accomplishment, WEYMANN became the only pilot able to lift off from a plowed field without any help other than that given by his passenger. And he did not hesitate to repeat this feat a third time to demonstrate that he had not benefitted from favorable circumstances.

The committee remarked on the ease with which the NIEUPORT lifted off the obligatory weight and noted that on landing, after flying 300 km, it still had 55 liters of gasoline and 18 liters of oil, or more than 50 kg.

It had, therefore, completed all the trials with 50 kg more than the 300 kg specified in the rules. Thus overloaded, it was the only plane to pass the altitude test straightaway, climbing to 500 meters in only 10 minutes.

By the end of the month, the eliminatory trials were over and the NIEUPORT "4 G" had come in first in all the events.

Preparations for take-off.

On November 20 there remained the 300 km course, in which only speed and the planes' efficiency would be compared. The final take offs were delayed because of bad weather, but this contest had, for all intents and purposes, been decided ten days earlier.

From the beginning the NIEUPORT plane had performed brilliantly, and it again proved its superiority by leaving its rivals far behind in this last event. The 300 km were covered by the NIEUPORT, piloted by Weymann, in 2 hours 36 minutes, which represented an average speed of around 116 km per hour.

The NIEUPORT, taking first place once again with the same ease it had displayed in winning the previous trials, had proved itself to be the best military plane.

The organizers of the Reims Competition had reached these reassuring conclusions: France was the country possessing the best airplanes for responding to military needs; and they were superior in both speed and safety.

It was to respond to these requirements that the competition had been held, and that such difficult conditions of landing, dismantling, and taking off with only the crew's assis-

Gunning the engine, ready for take-off!

Weymann being weighed before an event at the Reims competition.

Weymann overseeing the tuning of his engine.

The 4G in flight during military competition of Reims.

tance, of speed and altitude had been imposed. It was said that the demands made on even the best airplanes pushed them almost beyond their limits. That seems true, and only adds to the value of the success achieved by a craft that Edouard NIEUPORT had conceived already two years earlier.

The final trial (the cross country flight of three hundred kilometers) showed especially that his plane offered a primordial quality for a military craft: speed.

This inestimable advantage made it possible to carry out rapid reconnaissance missions and launch projectiles, and also to have a better chance of escaping enemy fire.

WEYMANN AU CONCOURS D'AVIATION MILITAIRE [1]

Le Concours d'aviation militaire touche à sa fin, tout au moins pour les épreuves éliminatoires. C'est, en effet, le 31 octobre que les opérations seront terminées. 31 concurrents avaient été admis à prendre part à cette compétition nationale. Les conditions étaient tellement rigoureuses, que bien peu d'appareils ont pu s'y soumettre. Ils se disputeront la première place dans la course de 300 kilomètres qui sera organisée dans le courant de novembre. C'est le monoplan Nieuport piloté par Weymann, qui est parvenu à passer le premier toutes les éliminatoires et à se qualifier pour l'épreuve finale. Ce succès était d'autant plus beau, que pas un monoplan n'avait encore réussi une seule épreuve. (Détails techniques : monoplan Nieuport, hélice intégrale Chauvière.)

Mes impressions sur le Concours Militaire

Par CHARLEY WEYMANN

Weymann va partir.

Le Concours d'aviation militaire a été remporté par Weymann, qui a accompli le parcours de 300 kilomètres sans escale, à une moyenne de 117 kilomètres à l'heure.

Charley Weymann.

Charley Weymann, qui a remporté cette année la coupe Gordon-Bennett et le Concours d'aviation militaire.

Nous avons demandé au vainqueur du Concours d'aviation militaire, Charley Weymann qui, cette année, s'est déjà attribué la victoire dans la Coupe Gordon-Bennett, de nous donner ses impressions sur la grande épreuve qui vient de faire faire un progrès important à la quatrième arme.

Mes impressions sur le concours militaire? Je dois vous dire que, vu les résultats pour moi, elles sont excellentes... Mais je ne pense pas que ce soit là ce que vous me demandez.

Parlons d'abord du règlement. On peut déclarer qu'il était aussi bon qu'il était possible de le faire il y a un an. Demander à un appareil d'emporter 300 kilos de charge utile, deux passagers et de l'essence pour 300 kilomètres, c'était, à cette époque, presque une utopie. Et c'est là le grand mérite de la commission, d'avoir courageusement posé un problème qui, résolu, devait et a fait faire un si grand pas à l'aviation.

Des résultats du concours, nous pouvons déduire que la France a maintenant — et cela très en avance sur tous les autres pays — un appareil qui porte très facilement, par n'importe quel temps, un observateur au moins et de quoi parcourir 5 à 600 kilomètres sans escale, à une vitesse moyenne dépassant le 100 à l'heure. C'est là un résultat splendide et presque inespéré. Pour ma part, j'ai effectué le trajet de 300 kilomètres avec, outre la charge réglementaire, de l'essence et de l'huile pour plus de 400 kilomètres.

Je dois avouer, qu'avant d'avoir eu en mains l'admirable engin qu'avait conçu le génial Nieuport pour le concours, j'étais un peu sceptique sur sa maniabilité. Je m'étais outrageusement trompé : jamais je n'ai éprouvé la moindre difficulté à le piloter et je suis certain que les officiers qui auront à le monter se montreront tout aussi enthousiastes que moi.

Weymann se fait peser.

Le lieutenant Ménard pèse Weymann qui suit les diverses phases de la manœuvre avec un certain intérêt.

Weymann félicité après la victoire.

Le commandant Labadie félicite Weymann qui, sur son monoplan Nieuport, vient d'accomplir les 300 kilomètres sans escale en 2 heures 34 minutes.

My Impressions of the Military Competition, by Charley Weymann.

ıvons dit hier l'exploit qu'avait accompli Weymann dans la seconde épreuve finale du ırs militaire d'aviation, à Reims. Il a couvert en deux heures et demie les 300 kilomètres du parcours imposé, soit une moyenne de 120 kilomètres à l'heure. C'est une des p formances que l'aviation ait jamais enregistrées. Nous publions ici des photograp mann et des autres concurrents de l'épreuve, prises à leur départ ou à leur arrivée.

: DÉPART DE WEYMANN SUR SON MONOPLAN, MOTEUR GNOME. LE SIGNAL DU DÉPART EST DONNÉ PAR UN OFFICIER AGITANT LE DRAPEAU TRICOLORE. — 2. PRÉVOST A SON ARRIVÉE. IL S'EST CLASSÉ SEC ERDUSSIN-GNOME. — 3. FISCHER. CLASSÉ TROISIÈME SUR SON BIPLAN MOTEUR GNOME. — 4. BARRA. QUATRIÈME SUR SON BIPLAN MOTEUR RENAULT. — 5. RENAUX. CLASSÉ CINQUIÈME SUR SON BIPLAN MOT

Weymann at the starting line with Prévost, Fischer, Barra, and Renaux.

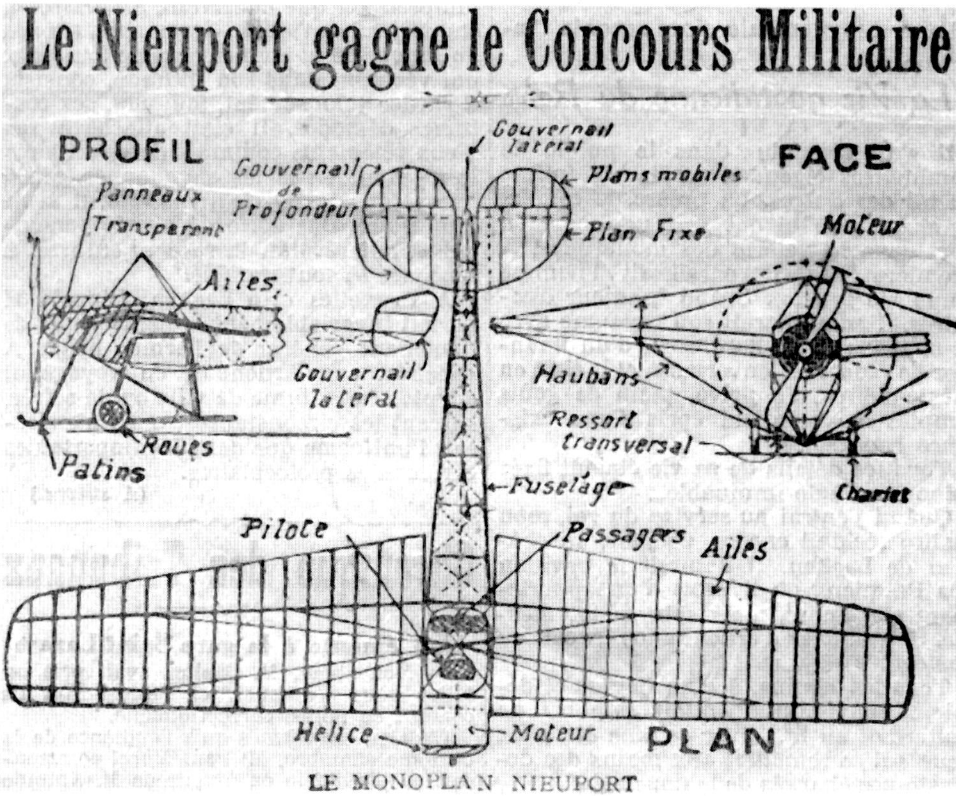

Two drawings: the NIEUPORT monoplane and the Gnome engine.

Le temps a bien voulu, hier, sinon s'apaiser complètement, du moins calmer ses fureurs, et les neuf appareils qualifiés pour la finale du concours d'aviation militaire ont pu partir de Reims et tenter le parcours Reims-Amiens-Reims, soit 300 kilomètres, sur lequel se disputait la finale.

Les temps mis par les appareils servant de base de classement, voici comme s'établit celui-ci :

Le Classement

1. Monoplan Nieuport (Gnome 100 chevaux), pilote Weymann. Temps : 2 h. 32 m.
2. Monoplan Deperdussin (Gnome 100 chevaux), pilote Prévost. Temps : 3 h. 15 m.
3. Biplan H. Farman (Gnome 100 chevaux), pilote Fischer.
4. Biplan M. Farman, pilote Barra.
5. Biplan M. Farman, pilote Renaux.

La vitesse moyenne de Weymann est de 120 kilomètres, avec un appareil pesant près de 1,000 kilos.

Voici quelques détails sur les appareils classés :

L'appareil vainqueur

Commençons par le vainqueur, le Nieuport. C'est un appareil monoplan, de 23 mètres de surface, de 12 mètres d'envergure. Longueur totale, 7 m. 50 ; profondeur des plans principaux, 2 m. 50 ; empennage, 3 m. et 1 m. 30.

Le chariot d'atterrissage est constitué par deux roues, reliées par un ressort à lames transversal, analogue aux ressorts de voitures, et formant essieu.

Le moteur, placé à l'avant, avec l'hélice montée directement et sans démultiplication sur l'axe, est un 14 cylindres Gnome, rotatif, d'une force nominale de 100 chevaux, avec bougies Oléo. Il y a deux rangs de sept cylindres, en étoile, et les cylindres du second rang sont placés entre les branches de l'étoile formée par le premier rang.

Les trois places sont en triangle, le pilote à l'avant, les passagers derrière. Le pilote commande avec le même levier, en laiton, les deux gouvernails, de profondeur et de direction latérale, placés à l'arrière.

Le fuselage est l'une des parties les plus originales et les plus réussies du Nieuport. Tout a été ramené le plus possible au centre, et la section de l'appareil figure assez bien un énorme poisson, où tout est dissimulé, de façon à réduire au minimum la résistance à l'avancement. Deux pédales indépendantes commandent le gauchissement des ailes, chaque déformation d'une aile amenant automatiquement une déformation de l'autre aile, [illegible] rétablit l'équilibre.

Le gouvernail de profondeur est formé de deux ailerons mobiles horizontaux, faisant suite à un empennage fixe, le tout de forme ellipsoïde. Le gouvernail latéral est un plan vertical, placé au-dessus du fuselage, à l'arrière.

Le poids total de l'appareil, tel qu'il a pris part au concours, en charge, est de 950 kilos environ, se décomposant en 470 kilos à vide et 480 kilos de poids utile transportable. Nous atteignons donc et nous dépassons même 40 kilos au mètre carré. Les ailes sont donc solides, malgré leur légèreté relative. A l'avant du fuselage sur l'aile, des panneaux transparents permettent d'observer le sol.

Le second

C'est encore un nouvel appareil, il date d'un an, le Deperdussin monté par Prévost, qui enlève la seconde place. L'appareil s'est montré un peu moins rapide que le Nieuport, c'est-à-dire que l'appareil le plus rapide du monde. Prévost s'est d'ailleurs égaré en route, ayant perdu sa carte, sinon l'écart eût été plus faible.

Nous avons donné déjà tous les détails de construction des Deperdussin, nous n'y reviendrons donc point. Ce bel et solide oiseau est le frère de celui que Vidart mena si souvent à la victoire dans le Circuit. Il est muni du même moteur Gnome à bougie Oléo.

Son ingénieur est M. Bechereau, un modeste qui est en train de devenir un des grands noms de l'aviation. M. Deperdussin, par son énergie et sa volonté, a placé sa jeune marque dans les premières du monde.

Les troisièmes

Du jour où trois monoplans furent qualifiés, disions-nous, la finale étant une course de vitesse, il était imposible que l'un d'entre eux ne fût pas vainqueur. Cependant les Farman n'en remportent pas moins un splendide succès. Ils ont trois appareils classés sur cinq, comme ils en avaient trois sur les neuf de la finale. Quand on songe qu'il y eut 31 appareils au début, qu'il en reste cinq et que les Farman en ont trois, on ne peut s'empêcher de dire que les champions du biplan se sont défendus en maîtres. Leurs moteurs plus faibles, leur voilure plus grande leur interdisaient tout autre espoir que celui de la régularité. L'équipe finit en position [illegible] perbe.

Les Prix

Voici la liste des prix gagnés par les trois maisons classées :

Maison Nieuport : achat de l'appareil vainqueur : 100,000 fr. Commande de 10 appareils à 40,000 fr., soit 400,000 fr. Prime de 10,000 fr. au maximum par appareil si la vitesse atteint 80 kilomètres à l'heure, soit 100,000 fr. Total : 600,000 fr.

Maison Deperdussin : commande de 6 appareils à 30,000 fr. et 10,000 fr. de prime par appareil, soit 240,000 fr.

Maison Farman : commande de 4 appareils dans les mêmes conditions, soit 160,000 francs.

Total : 21 appareils de commandés et 900,030 francs de prix.

C'est donc près d'un million de francs de subvention que la guerre vient de donner à l'aviation française qui, une fois de plus, a devancé toutes les autres en résolvant ce nouveau problème : le premier poids lourd de l'air. — GEORGES PRADE.

Newspaper article concerning Weymann's victory in the NIEUPORT monoplane.

What was remarkable about the NIEUPORT plane was that this superiority in speed had been obtained simply by studying the best shapes for improving efficiency, without sacrificing any of the plane's solidity. The victories won in the Gordon-Bennett Cup, the Michelin Cup, and many other competitions had already confirmed these qualities.

The triumph of the NIEUPORT in the final 300 km event at Reims had not surprised the insiders. They remembered that in the European Circuit, WEYMANN had flown non-stop from Paris to Utrech before abandoning the race so as to compete in the GORDON-BENNETT event in England, which he won. If the NIEUPORT Company had been able to finance the costly organization necessary for participating in the important cross country competitions taking place at the time, it would certainly have won many more prizes.

Humorous drawing of Weymann.

The Posthumus Triumph.

Even the best designed and built flying machine can do nothing extraordinary unless the engine gives it life. If it is to fly nonstop over hundreds of kilometers at fantastic speeds and run smoothly all the way, it needs an engine that can respond to the enormous demands made on it and function at full power without the slightest hitch as long as the pilot requires it. It was Edouard NIEUPORT who had chosen the 100 hp Gnome engine, and his successors never had reason to regret it.

This superb performance of the NIEUPORT monoplane with the GNOME engine, which WEYMANN had piloted to victory, created a considerable stir throughout the world and was going to have considerable commerical consequences for the two companies that had collaborated for this achievement, one in building the airplane, the other in providing its engine.

Foreign governments, keenly interested in the Reims competition, had sent representatives to follow all the events very closely.

After Reims, the NIEUPORT Company could hope to receive important orders, but admittedly under very painful and precarious circumstances, since only a few months earlier it had lost the young inventor of the airplanes that had just been recognized as the fastest and most manuverable in existence

Fortunately, in spite of its loss, the company maintained its standards of excellence and continued to gather new laurels:

- On December 24, 1911, GOBE broke the world record for distance in a nonstop circular flight, logging 740 km in 8 h 16'.
- On May 1, 1912, HELEN, piloting a NIEUPORT with a 70 hp Gnome engine, won the Deutsch de la Meurte Cup with a speed of 119,352 km per hour.

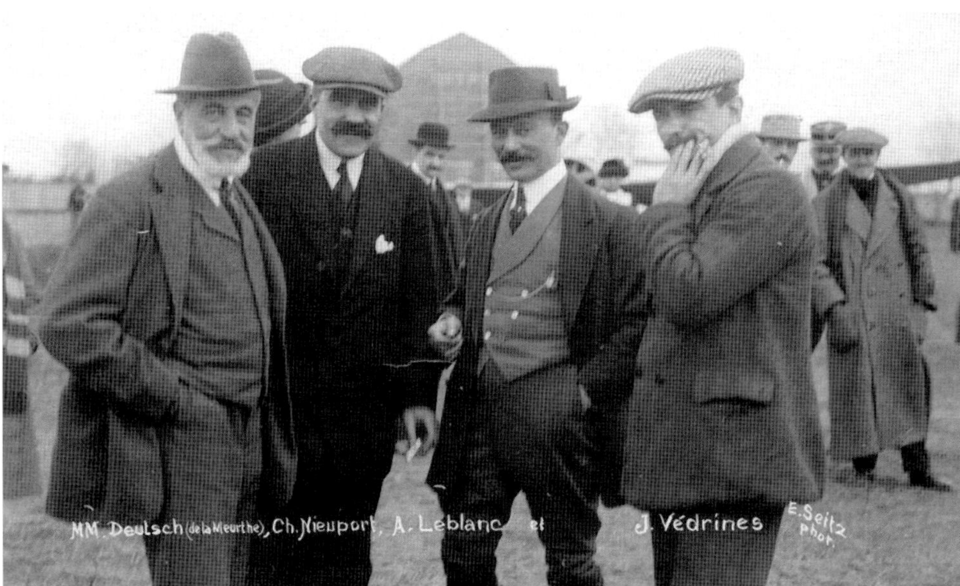

M. DEUTSCH de la MEURTHE and Charles NIEUPORT in discussion with Jules VEDRINES and A. LEBLANC at the end of the Reims military competition.

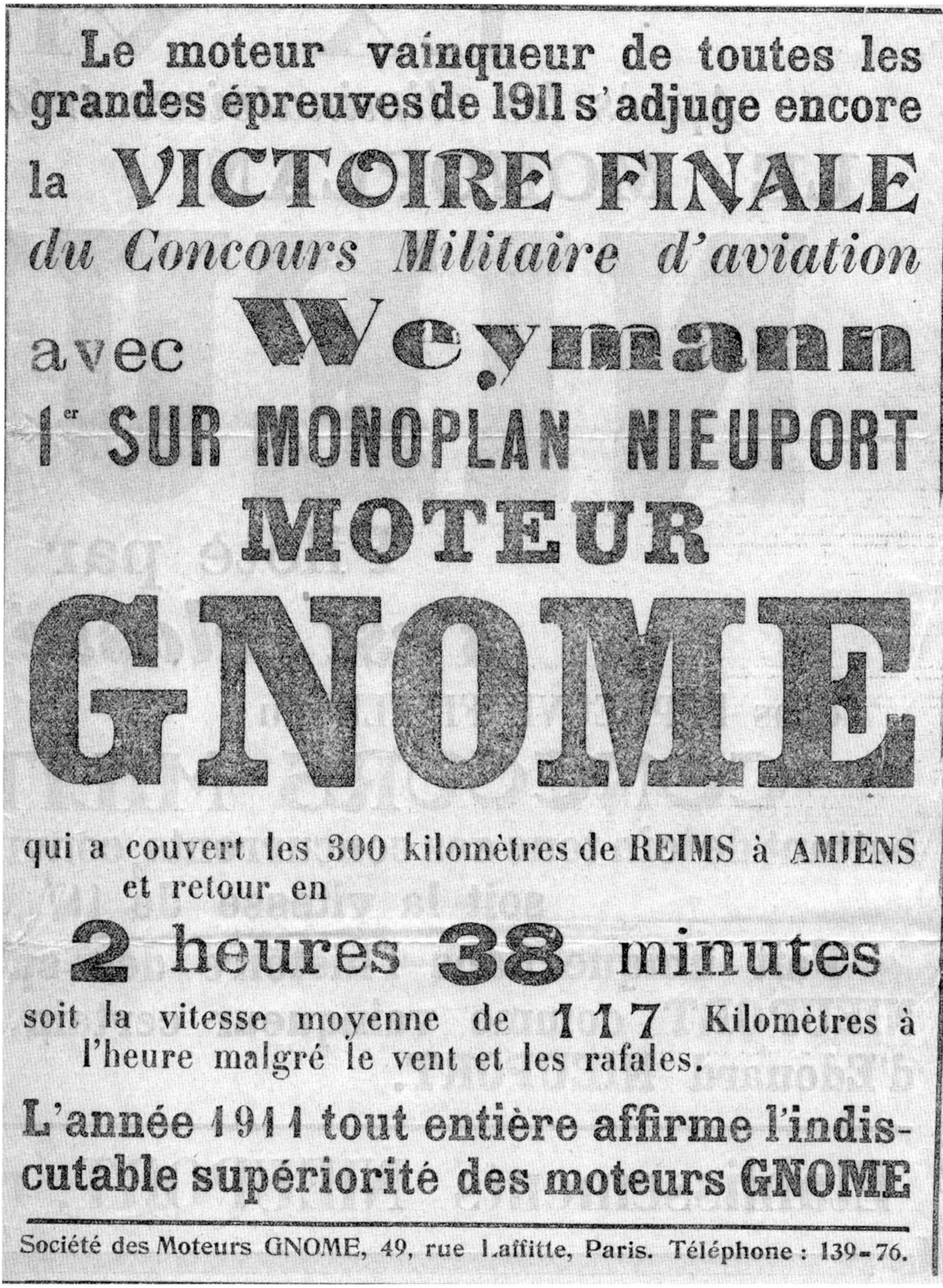

Advertisement for the Gnome engine.

The "Precursor," Edouard NIEUPORT, surrounded by photographs of the military pilots of his airplane.

- On June 17, 1912, Gérard ESPANET carried off the special prize at the Anjou Circuit Race.
- In August 1912 Weymann, flying a NIEUPORT monoplane with floats, placed fifth in the competition for hydroplanes in Saint Malo.

1912 was a remarkably good year for the NIEUPORT Company. Charles NIEUPORT, to whom his brother Edouard's torch had been passed, could be proud of the progress made. He had had his pilot's license since January 1912 and participated very actively in the air shows and meetings. Although he was not predisposed to flying, he gained experience and competence; however, he tended to ignore the dangers to which he was constantly exposed, as were all pilots in those days.

The Relentless Pursuit of Destiny

Charles NIEUPORT, along with his mechanic GUILLOT, was killed in a plane crash near Etampes on January 24, 1913. This terrible news produced profound and widespread grief. With this cruel misfortune, fate seemed to have struck the NIEUPORT family unmercifully.

It was only sixteen months after Edouard's death that Charles died in an almost identical accident, in the element that had become a part of them and for the conquest of which they had both given so much.

It is not exaggerated to speak of fatality, because Charles NIEUPORT was not on military duty and had taken along two of his pilots to carry out the delivery checks on the four planes ordered by the Army. It was probably to speed up these checks that he had taken the controls himself. The flight was to end in a terrible crash.

Charles NIEUPORT had arrived in Etampes that morning by train, accompanied by his pilots ESPANET and MANDELLI.

After lunch, they went to the hangar at the military airfield where the four three-seater 100 hp NIEUPORTs were to be *réceptionnés,* or checked out, before being accepted.

In the presence of Captain DESTOUCHES, president of the military commission, Charles NIEUPORT took off shortly afterwards with his mechanic GUILLOT as a passenger, and easily passed the altitude test, which consisted of climbing to 500 meters in less than a quarter of an hour with 500 kg of live load.

Taking off again almost immediately afterwards around three o'clock for the second trial, he soon disappeared in the direction of Orléans.

During a very steep turn NIEUPORT was making at around 300 meters between Mamerville and Méréville, so as to head back towards the airfield at Villesonnage, the craft lost speed, tilted to one side, and plunged at a breathtaking speed into a plowed field. The shock was so violent that the nose of the monoplane penetrated a meter and a half into the earth.

Members of the Méréville Gendarmerie were the first to reach the scene of the accident. They extricated the bodies of the two men, who had been killed instantly. Charles NIEUPORT had a fractured skull, and his pelvis and both legs were broken.

Méréville was eight kilometers from the airfield. Notified by telephone, the officers of the military base came to the spot immediately. The two bodies were then transported to the Etampes Hospital and left at the mortuary.

Comme son frère Edouard Charles Nieuport se tue en Aéroplane

Charles Nieuport s'est tué hier, en réceptionnant un aéroplane militaire, à l'aérodrome d'Etampes. Son mécanicien, René Guillot, est mort avec lui.

Hier après-midi, un peu avant trois heures, on réceptionnait, à l'aérodrome militaire, trois appareils Nieuport du type Concours militaire, des triplaces 100 chevaux, 14 cylindres, qui se comportèrent très bien aux manœuvres, et qui étaient devenus d'un type classique. Le premier était monté par Charles Nieuport, le second par le docteur Espanet et le troisième par le pilote Monelli. Chacun avait un mécanicien à bord. Celui de Nieuport était son compagnon habituel, René Guillot.

Ils firent un premier vol, puis atterrirent assez dur, mais sans inquiétude. Toutefois, un des mécaniciens fit observer à « Charles », on l'appelait ainsi familièrement, qu'une commande de gauchissement s'était légèrement faussée. Charles et Guillot l'examinèrent, n'y trouvèrent rien de particulièrement grave, et repartirent. L'appareil monta bien et, en arrivant au fond de l'aérodrome, entre Monnerville et Méreville, il était à 300 mètres environ. Le moteur s'arrêta tout à coup. Le pilote ne s'en émut guère et, suivant l'habitude, commença la descente en vol plané, en décrivant une longue spirale.

Que se passa-t-il à ce moment ? Nul ne le sait, la commande de gauchissement se bloqua-t-elle et la manœuvre ne se fit-elle pas, qui a pour but d'accrocher, pour ainsi dire, l'aile sur l'air, en en déformant le bout, pour empêcher de glisser dans le virage ? C'est probable, si l'on rapproche l'un de l'autre les quatre seuls faits qu'on connaisse : léger accident au gauchissement, arrêt du moteur, descente en vol plané en suivant une spirale, et chute en glissant sur l'aile.

Car la chute fut soudaine, brutale et effroyable. A 150 mètres de hauteur, on vit l'appareil glisser sur l'aile et tomber verticalement, une aile en l'air, l'autre en bas. Le tout s'écrasa sur le sol, et les deux hommes furent tués net, et littéralement aplatis et défigurés.

On les releva, et on conduisit les deux cadavres à l'hôpital d'Etampes.

Charles Nieuport, le cadet des deux frères, était né à Lagny (Marne), le 4 août 1878. Tant que vécut son frère, qui était pour lui, et à juste titre, un dieu, et le grand homme de l'aviation, il ne vola point, se consacrant entièrement à le soigner et à le suivre. Quand Edouard tomba, au champ d'honneur de la science implacable et cruelle, laissant une femme et deux enfants, le cadet jura qu'il remplacerait pour eux l'aîné, et que dans l'usine où étaient désormais leurs intérêts le nom de Nieuport serait toujours représenté. On essaya amicalement de l'en empêcher. Rien n'y fit. Il se dévoua tout entier à l'œuvre des siens. Huit jours après la mort de son frère, il volait, du premier coup, puis passait son brevet avec le numéro 742, les 20 et 22 janvier 1912, fit les manœuvres, et le jour anniversaire de la mort de son frère ramenait toute l'escadrille Nieuport de Sainte-Maure à Villacoublay, dans un vent si violent qu'il arrêta, en les clouant sur place, des appareils moins rapides, au-dessus de Tours.

Il est mort dans sa tâche pieuse et noble; saluons cet héroïque garçon dont la mort est un double deuil pour les siens.

15 Janvier

Georges Prade.

Newspaper article: **"Like His Brother Edouard, Charles NIEUPORT Dies in Plane Crash."**

The conjectures as to the causes of the accident were numerous, but it was noted that the wings had not given way. Could it be attributed to aeronautial phenomena whose laws were still undefined? The only plausible explanation is that Charles NIEUPORT was the victim of a failure of the alignment system.

SOLENNELLES OBSÈQUES DE CHARLES NIEUPORT

A seize mois d'intervalle, la dépouille mortelle de Charles Nieuport suivait hier, dans Paris, le même itinéraire que celle de son frère aîné, Edouard Nieuport ; qu'une foule énorme accompagnait, le 17 septembre 1911, au cimetière du Père-Lachaise.

Après la cérémonie religieuse à l'église Saint-Honoré-d'Eylau, trop petite pour la foule de personnalités et d'amis venus pour accompagner à sa dernière demeure Charles Nieuport, des discours furent prononcés sur le parvis de l'église. Le général Hirschauer, inspecteur permanent de l'aéronautique militaire, de sa voix vibrante, rappela qu'il venait précisément de demander au ministre la croix pour Edouard Nieuport au moment où la chute de Méréville se produisait. Hélas ! « C'est avec du sang qu'a été tracé le signe de l'honneur ! »

général Roques *colonel Boutteaux* *commandant Félix* *général Hirschauer* *M. H. Deutsch-de la Meurthe.* *Cl. Rapid*

Et après avoir, au nom du ministre de la guerre, adressé au colonel et à Mme Deniéport le témoignage de la douleur que cause au chef de l'armée la perte d'un soldat de l'air, le général termina en accentuant ces mots : « Chef de l'aéronautique militaire, c'est au soldat mort courageusement que j'adresse le dernier adieu ! »

M. Deutsch (de la Meurthe), au nom de l'Aéro Club de France, dit d'une voix émue combien grand était le culte voué par Charles à son frère Edouard, et insista sur le courage qu'il lui fallut pour prendre au volant la place du disparu. Puis, M. de la Fresnaye, administrateur de la Société Nieuport, retraça d'une voix brisée par l'émotion la carrière de Charles Nieuport, et adresse au compagnon de travail et de lutte un dernier adieu.

M. Quinton parla ensuite au nom de la Ligue Nationale Aérienne.

Les discours terminés, le corbillard se mit en route chargé de nombreuses couronnes parmi lesquelles on remarquait celles du ministre de la guerre, des ouvriers de la maison Nieuport, du personnel de l'école Nieuport à Villacoublay, des pilotes militaires de l'école Nieuport, de la Chambre Syndicale des Industries Aéronautiques, de l'Aé.C.F., de l'A.G.Aé., de la L.N.A., de la Stella, de la société Morane, de la société Gnome, de Audemars, Barrier et Garros, des camarades d'aviation de Sébastopol, du Syndicat des Aviateurs, etc.

Derrière le char funèbre suivaient les membres de la famille : le colonel Deniéport, père de la malheureuse victime ; son gendre, M. Guimet et MM. H. Depasse et Barbet-Massin, amis de la famille.

Venaient ensuite : le général Hirschauer, représentant le ministre de la guerre ; le général Roques, les capitaines Destouches, Michaud, les lieutenants de vaisseau Delevoye, Guillabert ; le lieutenant de vaisseau Dutertre, représentant le ministre de la marine ; les lieutenants de Montjone, de Lestrade, de Villepin, le sergent de Marmier, etc.

MM. Léon Barthou, Henry Deutsch (de la Meurthe), Esnault-Pelterie, Goupy, Kapférer, Paul Déroulède, Loreau, Bazaine, de la Fresnaye, Thomas, Quentin, Weymann, Dome, Espanet, Legros, Hélen, Gobé, Bertin, les deux frères Le Grand, etc., de la maison Nieuport ; MM. Bessonneau, Marcel Habert, Blériot, Robert Deperdussin, Pascal, Bechereau, Prévost, Jules Védrines, de Kergariou, Lamberjack, Emile Dubonnet, Saulnier, général de division Loupillard, Garros, Audemars, Barrier, de Maisonneuve, Collot, Perissé, Bielovucic, Gabriel Voisin, MM. Séguin frères, Luquet de Saint-Germain, Sarrault, colonel de Poumeyrac, Boillot, Leblanc, Lucien Millevoye, Léon et Robert Morane, Brindejonc des Moulinais, Martin, Labouret, Tabuteau, Brégi, comte de Lambert, Anzani, Grandseigne, Rousseau, Wimille, Sencier, Sue, Fafiotte, Thérould, etc.

Parti à 1 h. 15 de la place Victor-Hugo, le cortège arrivait à 3 heures au cimetière du Père-Lachaise, où avait lieu l'inhumation au milieu de l'émotion générale.

×

Aux générations futures, le nom glorieux de Nieuport, de ces deux frères qui ont sacrifié leur existence pour la conquête de l'air, apparaîtra comme synonyme de génie et de courage ! Génie, Edouard en avait fait preuve en créant son admirable appareil ; courage, Charles n'en a pas manqué en voulant, comme le rappelait le général Hirschauer : *qu'un Nieuport conduisît toujours à la victoire un appareil Nieuport !* Puisse cette pensée adoucir l'immense douleur des parents qui pleurent deux de leurs enfants si brutalement ravis à leur tendresse.

×

Alfred Leblanc, le glorieux vainqueur du Circuit de l'Est, vient de prendre l'excellente initiative d'une souscription permettant d'élever un monument aux frères Nieuport, morts tous deux pour l'aviation. Alfred Leblanc va demander à l'Aéro Club de France de s'occuper de cette belle œuvre à laquelle l'*Auto* s'associe de grand cœur.

G. Le Grand.

Newspaper clipping describing Charles NIEUPORT's funeral.

LES DRAMES DE L'AVIATION : CHARLES NIEUPORT

Le très remarquable pilote, Charles Nieuport, qui, par culte pour la mémoire de son frère, victime
l'aviation, avait voulu continuer son œuvre, a trouvé la mort avec son mécanicien, R. Guillot,
terrible chute.

***La Vie au Grand Air*, February 1, 1913: Charles NIEUPORT with Edouard in background.**

In any case, this brutal accident deprived the *Société NIEUPORT* of a dedicated and intelligent director who was also an excellent pilot. The bereavement experienced by Messieurs BAZAINE and de la FRESNAY, as well as the pilots, was overwhelming, because they had all transferred to Charles and his family the affection they had felt for Edouard.

The NIEUPORT Company was once again in mourning. Henry DEUTSCH de la MEURTHE, who had in the meantime taken over the Surcouf factories, which were building dirigibles, merged his various industrial holdings to form a new company, Astra. On May 29, 1912, it acquired a majority interest in the NIEUPORT Company, increasing the capital of 1,200,000 francs to 5,000,000 francs. The acquisition of holdings and the financial contribution of Astra would be of fundamental importance for the NIEUPORT Company, given the outbreak of the war and the considerable growth that ensued.

The production of the NIEUPORT airplanes went on, and the 4G continued to achieve success:

- Marc BONNIER and his mechanic BARNIER left Paris on November 10, 1913, and arrived in Cairo after a voyage of 5,400 km in a NIEUPORT equipped with an 80 hp Gnome engine.
- Reaching an altitude of 6,120 meters on December 28, 1913, Georges LEGANEUX broke the world record.

As for technological development, DEUTSCH de la MEURTHE gave wide leeway to Gustave DELAGE when he appointed him to replace Charles NIEUPORT as director of the company.

DELAGE, a former military pilot of NIEUPORT planes with the rank of captain, took over the management on January 1, 1914, bringing with him an impressive technical competence.

Shortly after arriving he designed the company's first biplane, the NIE -10B, having in mind the 1914 Gordon Bennett Cup. From this aircraft was born a whole family of planes built between 1915 and 1918 following the idea of the original, which was intended to combine the sturdiness of a biplane with the advantages (visibility, in particular) of the monoplane.

The sesquiplane is thus a monoplane with an upper "parasol" wing, having a normal bilongeron structure, and with a stump of a lower wing with one spar of depth. DELAGE's merit is to have based himself on the original discoveries of Edouard NIEUPORT in the conception of light aircraft requiring only a minimum motorization and offering a surprising maneuverability.

NIEUPORT had started out with the monoplane, which unquestionably lacked the solidity required for fighters. At the time, the materials used could not combine, in a single wing, both the flexibility and resistance needed in an aircraft carrying out radical movements.

Before his death, NIEUPORT had become aware of the problems of lift associated with motorization. At the time, engines were weak. The challenge was to maintain an overall lightness in the structure while making it solid. Edouard did not have time to implement the solution to this problem, but he undoubtedly paved the way.

The first triplane designed from the Nie 10B, designed by Delage.

The declaration of war in August 1914 broke off all activity at the factory. DELAGE, mobilized at the beginning of the hostilities, was very soon enjoined to return to his post, where he resumed work on his projects.

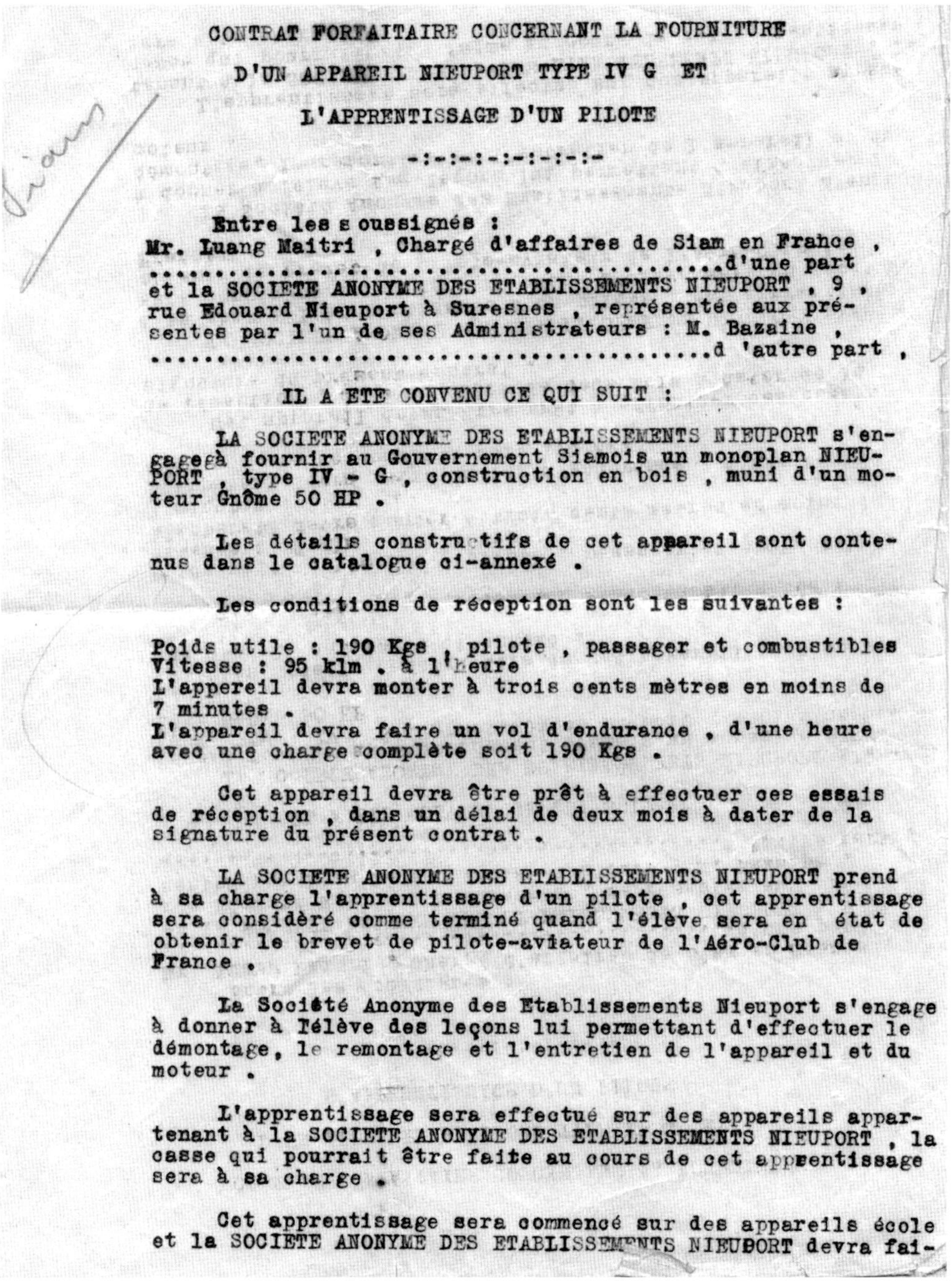

CONTRAT FORFAITAIRE CONCERNANT LA FOURNITURE

D'UN APPAREIL NIEUPORT TYPE IV G ET

L'APPRENTISSAGE D'UN PILOTE

-:-:-:-:-:-:-:-

Entre les soussignés :
Mr. Luang Maitri , Chargé d'affaires de Siam en France , ...d'une part
et la SOCIETE ANONYME DES ETABLISSEMENTS NIEUPORT , 9 , rue Edouard Nieuport à Suresnes , représentée aux présentes par l'un de ses Administrateurs : M. Bazaine , ...d 'autre part ,

IL A ETE CONVENU CE QUI SUIT :

LA SOCIETE ANONYME DES ETABLISSEMENTS NIEUPORT s'engageà fournir au Gouvernement Siamois un monoplan NIEUPORT , type IV - G , construction en bois , muni d'un moteur Gnôme 50 HP .

Les détails constructifs de cet appareil sont contenus dans le catalogue ci-annexé .

Les conditions de réception sont les suivantes :

Poids utile : 190 Kgs , pilote , passager et combustibles
Vitesse : 95 klm . à l'heure
L'appereil devra monter à trois cents mètres en moins de 7 minutes .
L'appareil devra faire un vol d'endurance , d'une heure avec une charge complète soit 190 Kgs .

Cet appareil devra être prêt à effectuer ces essais de réception , dans un délai de deux mois à dater de la signature du présent contrat .

LA SOCIETE ANONYME DES ETABLISSEMENTS NIEUPORT prend à sa charge l'apprentissage d'un pilote , cet apprentissage sera considéré comme terminé quand l'élève sera en état de obtenir le brevet de pilote-aviateur de l'Aéro-Club de France .

La Société Anonyme des Etablissements Nieuport s'engage à donner à Télève des leçons lui permettant d'effectuer le démontage, le remontage et l'entretien de l'appareil et du moteur .

L'apprentissage sera effectué sur des appareils appartenant à la SOCIETE ANONYME DES ETABLISSEMENTS NIEUPORT , la casse qui pourrait être faite au cours de cet apprentissage sera à sa charge .

Cet apprentissage sera commencé sur des appareils école et la SOCIETE ANONYME DES ETABLISSEMENTS NIEUPORT devra fai-

(Above and following) Delivery contract of a NIEUPORT IV G.

- 2 -

re l'apprentissage de l'élève jusqu'au moment où il aura obtenu le brevet de l'Aéro Club de France .

Monsieur Maitri sera responsable des accidents causés aux tiers et devra s'assurer en conséquence .

En aucun cas, la SOCIETE ANONYME DES ETABLISSEMENTS NIEUPORT ne sera responsable des accidents de quelque nature que ce soit , qui pourront survenir à l'élève .

LA SOCIETE ANONYME DES ETABLISSEMENTS NIEUPORT se réserve le droit , dans un délai de huit jours à dater de la première leçon , de résilier le présent contrat , si l'élève ne lui semble pas possèder les qualités nécessaires pour faire un pilote .

Le Gouvernement siamois aura le droit de demander la résiliation du présent contrat , dans un délai de huit jours à dater du jour de la première leçon , étant entendu que l'élève devra se tenir à la disposition de la SOCIETE DES ETABLISSEMENTS NIEUPORT pour prendre cette première leçon , dès que la SOCIETE ANONYME DES ETABLISSEMENTS NIEUPORT le lui demandera .- Dans ce cas , il devra payer à la SOCIETE ANONYME DES ETABLISSEMENTS NIEUPORT :

1°.- Le montant des leçons qu'elle aurait pu donner à l'élève , chaque leçon d'un quart d'heure étant de cinquante frs . mais étant en tous cas entendu , que la SOCIETE ANONYME DES ETABLISSEMENTS NIEUPORT ne pourra réclamer de ce chef au Gouvernement Siamois, pour chaque journée de vol , une somme supèrieure à cent francs .

2°.- Le montant de la casse entraînée par cet apprentissage pendant ces huit jours , s'il y a lieu Le prix de l'appareil , y compris les frais d'apprentissage de l'élève et de casse s'il y a lieu sera de vingt huit mille c nq cents frs (28.500 frs ."") .nets , s'entandant pour appareil livrable dans un des parcs de la Société Anonyme des Etablissements Nieuport , non emballé

Le Paiement devra avoir lieu de la manière suivante : Un tiers (1/3) du montant à la signature du contrat les deux autres tiers à la livraison dans un des parcs de la SOCIETE ANONYME DES ETABLISSEMENTS NIEUPORT .

En cas de contestation , les parties déclarent que les Tribunaux de la Seine seront seuls compètents .

Fait en double exemplaire , à Suresnes

Le 25 Juillet 1912
Lu et approuvé :
Luang Maitri

Lu et approuvé
Léon Bazaihe

L'appareil sera livré avec les accessoires d'usage

Nos Grands Oiseleurs

Morane

Sommer

AU Grand-Palais. Deux gardiens. L'un est un vieil habitué des expositions. Il faisait jadis le Palais de l'Industrie, quand il y avait encore un Palais de l'Industrie. Il faisait le Concours hippique et le Mobilier. Il a fait l'Automobile et il fait maintenant le Salon de l'Aéronautique. Il a la médaille militaire et a eu trois fois déjà la main serrée par M. Dujardin-Beaumetz. C'est un gardien arrivé. L'autre est un novice. Il était dans l'épicerie et depuis la vie chère, l'épicerie ne va plus. Il s'est mis gardien d'exposition, grâce à une cousine de ses anciens patrons qui connaît beaucoup M. Dufayel. Mais il a encore peu d'expérience. Il a seulement fonctionné au Salon d'Automne. Aussi tous les engins aériens l'effraient.

Les deux hommes assistent à la visite de M. le président de la République qui a couru les stands avec un visible intérêt et a fait de judicieuses réflexions.

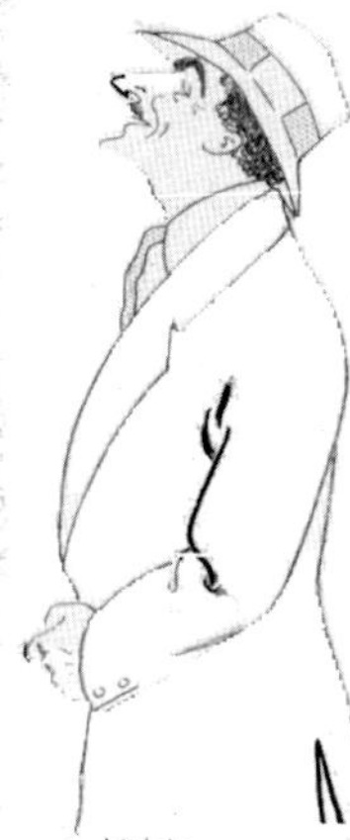

VOISIN

LE JEUNE GARDIEN, *goguenard.* — Il est plus lourd que l'air, le chef de l'Etat.

LE VIEUX GARDIEN, *sévère.* — Dans le service il ne faut jamais blaguer le gouvernement. C'est un cas de mise à pied.

LE JEUNE. — Suffit, suffit! Et les types poilus qui l'accompagnent, c'est y des gens du gouvernement?

LE VIEUX. — Espèce de bleu, ce sont les princes de l'aviation.

LE JEUNE. — Pas possible! Non mais des fois! J'connais Védrines, même qu'à Saint-Denis j'ai pris un verre avec lui. J'connais Weymann, qu'est haut comme une botte et qu'a une bobine de jockey.

LE VIEUX. — Tu ne connais rien. T'es une mazette en matière d'aviation. Ces gens qui font cortège à Fallières, ce sont les princes de l'aviation, je te dis, ceux qui gagnent la grosse galette avec les appareils.

LE JEUNE. — C'est donc pas les aviateurs qui gagnent?

LE VIEUX. — Non mais des fois! C'est ceux qui construisent... Ouvre tes mirettes, ouvre-les bien, si tu veux les connaître. Moi, je m'y suis fait à leur visage, fallait bien, puisque je dois avoir l'œil aux stands... écoute et zyeute... C'est comme qui dirait une leçon que tu vas prendre... Tiens... Tu vois le grand maigre au milieu qui a l'air tout triste et dont la petite moustache brune est coupée comme une brosse à dents?

LE JEUNE. — Oui...

LE VIEUX. — C'est Esnault-Pelterie, un brave et digne jeune homme. Il a monté dans le temps. Un jour, sans savoir ce qu'il faisait, il a atteint 30 mètres de haut. Jamais on n'avait encore vu ça. Du coup, ça la lui a coupé net. Il n'est plus remonté. C'est un savant tout de même. Il fait de bons appareils, seulement il n'a pas la veine. Il a fallu qu'il attende le Circuit européen pour voir bien voler sur un de ses monoplans. C'était Gibert, qui fit merveille. Esnault-Pelterie est le grand manitou de cette exposition. Il est dans les huiles, serre la main au président de la République, et pourtant, regarde comme il a l'air de s'embêter!

LE JEUNE. — Ça ne serait-il pas des fois parce que le petit vieux qui lui parle gueule comme un âne, qu'il s'embêterait?

LE VIEUX. — Quel petit vieux?

LE JEUNE. — Celui qui a des cheveux gris et qui fait un foin de tous les diables.

LE VIEUX. — Celui qui dit qu'il a un rendez-vous dans une demi-heure pour aller toucher 200 000 francs et un autre cet après-midi pour s'en voir verser 500 000?

LE JEUNE. — Tout juste!

LE VIEUX. — C'est Deperdussin, la pâte des constructeurs. Le seul qui laisse quelquefois à ses pilotes tout ce qu'ils gagnent comme prix. Il n'a jamais su ce qu'était un aéroplane. Le plus haut qu'il s'est élevé c'est sur une impériale et il a eu le vertige, mais il s'est attaché les services d'un excellent ingénieur, Béchereau. Il a des capitaux importants, aussi sa maison marche bien.

LE JEUNE. — Il a l'air moins rêveur que le type qui a des grands cheveux graisseux.

LE VIEUX. — Celui qui ressemble à un poète?

LE JEUNE. — Poète si vous voulez, on croirait plutôt qu'il a besoin d'aller chez le coiffeur.

LE VIEUX. — Ne te moque pas! C'est un grand inventeur: c'est M. Coanda. Son appareil n'a jamais pu voler. On fait des démarches en ce moment pour l'exposer au prochain Salon culinaire comme sorbétière. C'est la grâce que tout le monde lui souhaite.

LE JEUNE. — Il ferait un joli numéro d'excentriques au cirque avec le vieux qui a une barbe d'Auvergnat!

LE VIEUX. — Comment, tu oses insulter M. Levavasseur, le père de l'*Antoinette?*

LE JEUNE. — Eh bien! j'espère pour Antoinette qu'elle ne ressemble pas à son père. On dirait Balaoo.

LE VIEUX. — S'il avait construit un moteur aussi épatant que son monoplan, ce monsieur-là aurait pu conquérir le monde aérien, grâce à son pilote Latham. Pour le moment, il fabrique des aéroplanes dits de guerre qui ne peuvent monter et semblent de vastes voitures de déménagements or-

Deperdussin

Blériot

(Above and following) Article from *Fantasio:* "Our Great Bird-Catchers."

FANTASIO 382

Bréguet

nées de crinolines.

Le Jeune. — Oh ! dites, regardez celui qui enlève son chapeau haut de forme et met un melon à la place !

Le Vieux. — C'est Paulhan. Il fait ça chaque année : le tube c'est pour l'inauguration officielle ; une fois le président parti, il pense qu'il est temps d'arrêter les frais et se coiffe comme tout le monde.

Le Jeune. — Il est tout jeune. N'était sa petite moustache brune, on le prendrait pour son fils... Et celui qui a traversé la Manche, le fameux Blériot, il n'est pas là ?

Le Vieux. — Je ne le vois pas... Attends... Ah ! si, là-bas, le grand qui a l'air de revenir d'un enterrement avec les moustaches tombantes d'un fier Gaulois. Il parle avec un petit dont les yeux rieurs semblent peu en rapport avec le sinistre personnage qui l'accompagne. Le grand c'est Blériot, le petit c'est Alfred Leblanc.

Le Jeune. — Le vainqueur du Circuit de l'Est ? Comme il a l'air bon type ! Il ne doit pas être fier, celui-ci !

Le Vieux. — Oui, mais il ne faut pas qu'on l'embête. En voilà un homme calé. C'est le bras droit de Blériot.

Le Jeune. — Il ne vole plus, Blériot ?

Le Vieux. — Plus souvent qu'il volerait... Il aime bien mieux vendre ses appareils. Il ne lui en resterait pas un pour lui et puis au moins quand c'est les autres qui cassent, c'est à lui qu'on paye, tandis que s'il volait pour son compte et s'il brisait quelque chose ce serait à ses frais. Oh ! pour ça, il est pratique. D'ailleurs il est dans le même cas que tous ses confrères, mais surtout que les deux frères qui se balladent dans la rangée du milieu. Celui qui a le bouc et qui est en cycliste, c'est Henry ; l'autre, le blond, l'air d'un bull-dog, c'est Maurice Farman. Autrefois ils fabriquaient chacun de leur côté, maintenant ils sont ensemble. Je te prie de croire qu'ils n'attachent pas leurs chiens avec des saucisses. Et puis dans les courses et concours, ils n'ont jamais fini de réclamer, d'ergoter et de faire des chichis. Tiens, tu vois celui qui passe à côté d'eux sans avoir l'air de les voir, mais qui les a très bien vus ? C'est Gabriel Voisin. Tout jeune et décoré de la Légion d'honneur ! Eh bien ! Henry Farman a commencé avec lui. Il était son pilote, puis il a plaqué Voisin, s'est fait constructeur en imitant d'abord, en perfectionnant ensuite et en laissant son ex-ami dans les choux. Voisin aurait pu être à la tête de l'aviation comme il était à son origine, mais il a un sale caractère, se brouille avec tout le monde et ne veut jamais rien modifier à ses appareils tant que ce n'est pas sorti de son idée.

Le Jeune. — Alors quoi, ils se copient donc tous ?

Le Vieux. — Souvent. Il n'y a pas plus de deux ou trois types d'appareils vraiment originaux. Ainsi Sommer, le petit qui a la barbiche blonde et l'air rigolo, qui cause à ta droite avec le grand et robuste Kimmerling...

Le Jeune. — Le fameux Ki-Ki ?

Le Vieux. — Oui. Eh bien ! au commencement il a fabriqué un biplan qui ressemblait au *Farman* et un monoplan pareil au *Blériot*. Or, maintenant ces deux engins sont devenus presque différents des autres et si ses monoplans filent vite, par contre ses biplans peuvent emporter des charges considérables... Mais voilà un groupe imposant qui arrive par là. Regarde.

Le Jeune. — Je zyeute !

Le Vieux. — Le grand c'est le père du fils. C'est Hanriot qui a fabriqué un monoplan que seul son gosse sait conduire. Il l'emmène dans tous les patelins pour donner des exhibitions et son garçon, le benjamin, comme on l'appelle, a toujours quinze ans depuis une éternité. Celui qui a une bonne balle toute rasée, c'est Borel qui s'est endormi un soir associé de Morane et réveillé le lendemain constructeur d'appareils. D'ailleurs tout le monde peut être constructeur, pourvu qu'on ait un ingénieur. N'importe : ce pauvre Borel a été plaqué successivement par Morane, Saunier, son ingénieur, son dessinateur, Védrines, Tabuteau, etc...

Le Jeune. — Alors qu'est-ce qu'il devient, Morane ?

Le Vieux. — Tiens, c'est celui qui traîne la jambe et qui n'a jamais l'air de s'amuser, celui qui a de bons yeux tristes, là, dans le stand. Tu vois ?

Le Jeune. — Oui. Il construit encore ?

Le Vieux. — Mais de son côté. Et il y a deux marques Morane en même temps. Par contrat, Borel peut appeler pendant six mois ses appareils monoplans Borel-Morane et Morane en fait d'autres qui se nomment tout simplement Morane.

Le Jeune. — Drôle de métier tout de même où on ne fait que se brouiller et se raccommoder !

Le Vieux. — En voilà qui ne se brouillent jamais avec personne, les deux qui arrivent ensemble par ici. Ce sont Louis et Jacques Bréguet, des hommes de valeur. Ils font leur travail à Douai, ne fréquentent jamais leurs confrères et ne les voient que dans les concours où on les observe d'un mauvais œil parce que leurs biplans avancent plus vite que bien des monoplans. Mais on ne peut leur en vouloir, car dès qu'il y a une réclamation dont ils pourraient profiter, ils se désistent très chiquement. Ils causent dans ce moment avec Savary, l'obstiné qui s'imagine qu'avec deux hélices on peut mieux voler qu'avec une. C'est son affaire après tout, mais c'est un bon gars tout de même. Tu vois, je t'ai fait faire la tournée des grands constructeurs, tu les connais tous maintenant. Le malheur c'est que le plus remarquable, le plus génial, le plus modeste ne soit plus là.

Le Jeune. — Qui ça ? Nieuport ?

Le Vieux. — Oh ! mais tu es au courant, toi.

Le Jeune. — Dame, qu'est-ce qui ne connaissait pas Nieuport ? Et, quoique pas dessalé, je vous assure que j'y suis allé de ma larme le jour où le pauvre bougre est mort.

Le Vieux. — Et ce n'était pas de sa faute. Il ne voulait pas voler. C'est un officier qui l'a obligé à évoluer dans la tempête. Par ordre il s'est envolé ; par ordre, peut-on dire, il s'est tué. Pauvre gars ! Si bon, si honnête, si doux ! C'est peut-être cette fois-là que la France a fait la plus grande perte...

M. Granet, *secrétaire du Salon, s'adressant aux deux gardiens.* — Eh bien ! les causeurs, vous vous imaginez peut-être que vous êtes là pour vous promener et bavarder ? Voulez-vous aller à vos postes respectifs ?

Le Vieux, *à part.* — Crâneur !

(*Les deux gardiens se séparent.*)

Jacky.

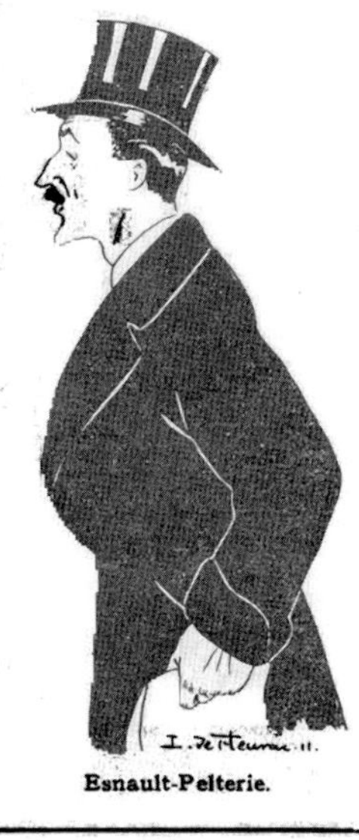

Esnault-Pelterie.

6

The Nieuport Planes in the War

The Declaration of War

It is easy to imagine the disruption caused at the NIEUPORT factory in Issy-les-Moulineaux by the general mobilization on August 2, 1914. Gustave DELAGE was among the first to be recruited, followed soon afterwards by practically all the company's engineers and nearly half of its employees.

The government was worried about security, so it had the remaining personnel and a part of the equipment transferred to Tours.

But shortly before Gustave DELAGE was returned to his post, the factory had been moved back to Issy-les Moulineaux after it was decided that it was not under risk from German bombs. Needless to say, these transfers had brought an almost total halt to production.

Increasing Production

It was at this point that the NIEUPORT Company would undergo considerable growth. The demand for manpower was urgent, and the factory soon had 2,000 workers, both men and women, and the subcontractors employed almost as many.

Drawing of the NIEUPORT factory in Issy-les-Moulineaux. The number of buildings was perhaps overestimated, since this document comes from the company's catalogue.

Prototype of the NIEUPORT Nie 10.

The NIEUPORT Nie 10, equipped with a Hotchkiss machine gun. The pilot is seated behind the observer.

The NIEUPORT Nie 10 with the cockpit in front.

The premises were expanded to contain the six buildings necessary for the creation of new workshops. A succession of various types of airplanes, using as many fixed as rotary engines, was produced.

DELAGE returned to his project to design a plane for competitions (a Type X), and built the NIE 10, equipping it with an 80 hp CLERGET engine.

New models were being tested every day. (Cf. Annex 1). A two-seater observation craft, the Nie-10-A2, was presented to the Aeronautical Manufacturing Service in May 1915. This plane, with a wooden frame reinforced with canvas, and having an airfoil of 18,60 m^2, was fitted out with an 80 hp Rhône engine. It was armed with a Hatehkin heavy machine gun mounted behind the pilot for the observer's use.

The Nie 12 equipped with two machine guns.

It was soon followed by the 12 A2 model (Cf. Annex 1), powered by a 130 hp Clerget engine and having an airfoil of 22m^2.

On October 1, 1914, the Army possessed only a reconnaissance squadron made up of NIEUPORT N 12s, and the Navy had only a few 6H hydroplanes with floats that had been ordered by the Turks but were requisitioned.

The need for new and more "high performance" airplanes was becoming painfully apparent. While producing a limited series of these N10 reconnaissance planes, DELAGE was simultaneously seeking to transform them into single-seater fighters. This was an attempt to offset the weight of the machine gun, which was mounted on a carriage, allowing it to fire directly ahead as well as to be tilted, so that it could be fired upwards and reloaded with relative ease.

When the Nie-10 failed to give the desired results, its airfoil was reduced to 13 m^2. This minuscule plane, whose dimensions (a wingspan of 7.65 and a width of 5.80) caused it to be named "*le bébé*," or "Baby," achieved the surprising performance of 156 km per hour and a maximum altitude of 4,600 meters. In the beginning, however, certain defects due to the fragility of the wings were noticed in "le Bébé." DELAGE corrected them by reinforcing the structure, increasing the power, and progressively refining the aerodynamics of the craft.

Thus was born the celebrated fighter, the "Baby NIEUPORT," which incontestably brought glory to the company (cf. Annex 1).

NIEUPORT 12 bis.

Prototype of the NIEUPORT 11 called "Bébé NIEUPORT."

The Nie-11, or "Baby, " was equipped with an 80 hp Rhône engine and armed with a machine gun placed above the wing so as to shoot over the propeller. Given its success, it was immediately produced in large numbers.

The NIEUPORT 11 was placed in service by the end of summer of 1915 when it joined the fighter squadrons of the French Air Force, as well as those of the British Royal Naval Air Service (RNAS) and the Royal Flying Corps (RFC).

It should be pointed out that even before the United States entered the war, "Yankee" volunteers joined the N124 Squadron, flying NIEUPORT 11s. Subsequently, the American Army bought 75 airplanes of this type for training future pilots.

The "Baby NIEUPORT" was the champion of the French fighters and was to ensure the Allies' control of the skies over Verdun. "Bébé NIEUPORT," the fighter flown by all the

The Top Seeded Airplane of the NIEUPORT 11.

(This page and following) The NIEUPORT factory.

The NIEUPORT 17.

aces, also received the accolades of the armies at the front, notably at Verdun. It was later used in flight schools.

The plane was made almost entirely of wood, notable exceptions being the forward section of the airframe and a few minor elements:

- The engine, covered by an aluminium cowling, was attached to the forward section, which was made from steel tubes.
- The sides of the forward fuselage were covered by aluminium sheets, across which large *portes de visite* (doors) gave access to the interior equipment.
- A caisson, or rectangular section, with ash or fir longerons reinforced by steel wires covered with canvas and plywood, was behind the fuselage.

NIEUPORT 17 bis.

- The wing spars were made of fir, while the ribs were of ash or linden, and everything was covered with canvas.
- The uprights (*montants de liaison*) connecting the two wings were made of fir, but the stabilizer was formed from steel tubes covered in canvas.
- The landing gear had streamlined wheels and catapulting shock absorbers. The controls for direction and depth were flexible, whereas the wing control was rigid.

It was the airplane of the aces. While flying it GUYEMER had his first fourteen victories, and with it the finest fighter pilots, including NUNGESSER, NAVARRE, PELLETIER, DOIRY, DORME, HOURTAUX, and PINSARD, became the masters of the sky and the terror of the German Fokkers.

Encouraged by these results, DELAGE tried a 110 hp Rhône engine on this airframe to produce a new model, the Nie 16. The Germans, realizing the qualities of the plane, produced a copy based on a captured craft. It was the Siemens-Schukert, identical to the NIEUPORT 16 except that the engine and propeller turned in opposite directions.

DELAGE obtained still better results by extending the airfoil to 14.75 m^2. This modification gave birth to the Nie 17-C1, which could reach a speed of 162 km per hour at 2,000 meters. It was initially equipped with a 110 hp Rhône 9J engine, which was replaced on the last models of the series by a Clerget 9B or Bentley AR1 engine, both producing 130 hp. This new motorization made it possible to reach a speed of 175 km/h.

The NIEUPORT 17 deserves particular mention because it had a determining role in the development of fighter planes. It had a range of two hours and could climb to a ceiling of 5,000 meters.

The NIEUPORT 17 CI was put into service at the end of 1916 and remained on the front line until its replacement by the SPAD VII. It was widely used by the Belgian Air

NIEUPORT 27.

The NIEUPORT derived from the Nie 24 and 27.

Force, whose Squadrons 1 through 5, based in Coxide, had outstanding pilots, such as André de MEULEMEESTER, Francis JACQUET, Jean OLIESLAGERS, and Edmond THIEFFRY. The N17 was even sold to the non-belligerent countries of Finland, the Netherlands, and Switzerland at the end of the war.

Other types of airplanes, such as the Nie 24 and 27, were tested, but were not built in large numbers.

The Nie 28 biplane had its inaugural flight on June 14, 1917. With a wingspan of 8.15 m, it had an upper wing that tilted forward and an airfoil shrouded by a pair of parallel streamlined masts. Remarkably light, it had a ringlike cowling that entirely covered the 180 hp Rhône engine, achieving a perfect aerodynamic form.

One of the prototypes of the NIEUPORT 28.

At the first test in Villacoublay, the plane flew at a speed of 209 km/h and climbed to 5,000 meters in 16'30". Following certain modifications it performed exceedingly well: its ground speed of 212 km/h and exceptional maneuverability made it an excellent fighter plane.

But before incorporating the airplane into the various squadrons, some modifications had to be made to the exhaust pipe. Accumulated gases that were carbureted but unburned could, on reaching a certain volume, ignite and provoke an explosion. In March 1918 it was ready for service, and 297 of these planes would be used by the 27th, 94th, 95th, and 147th squadrons made up of American pilots.

The Nie 28 monoplane was also an airplane flown by the LAFAYETTE Escadrille. During the war the factory produced a total of 7,200 NIEUPORT fighter and reconnaissance planes. 1,733 would be used by the American Expeditionary Force, notably in the celebrated LAFAYETTE Escadrille.

Air Supremacy

There is no doubt that when war broke out the various existing aircraft were unprepared to engage in combat and fell short of military requirements.

In the first place, they were exceedingly vulnerable. This pathetic "military hardware" was initially used for observation and pinpointing targets for artillery fire. Their wings were either too large or poorly disposed.

It was not until the Battle of Verdun that the role and importance of aviation was truly understood. Until then, there had been mainly individual skirmishes between pilots armed with rifles and revolvers.

Afterwards, an enormous effort was undertaken. The number of planes was greatly augmented, as was the number of pilots, who were instructed in special schools teaching the techniques of combat in the air. The armament was strengthened, and different types of machine guns appeared. It was only then that the aerial fighter was born.

The first NIEUPORT plane to engage in hostilities had been the "Destroyer." It was a two-seater monoplane equipped with a powerful 160 hp rotary engine.

The fuselage and the engine cowling were armor-plated. The pilot sat in front with the machine gun behind him. It was an aircraft conceived for destroying dirigibles, but the results were not very encouraging. The weight of its armor was undoubtedly a great handicap. It saw action from June to October 1914.

The Destroyer.

A new monoplane, a "Type X" with a 80 hp CLERGET radial engine, was produced soon afterwards. Unfortunately, there is very little documentation concerning this plane, which had a brief career. It is known only that it was very easy to maneuver and that the pilot had a much greater visibility than in the "Destroyer." Used by the Army for observation, it was built by the Italian firm Machi as a "licensed product."

With the development of the air war, a generation of biplanes was born. The first NIEUPORT biplane, which appeared in 1914, was called the Nie XB, but was later known as the Nie 10. It was intially intended for surveillance. The pilot was seated behind the machine gun, but this arrangement, which was quite uncomfortable for the pilot, was subsequently reversed. It had an 80 hp Rhône engine and could reach a speed of 140 km per hour with a ceiling of 3,800 meters. It was used in the French, British, Belgian, and Russian squadrons until July 1916, after which it was replaced by the more powerful Nie 12.

On April 22, 1915, the German Fokker appeared. It was the first fighter to fire across the propeller, and its firing power was much superior to that of the Allied fighters. It was Anthony FOKKER who achieved the true synchronization of the machine gun with the propeller's rotation.

In fact, he exploited the invention of Roland GARROS, who had perfected a streamlined propeller with steel deflectors. By stalling the firing adjustment of the machine gun, it became possible to fire through the propeller. This rudimentary system had been discovered by the Germans when they seized what was left of Roland Garros's *Morane Saulnier*, which he had landed behind German lines. FOKKER, basing himself on Frantz SCHNEIDER's work, placed a deflector in front of the machine gun barrel so that when the propeller passed, it was possible to fire rapidly without having any bullets touch the propeller.

This ingenious idea established German superiority in the air from the fall of 1915. The French did not resolve the problem of synchronization until the beginning of 1916.

In February 1916 certain steps, marking the beginning of a recovery from this desperate situation, were taken at French Air Force headquarters. Also at that time, the best pilots from all the squadrons were selected to form the *1er groupement d'aviation de chasse* (the First Squadron of Aviation Fighters), with DE ROSE as their leader. It was then that the first aces, namely GUYNEMER, NAVARRE, and NUNGESSER, emerged.

It was to respond to the incontestable superiority of the Fokker that the NIEUPORT Nie 11, or "Baby," had appeared in autumn 1915.

As was stated earlier, the "Baby NIEUPORT" was very close to the Nie 10 in form. But its airfoil had been reduced to 13 m^2 from the 18 m^2 of its predecessor. Using the same engine (80 hp Rhône), its weight was decreased from 680 kg to 480 kg, which gave it a superior performance and, especially, made it much easier to handle.

With DE ROSE as its head, a spectacular turnabout took place in the French Air Force, thanks to better organization and new aerial tactics.

The French Air Force was able to reverse the situation only at the beginning of 1916 with the introduction of the Nie 11, at first equipped with a Hotchkiss machine gun and, later, by the more rapid Lewis. The weapon was mounted on the wing and fired a magazine of 47 bullets above the propeller. Taken as a whole, the armament of this aircraft remained inferior to that of the Fokker E III, but from February 1916 this plane played an outstanding role in the sky over Verdun, where it emerged as the best of the Allied fighters. It was built as a "licensed product" in Italy and Russia.

Georges Guynemer.

Navarre.

An "Aviatik" brought down by Navarre near Jonchery in April 1915.

DE ROSE

Le commandant de Rose fut reçu pilote en 1910, comme lieutenant et il se signala immédiatement par une maîtrise et une hardiesse qui l'ont fait longtemps considérer comme téméraire, mais maîtrise et hardiesse raisonnées, car, technicien remarquable, il ne demandait jamais à son appareil que ce que son appareil pouvait donner, et ce que l'on a longtemps appelé sa chance n'était que la récompense de son savoir et de son courage. Entré dans l'aviation, il ne la quitta plus et c'est comme chef d'escadrille de la 5e armée qu'il mourut au champ d'honneur. Il avait, au début de la guerre, donné des preuves de son extraordinaire sang-froid. Ayant dû atterrir, faute d'essence, aux abords d'un village belge, il commençait à remplir son réservoir, les paysans lui ayant apporté tout ce qu'ils avaient trouvé, quand des enfants accoururent effarés, criant : « Voici ulhans!» En un clin d'œil tout le monde s'est enfui. De Rose, tout en eillant l'approche des cavaliers, continue son ouvrage avec un tel calme que ıhlans inquiets et craignant une embuscade, s'arrêtèrent. Ayant terminé, ose mit l'hélice en mouvement, sauta dans son appareil et s'envola, poursuivi ın violent feu de mousqueterie qui, heureusement, ne l'atteignit pas. Quelques nts après, il rentrait dans nos lignes avec de précieux renseignements.

The 80 hp Nie 11 reached the front only in 1916. In May 1916, six NIEUPORT squadrons were present at Verdun.

The problem of synchronized firing had been solved at the beginning of 1916, and the new synchronized Vickers were brought into service in May. On May 2, 1916, the first NIEUPORT fighter—the new 110 hp Nie XVII—to be equipped with this weapon was entrusted to Lieutenant Chaput.

Chaput.

In July, August, and September 1916 the situation was dramatically reversed. The French Air Force gained total control of the skies. Cachy became the Mecca of these fighter pilots, since it was the base of the two most celebrated squadrons, the N3 and N65.

At the same time there appeared the new NIEUPORT fighter, the Nie 17, with a 110 hp Rhône engine and a Lewis machine gun, of which the magazine could spew forth 100 bullets rather than 47. Still less powerfully armed than the Fokker, it neverthelss became redoubtable for the German fighers.

The Nie 17, which was a remarkably tough fighter, equipped most of the French and Allied squadrons, in particular the famous LAFAYETTE Escadrille made up of Americans and named for the revered French general who participated in the American War for Independence as an aide to George WASHINGTON. This squadron covered itself in glory.

The NIEUPORT 17, called "*le super Bébé*" or "Super Baby," was undoubtedly one of the most acclaimed fighters in the Allied camp, especially since it played a determining role in the development of the fighters that came later. Its victories stimulated the imagination. Combining the unequaled qualities of durability, extraordinary maneuverability, and an impressive climbing speed, it was the plane that everyone wanted to fly. Its remarkable maneuverability was combined with a speed that was just as great in horizontal flight as in climbing, thanks to its very clean lines and the relationship of weight, power, and airfoil surface.

It was an airplane piloted by the Frenchmen George GUYNEMER, Charles NUNGESSER, Jean NAVARRE, CHAPUT, René FONCK, Armand PINSARD, and many others. Among the Allied aces who fought with the NIEUPORT 17 were the British Albert

Nungesser in his NIEUPORT 17.

BALL, the Canadian William Avery BISHOP, and the Italian Francesco BARACCA.

On the French side, the best known of all the aces was Georges GUYNEMER, whose first missions in November 1915 were carried out in a NIEUPORT 10, and subsequently in a NIEUPORT 11 and a Nie 17, respectively. He achieved a total of 53 victories, 24 of which were in NIEUPORT planes that he had named "*le Vieux Charles*" ("Old Charles") for his mechanic Charles GUERDER, which he thought would bring him luck.

In April 1916 Captain Antonin BROCARD commanded the N3 Squadron, which was composed of Nie 16s. It was the famous "Swan Squadron," in which each pilot had a stylized swan painted on the fuselage of his aircraft. A single order had been given to them: sweep the skies clean of all enemy planes over Verdun. This squadron brought together the pride of the French Air Force: GUYNEMER; NUNGESSER; CHAPUT; DELLIN; and NAVARRE, who was called "*la sentinelle de Verdun*" ("The Sentry of Verdun").

That this formation of talented pilots flew with extraordinary bravery is illustrated by a rather unusual anecdote. On September 30, 1915, a complaint was lodged against the N3 Squadron by a game warden's wife, stating that "the aviators had been seen shooting from their planes at a covey of young partridges, and then landing to gather up the dead game!"

This elite squadron distinguished itself throughout the war, and not a day passed without a pilot coming in to land while revving his engine three times as a sign of victory.

It seems that about this time the German Air Force began to realize the superiority that had been acquired by the Allied fighters. The NIEUPORT became much feared, and combat

Deullin, an outstanding pilot thanks to strong powers of concentration and a rare visual acuity.

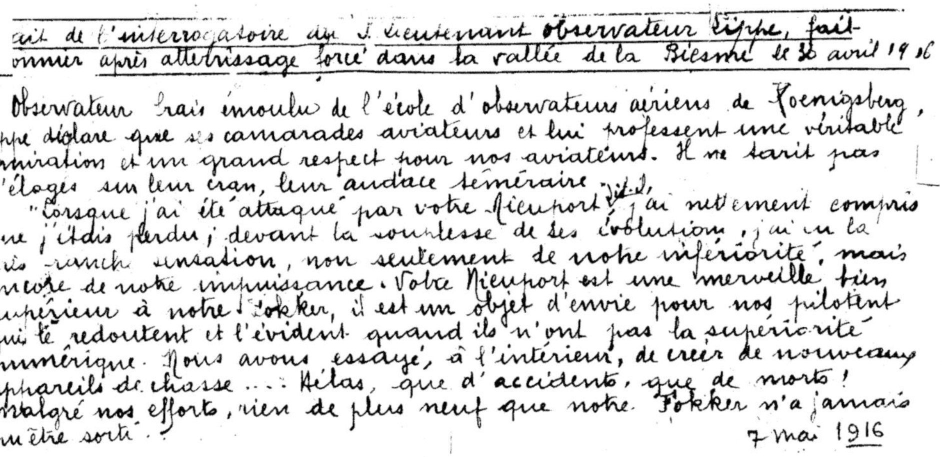

ait de l'interrogatoire du S. Lieutenant observateur Lippe, fait
onnier après atterrissage forcé dans la vallée de la Biesme le 30 avril 1916

Observateur frais émoulu de l'école d'observateurs aériens de Koenigsberg, Lippe déclare que ses camarades aviateurs et lui professent une véritable admiration et un grand respect pour nos aviateurs. Il ne tarit pas d'éloges sur leur cran, leur audace téméraire...

"Lorsque j'ai été attaqué par votre Nieuport, j'ai nettement compris que j'étais perdu; devant la souplesse de ses évolutions, j'ai eu la très franche sensation, non seulement de notre infériorité, mais encore de notre impuissance. Votre Nieuport est une merveille bien supérieur à notre Fokker, il est un objet d'envie pour nos pilotes qui le redoutent et l'évitent quand ils n'ont pas la supériorité numérique. Nous avons essayé, à l'intérieur, de créer de nouveaux appareils de chasse...: Hélas, que d'accidents, que de morts! Malgré nos efforts, rien de plus neuf que notre Fokker n'a jamais pu être sorti."

7 mai 1916

A written account of the questioning of a German observer who was captured after a forced landing in the Biesme Valley on April 30, 1916.

was intentionally avoided by the German pilots, who were flying Rumplers or Albatrosses and defended themselves from the NIEUPORT's attacks by using as best they could their machine guns, which remained more effective.

Lippe, a recent graduate of the School for Aerial Observation in Koenigsberg, stated that he and his fellow pilots had a genuine admiration and great respect for our pilots. He could not say enough in praise of their guts, their reckless daring:

> "When I was attacked by your NIEUPORT, I clearly understood that I was lost. Faced with the flexibility of its movements, I had the sensation, not only of our inferiority, but also of our helplessness. Your NIEUPORT is a marvel, much superior to our Fokker. It is an object of envy for our pilots, who fear and avoid it when they do not have superiority in numbers. We have tried to create new fighters... Alas, so many accidents, so many deaths! Despite our efforts, nothing newer than our Fokker has ever been produced." May 7, 1916.
>
> Interrogation of a German pilot giving his impressions of the NIEUPORT's qualities.

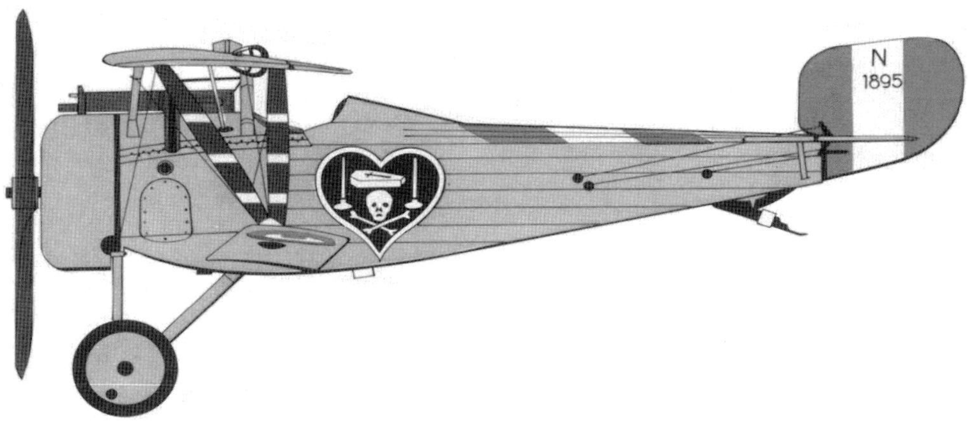

Drawing of Nungesser's NIEUPORT 17.

GUYNEMER standing beside his NIEUPORT 10, "Old Charles."

Senior Master Sergeant CHAINAT, eleven victories.

Pilot Officer DORME, 23 victories. He lost his life in aerial combat on May 25, 1917.

At Cachy, General JOFFRE inspecting Dorme's NIEUPORT.

In 1916, the French Air Force acquired a redoubtable new weapon in the struggle against the German observation balloons: the Le Prieur rocket. This amazing advance was made by a naval officer, Lieutenant Le PRIEUR, who had the idea of equipping a NIEUPORT with eight rockets that could be fired electrically. On May 22, virtually all the enemy balloons on the right bank of the Meuse were set on fire by eight NIEUPORT fighters. Up to then, the Germans' success in ground combat could be attributed in large part to their ability to observe Allied troop movements. But the new weapon changed all that, because it prevented surveillance of the French front by the "Drachen," which invariably risked being shot down by the NIEUPORTs.

Captain BROCARD, leader of Squadron 3, in the cockpit of his NIEUPORT 17 in May 1916.

Lieutenant Paul TARASCON, instructor of GUYNEMER, HEURTAUX, and DORME, 12 victories.

A Nie 17 armed with Le Prieur rockets.

On June 21, 1916, a Frenchman, Lieutenant Anselme MARCHAL, achieved an incredible feat in his NIEUPORT 11. After having equipped his craft so that it could remain airborne for fourteen hours, he took off in the evening from the Nancy Airport, heading towards Germany. At three in the morning he flew over Berlin, dropping tracts, then continued in the direction of Russia. Unfortunately, an engine failure forced him to land near Chelm, at least 100 kilometers from the Russian border. He was taken prisoner, but he had broken the world record for distance, having flown 389 km.

A close-up showing the installation of the Le Prieur rockets.

On August 31, 1916, Captain BALL of the Royal Flying Corps, alone and facing twelve enemy planes, fought one of the most heroic battles of the air war in a NIEUPORT, demonstrating that he had the makings of an ace. Setting off to patrol across the German lines at 18:30, he spotted twelve Rolands flying over their terrain at Cambrai. Diving 3,350 m in his monoplane, he shot back up like an arrow and opened fire on one of the planes at less than 50 meters. He forced a second plane to land, but then ran out of ammunition. His plane was hit by enemy fire, but, imperturbable, BALL took out his Colt and started firing back at his adversary. Despite all, he succeeded in returning to his base safe and sound. On May 17, 1917, at the age of twenty and after 43 victories, Albert BALL was shot down by the brother of the RED BARON, Lothar von RICTHOFEN, who himself was forced to land after his gasoline tank was hit.

In the spring of 1916, just about the time when the first American volunteers were arriving at the front, a new series of NIEUPORT fighters (Nie 17) emerged from the factories. They were to equip the American Squadron N 124, which took the name LAFAYETTE Escadrille on December 6, 1916. The squadron had three main bases: Cachy, Bar le Duc, and Luxeuil. The training camps were located in Avord and Pau.

(Top) A french squadron, perhaps N 313. (Bottom) The N1 Squadron of the Royal Flying Corps, equipped with NIEUPORT 27s.

Training American pilots with a NIEUPORT 10 at Camp d'Avord.

On April 18, 1916, seven very determined American volunteers formed the N 124 Squadron. They could have stayed quietly at home, but they were fascinated by aviation and their spirit of adventure took precedence over everything else.

The volunteers were Norman PRINCE, ELLIOT C. COWDIN, William THAW, Weston BERT HALL, Kiffin Y. ROCKWELL, James R. McCONNELL, Victor E. CHAPMANN, Bert HILL, and Raoul LUFBERY. They were later joined by others, including Eddie RICKENBACKER, who was going to become the leading American ace of the First World War. All of them wanted to engage in air battle with the Germans, and they were equipped with NIEUPORT 17s. During the hostilities 267 Americans volunteered to serve in this squadron without thinking about the dangers to which they would be exposed. 69 lost their lives in this courageous commitment: 42 were killed in action; 21 died in airplane accidents; 4 succumbed to illnesses; and 2 committed suicide.

On May 18, Kiffin Y. ROCKWELL achieved the first victory of an American pilot by downing a German LVG over Alsace.

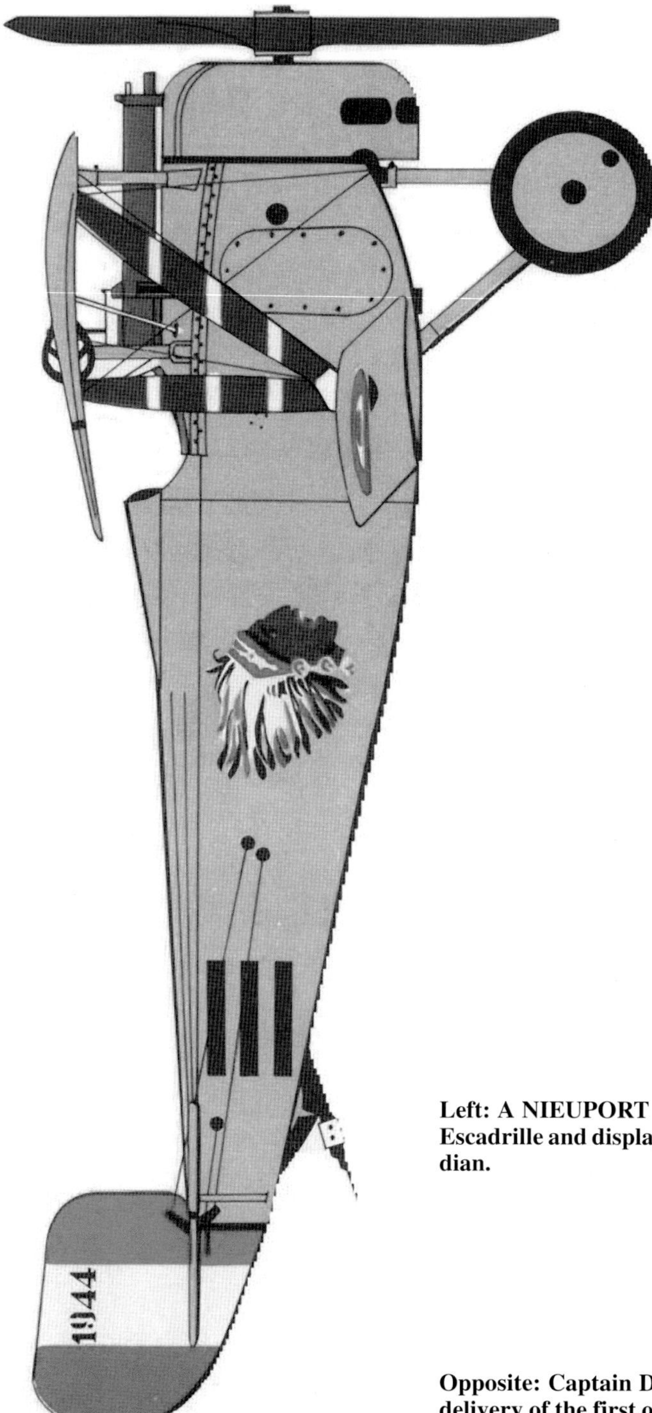

Left: A NIEUPORT 17 belonging to the Lafayette Escadrille and displaying the head of a Seminole Indian.

Opposite: Captain DAVID PETERSON, accepting delivery of the first of the Nieuport 28 fighters allocated to the Lafayette Escadrille.

American postage stamp honoring RICKENBACKER.

(Above) Captain Eddie RICKENBACKER, "Ace of the American Aces" with 26 victories, beside his NIEUPORT 28. (Opposite) Captain David PETERSON accepting delivery of the first NIEUPORT 28 fighters allocated to the Lafayette Escadrille.

The Canadian Billy Bishop beside his NIEUPORT 17.

On October 31, 1916, the first 25 SPAD VIIs were delivered to the French Air Force. They were initially used by the N3 Squadron known as "The Swans." This remarkable aircraft, designed by the engineer Bechereau, performed only modestly at the beginning, evoking only mitigated enthusiam. But it evolved rapidly and was to become the best of the Allied fighters.

Orignially, pilots such as NUNGESSER, who had grown used to the agility of the little NIEUPORTs, preferred to stay with the NIEUPORT 17 rather than fly the SPAD VII. Nevertheless, the majority of flyers were not long in changing their minds, appreciating the sturdiness and reliability of the SPAD, which allowed them to make steep and prolonged dives safely.

The 95th Squadron of the American Air Force with NIEUPORT 28s.

Meanwhile, some pilots continued their exploits with NIEUPORT 17s and 24s.

On March 25, 1917, flying a Royal Flying Corps NIEUPORT 17, the Canadian Ace William Bishop shot down his first Albatros. At Cambrai on June 2, 1917, he attacked an airfield and destroyed seven German planes on the ground before bringing down three in an aerial battle.

The SPAD XIII, which began to see action in May 1917, definitely outclassed the NIEUPORTs, which were still being flown by the American Expeditionary Force and the Royal Flying Corps.

By October 1917, the French command had become aware of the fact and gradually relegated the NIEUPORTs to the role of training craft. 71 Nie 27s would be delivered to the RFC and 287 to the American Forces. Subsequently, the American Army, appreciating the qualities of the new NIE 28, would order 600.

By April 1, 1918, there remained, it seems, only 56 NIEUPORT planes of various types on the battlefront.

Reception of Aces at the Aéro-club de France on 14 June 1917. Standing from left to right: JAILLER; Walter LOWEL; Raoul LUFBERY; Archibald JOHNSON; Willis HAVILAND; Georges THENAUD; Harold WILLIS; Henri LANGUEDOC; TOURDAY; Hector VARCIN; and William THAW. Sitting from left to right: Albert DEULLIN; Alfred HEURTAUX; Georges GUYNEMER; Paul TARASCON; and André WATTEAU.

Les ORGANISATEURS de la VICTOIRE

Louis BLÉRIOT, ingénieur de l'Ecole Centrale de Paris, dès 1900 chercha à résoudre le problème du plus lourd que l'air. Héros de la première traversée de la Manche en aéroplane, son nom est intimement lié à l'histoire de l'Aviation.

Louis Blériot est Président d'Honneur de la Chambre Syndicale des Industries Aéronautiques, il est chevalier de la Légion d'Honneur depuis 1909.

Gabriel VOISIN créa en France la première entreprise industrielle d'aviation.

Il partagea avec Blériot le prix Osiris (100.000 fr.). Chercheur infatigable, il a créé le premier appareil en tubes métalliques et le premier avion-canon. Gabriel Voisin est chevalier de la Légion d'Honneur depuis 1910.

Nieuport. Dès 1902, Nieuport étudia, et résolut le problème difficile de l'allumage du moteur à explosion. C'est avec sa magnéto, que la Darracq atteignit, pour la première fois, les 200 kilomètres dans l'heure.

Les premiers vols Santos Dumont et de Farman furent effectués sur moteurs à magnéto Nieuport. Nieuport venu à l' aviation, construisit un appareil qui fit sensation, quoique muni d'un petit moteur il conquit les records les plus enviés. Pendant la guerre les meilleurs aviateurs se sont signalés sur appareil Nieuport.

Pierre CLERGET, né à Dijon en 1875, diplômé du Jury d'Etat en 1895, s'occupa d'abord des moteurs fixes. Il créa le premier type de moteur automobile à 4 cylindres, Sultan. En 1890, Pierre Clerget s'associa avec M. E. Archdeacon et établit en 1907, un moteur d'aviation 7 cylindres rayonnant.

Associé avec M. Blin, Pierre Clerget a construit des moteurs d'aviation ; le type actuel, le 130 HP, est adopté par tous les alliés.

Pierre Clerget est l'un de nos plus importants constructeurs de moteurs d'aviation.

Louis et Laurent SEGUIN, inventeurs du moteur rotatif Gnôme, grâce auquel l'Aviation a eu un si rapide essor.

The Organizers of the Victory.

The Final Exploit of a Nieuport Fighter

It was in a "*Bébé*" NIEUPORT with a 120 hp Gnome engine that Charles GODEFROY flew under the Arc de Triomphe in Paris on August 7, 1919, to protest the absence of the Air Force in the Victory Parade that followed the Armistice.

NIEUPORT 29 CI.

The Nie 29 appeared only after the end of the war. Its career would span eleven years, during which numerous examples were delivered to allies of France, including Russia, Japan, and Siam.

Despite the success of its models, the NIEUPORT factory had to be converted to a new type of production. The need for military planes was obviously not the same, and the significant decrease in orders was felt. The factory at Issy-les-Moulineaux began to design extremely rapid airplanes for competitions, and they won many prizes in the '20s. Several models were built as licensed products in Belgium, Spain, Italy, and Japan.

The industrial adventure of the NIEUPORT factory continued, following much restructuring and much posturing, until 1949, when the final prototype was produced.

PALMARÈS 1920 ET 1921

CHALLENGE LÉON MORANE

COUPE DEUTSCH DE LA MEURTHE (1920)

COUPE DES OLYMPIADES

COUPE GORDON-BENNETT

TRAVERSÉE DE LA MÉDITERRANÉE

RECORDS DU MONDE DE HAUTEUR

RECORDS DU MONDE DE VITESSE

GRAND PRIX D'ITALIE (MEETING DE BRESCIA)

COUPE DEUTSCH DE LA MEURTHE (1921)

Record of Prizes Won in 1920 and 1921.

RECORDS DU MONDE DE VITESSE

RECORDS DE VITESSE SUR BASE DE 1 KILOMÈTRE PARCOURUE DEUX FOIS DANS CHAQUE SENS

7 FÉVRIER 1920. — Sadi-Lecointe, sur Nieuport-Delage. Vitesse = 275 kilom. 862.

10 OCTOBRE 1920. — Sadi-Lecointe, sur Nieuport-Delage. Vitesse = 296 kilom. 694.

12 DÉCEMBRE 1920. — Sadi-Lecointe, sur Nieuport-Delage. Vitesse = 313 kilom. 043.

26 SEPTEMBRE 1921. — Sadi-Lecointe, sur Nieuport-Delage. Vitesse = 330 kilom. 275.

RECORD DU MONDE DE VITESSE SUR UNE DISTANCE DONNÉE DE 100 KILOMÈTRES

25 SEPTEMBRE 1920. — Sadi-Lecointe, sur Nieuport-Delage, en 21' 28". Vitesse = 281 kilomètres.

RECORD DU MONDE DE VITESSE SUR UNE DISTANCE DONNÉE DE 200 KILOMÈTRES

28 SEPTEMBRE 1920. — Sadi-Lecointe, sur Nieuport-Delage, en 43' 42" 3/5. Vitesse = 275 kilom. 800.

1er OCTOBRE 1921 — Kirsch, sur Nieuport-Delage, en 42' 39" 4/5. Vitesse = 282 kilom. 200.

RECORDS DU MONDE D'ALTITUDE

24 JUIN 1921. — Kirsch, sur Nieuport-Delage, type 29 C 1. 8.900 mètres.

15 JUILLET 1921. — Kirsch, sur Nieuport-Delage, type 29 C 1. 10.300 mètres.

World Speed Records.

Tropies won with NIEUPORT planes.

Aviators' memorial to Edouard NIEUPORT and the pilots killed during the First World War.

Monument to Edouard NIEUPORT in Villacoublay.

Pauline POMMIER, daughter of Edouard NIEUPORT, at a memorial luncheon in the 1960s. Armand Gobé is to her right, and Dr. Espanet to her left.

Edouard NIEUPORT.

Edouard NIEUPORT, his son.

Pauline POMMIER, his daughter.

Appendix 1

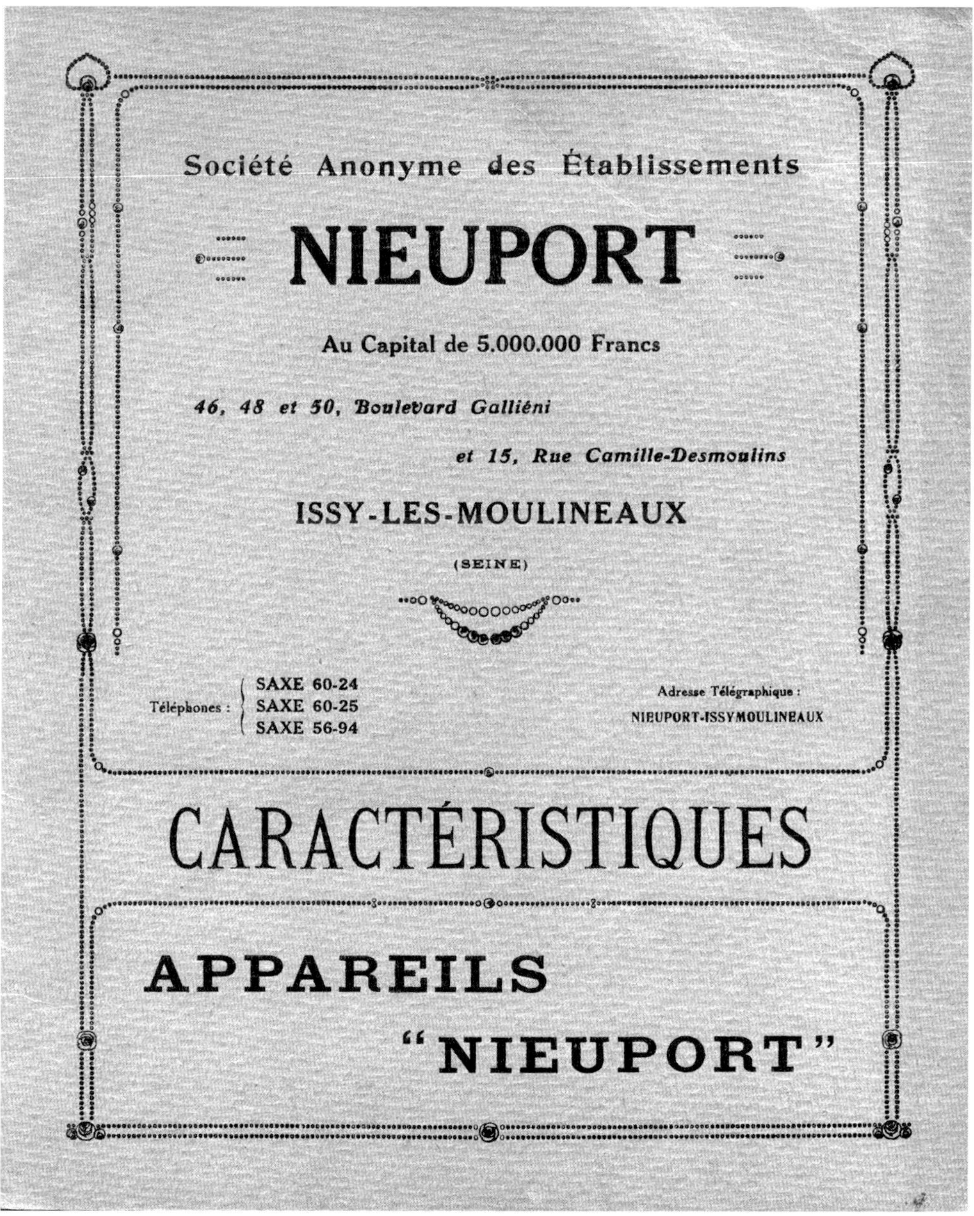

Société Anonyme des Établissements

NIEUPORT

Au Capital de 5.000.000 Francs

46, 48 et 50, Boulevard Galliéni

et 15, Rue Camille-Desmoulins

ISSY-LES-MOULINEAUX

(SEINE)

Téléphones : SAXE 60-24, SAXE 60-25, SAXE 56-94

Adresse Télégraphique : NIEUPORT-ISSYMOULINEAUX

CARACTÉRISTIQUES

APPAREILS

"NIEUPORT"

3

APPAREIL Type X - BIPLACE

Rhône 80 HP

2 roues de 650 × 80
Voie de 1 m. 600
Courbure d'ailes type N
Flèche maxima courbure d'ailes : 46
Angle poutre et caisson de tête : 90°

RÉGLAGE — INCIDENCE DES PLANS

SUPÉRIEUR		INFÉRIEUR			
		DROIT		GAUCHE	
Fuselage	Extrémité	Fuselage	Extrémité	Fuselage	Extrémité
2°30	2°30	4°	4°	4°	5°

Surface : 18 m²

CABLES

		Diamètre	Résistance
Porteurs	AV	4	1800
	AR	5	2800
Non porteurs	AV	3	1100
	AR	3	1100

HÉLICES

Marque	RÉGY	CHAUVIÈRE
Série	155	2219

CARACTÉRISTIQUES SPÉCIALES : Béquille rigide
Biplace pilote AV

APPAREIL Type X - MONOPLACE

Mêmes caractéristiques que TYPE X BIPLACE sauf :

RÉGLAGE — INCIDENCE DES PLANS

SUPÉRIEUR		INFÉRIEUR			
		DROIT		GAUCHE	
Fuselage	Extrémité	Fuselage	Extrémité	Fuselage	Extrémité
2°15	2°15	4°	4°	4°	5°

APPAREIL Type XI - MONOPLACE

Rhône 80 HP

2 Roues de 650 × 80

Voie de 1 m. 600

Courbure d'ailes type N

Flèche maxima courbures d'ailes : 34

Angle poutre et caisson tête : 86°30

RÉGLAGE — INCIDENCE DES PLANS

SUPÉRIEUR		INFÉRIEUR			
		DROIT		GAUCHE	
Fuselage	Extrémité	Fuselage	Extrémité	Fuselage	Extrémité
2° 30	2° 30	4°	4°	4°	5°

Surface 13 m²

CABLES

		Diamètre	Résistance
Porteurs	AV.	3	1100
	AR.	4	1800
Non porteurs	AV.	3	1100
	AR.	3	1100

HÉLICES

Marque	LEVASSEUR
Série	450

CARACTÉRISTIQUES SPÉCIALES : Béquille rigide

7

APPAREIL Type XVI - MONOPLACE

Rhône 110 HP

2 Roues de 650 × 80

Voie de 1 m. 600

Courbures d'ailes type N

Flèche maxima courbure d'ailes : 34

Angle poutre et caisson tête : 86°30

RÉGLAGE — INCIDENCE DES PLANS

SUPÉRIEUR		INFÉRIEUR			
		DROIT		GAUCHE	
Fuselage	Extrémité	Fuselage	Extrémité	Fuselage	Extrémité
2° 30	2° 30	4°	4°	4°	5°

Surface : 18 m²

CABLES

		Diamètre	Résistance
Porteurs	AV.	3	1100
	AR.	4	1800
Non porteurs	AV.	3	1100
	AR.	3	1100

HÉLICES

Marque	LEVASSEUR
Série	482

CARACTÉRISTIQUES SPÉCIALES : Béquille rigide

2287

9

APPAREIL Type XVII bis - MONOPLACE

Clerget 130 HP

2 roues de 650 × 80
Voie de 1 m. 600
Courbure d'ailes type N
Flèche maxima courbure d'ailes : 34
Angle poutre et caisson tête : 86°40

RÉGLAGE — INCIDENCE DES PLANS

SUPÉRIEUR		INFÉRIEUR			
		DROIT		GAUCHE	
Fuselage	Extrémité	Fuselage	Extrémité	Fuselage	Extrémité
2°50	2°50	4°	4°	4°	5°

Surface : 15 m²

CABLES

		Diamètre	Résistance
Porteurs	AV	4	1800
	AR	4	1800
Non porteurs	AV	3	1100
	AR	3	1100
De retenue		3	800

HÉLICES

Marque	LEVASSEUR
Série	802

CARACTÉRISTIQUES SPÉCIALES : Béquille rigide

11

APPAREIL Type XVII - MONOPLACE

Rhône 110 HP

2 Roues de 650 × 50
Voie de 1 m. 600
Courbures d'ailes type N
Flèche maxima courbure d'ailes : 34
Angle poutre et caisson tête : 87°40

RÉGLAGE — INCIDENCE DES PLANS

SUPÉRIEUR		INFÉRIEUR			
		DROIT		GAUCHE	
Fuselage	Extrémité	Fuselage	Extrémité	Fuselage	Extrémité
2°50	2°50	4°	4°	4°	5°

Surface : 15 m^2

CABLES

		Diamètre	Résistance
Porteurs	AV	4	1800
	AR	4	1800
Non porteurs	AV	3	1100
	AR	3	1100
De retenue		3	800

HÉLICES

Marque	LEVASSEUR	ÉCLAIR
Série	484	4

CARACTÉRISTIQUES SPÉCIALES : Béquille rigide
Mitrailleuse Wickers dans l'axe

1465

15

APPAREIL Type XXI - MONOPLACE

Rhône 80 HP

2 Roues de 650 × 80

Voie de 1 m. 600

Courbure d'ailes type N

Flèche maxima courbure d'ailes : 34

Angle poutre et caisson de tête : 86°40

RÉGLAGE — INCIDENCE DES PLANS

SUPÉRIEUR		INFÉRIEUR			
		DROIT		GAUCHE	
Fuselage	Extrémité	Fuselage	Extrémité	Fuselage	Extrémité
2°40	2°40	4°	4°	4°	5°

Surface : 15 m²

CABLES

		Diamètre	Résistance
Porteurs	AV.	4	1800
	AR.	4	1800
Non porteurs	AV.	3	1100
	AR.	3	1100
De retenue		3	800

HÉLICES

Marque	LEVASSEUR
Série.	450

CARACTÉRISTIQUES SPÉCIALES : Béquille rigide

APPAREIL Type XXIV

Mêmes caractéristiques que type XXVII sauf :

CARACTÉRISTIQUES SPÉCIALES : Béquille rigide
Essieu en une seule pièce

APPAREIL Type XXIV bis

Mêmes caractéristiques que type XXVII sauf :

CARACTÉRISTIQUES SPÉCIALES : Béquille rigide
Essieu en une seule pièce
Empennage en tubes

19

APPAREIL Type XXVII - MONOPLACE

Rhône 120 HP

2 roues de 650 × 80

Voie de 1 m. 600

Courbures d'ailes type N° 5

Flèche maxima courbure d'ailes : 14

Angle poutre et caisson de tête : 86°40

RÉGLAGE — INCIDENCE DES PLANS

SUPÉRIEUR		INFÉRIEUR			
		DROIT		GAUCHE	
Fuselage	Extrémité	Fuselage	Extrémité	Fuselage	Extrémité
2°40	2°40	3°	3°	3°	4°

Surface : 15 m²

CABLES

		Diamètre	Résistance
Porteurs	AV.	4	1800
	AR.	4	1800
Non porteurs	AV.	3	1100
	AR.	3	1100
De retenue		3	800

HÉLICES

Marque	LEVASSEUR	RÉGY	CHAUVIÈRE
Série	549	354	2228

CARACTÉRISTIQUES SPÉCIALES : Essieu en 2 parties
Béquille souple
Empennage en bois

N

21

APPAREIL Type XII - BIPLACE

Clerget 110 HP

2 Roues de 700×100

Voie de 1 m. 800

Courbures d'ailes type N

Flèche maxima courbure d'ailes : 54

Angle poutre et caisson de tête : 90°

RÉGLAGE — INCIDENCE DES PLANS

SUPÉRIEUR		INFÉRIEUR			
		DROIT		GAUCHE	
Fuselage	Extrémité	Fuselage	Extrémité	Fuselage	Extrémité
3°30	3°30	4°	4°	4°	5°

Surface : 23 m²

CABLES

		Diamètre	Résistance
Porteurs	AV	4	1800
	AR	5	2800
Non porteurs	AV	4	1800
	AR	4	1800

HÉLICES

Marque	RÉGY	ÉCLAIR
Série	274	2

CARACTÉRISTIQUES SPÉCIALES : Biplace pilote AV
Béquille rigide

23

APPAREIL Type XII bis - BIPLACE

Clerget 130 HP

2 Roues de 700 × 100
Voie de 1 m. 800
Courbure d'ailes type N
Flèche maxima courbures d'ailes : 54
Angle poutre et caisson tête : 90°

RÉGLAGE — INCIDENCE DES PLANS

SUPÉRIEUR		INFERIEUR			
		DROIT		GAUCHE	
Fuselage	Extremité	Fuselage	Extrémité	Fuselage	Extrémité
3°	3°	4°	4°	4°	5°

Surface : 23 m²

CABLES

		Diamètre	Résistance
Porteurs	AV.	4	1800
	AR.	5	2800
Non porteurs	AV.	4	1800
	AR.	4	1800

HÉLICES

Marque	ÉCLAIR
Série	20

CARACTÉRISTIQUES SPÉCIALES : Biplace pilote AV
Béquille rigide

25

APPAREIL Type XX - BIPLACE

Rhône 110 HP

2 Roues de 700 × 100
Voie de 1 m. 800
Courbure d'ailes type N
Flèche maxima courbure d'ailes : 54
Angle poutre et caisson tête : 90°

RÉGLAGE -- INCIDENCE DES PLANS

SUPÉRIEUR		INFÉRIEUR			
		DROIT		GAUCHE	
Fuselage	Extrémité	Fuselage	Extrémité	Fuselage	Extrémité
3°	3°	4°	4°	4°	5°

Surface : 23 m²

CABLES

		Diamètre	Résistance
Porteurs	AV.	4	1800
	AR.	5	2800
Non porteurs	AV.	4	1800
	AR.	4	1800

HÉLICES

Marque	RÉGY	ÉCLAIR
Série	151	2

CARACTÉRISTIQUES SPÉCIALES : Biplace pilote AV
Béquille rigide

677

27

APPAREIL Type XIV - BIPLACE

Hispano 150 HP

2 Roues de 700 × 100

Voie de 2 mètres

Courbure d'ailes type N

Flèche maxima courbures d'ailes : 53

Angle poutre et caisson tête : 90°

RÉGLAGE — INCIDENCE DES PLANS

SUPÉRIEUR		INFÉRIEUR			
		DROIT		GAUCHE	
Fuselage	Extremité	Fuselage	Extremité	Fuselage	Extremité
4°	4°	5° 30	5° 30	5° 30	6°

Surface : 30 m²

CABLES

			Diamètre	Résistance
1° CELLULE . . .	Porteurs	AV.	5	2800
		AR.	6	4000
	Non porteurs . .	AV.	3	1100
		AR.	4	1800
2° CELLULE . . .	Porteurs	AV.	3	1100
		AR	4	1800
	Non porteurs . .	AV.	3	1100
		AR.	3	1100

HÉLICES

Marque	ÉCLAIR
Série	8

CARACTÉRISTIQUES SPÉCIALES : Biplace pilote AV

Béquille rigide

N

29

APPAREIL Type 80 - BIPLACE

Rhône 80 HP

2 Roues de 700 × 100
Voie de 1 m. 800
Courbure d'ailes type N
Flèche maxima courbure d'ailes : 54
Angle poutre et caisson tête : 88°55

RÉGLAGE — INCIDENCE DES PLANS

SUPÉRIEUR		INFÉRIEUR			
		DROIT		GAUCHE	
Fuselage	Extremité	Fuselage	Extremité	Fuselage	Extremité
2°	2°	5°	5°	5°	6°

Surface : 23 m²

CABLES

		Diamètre	Resistance
Porteurs	AV	4	1800
	AR.	5	2800
Non porteurs	AV.	4	1800
	AR.	4	1800

HÉLICES

Marque	RÉGY
Série	230 blindée

CARACTÉRISTIQUES SPÉCIALES : Biplace école pilote AR
Simple commande
Béquille souple

APPAREIL Type 81

Mêmes caractéristiques que type 80 sauf :

CARACTÉRISTIQUES SPÉCIALES : Biplace école double commande

APPAREIL Type 82 - BIPLACE

Rhône 80 HP

4 Roues { 2 Roues AV de 650 × 80
2 Roues AR de 700 × 100

Voie de 2 m. 600

Courbure d'ailes type N

Flèche maxima courbure d'ailes : 53

Angle poutre et caisson tête : 88°40

RÉGLAGE — INCIDENCE DES PLANS

SUPÉRIEUR		INFÉRIEUR			
		DROIT		GAUCHE	
Fuselage	Extrémité	Fuselage	Extrémité	Fuselage	Extrémité
3° 50	3° 50	4° 30	4° 30	4° 30	5° 30

Surface : 30 m²

CABLES

			Diamètre	Résistance
1re CELLULE . . .	porteurs	AV.	5	2800
		AR.	6	4000
	non-porteurs . .	AV.	3	1100
		AR.	4	1800
2e CELLULE . . .	porteurs	AV.	3	1100
		AR.	4	1800
	non-porteurs . .	AV.	3	1100
		AR.	3	1100

HÉLICES

Marque	RÉGY
Série	230 blindée

CARACTÉRISTIQUES SPÉCIALES : Biplace, Ecole double commande

Béquille rigide

N

33

APPAREIL Type 83

Rhône 80 HP

2 Roues de 700 × 100

Voie de 1 m. 800

Courbure d'ailes type N

Flèche maxima courbure d'ailes : 46

Angle poutre et caisson tête : 90°

RÉGLAGE — INCIDENCES DES PLANS

SUPÉRIEUR		INFERIEUR			
		DROIT		GAUCHE	
Fuselage	Extrémité	Fuselage	Extrémité	Fuselage	Extrémité
3°	3°	3° 20	3° 20	3° 20	4° 20

Surface : 18 m²

CABLES

		Diamètre	Résistance
Porteurs	AV.	4	1800
	AR.	5	2800
Non porteurs	AV.	4	1800
	AR.	4	1800

HÉLICES

Marque	RÉGY
Série	230 blindée

CARACTÉRISTIQUES SPÉCIALES : Biplace école pilote AR
Simple commande
Béquille souple

NIEUPORT-ASTRA

NIEUPORT, ASTRA
ET COMPAGNIE GÉNÉRALE TRANSAÉRIENNE
RÉUNIES

SOCIÉTÉ ANONYME AU CAPITAL DE 38.000.000 DE FRANCS

SIÈGE SOCIAL :
46, 48, 50, Boulevard Gallieni
ISSY-LES-MOULINEAUX (SEINE)

CONSTRUCTIONS AÉRONAUTIQUES

USINES :
ISSY-LES-MOULINEAUX — BILLANCOURT — ARGENTEUIL
ILE DE LA JATTE (Levallois-Perret) — HÉRICOURT (Vosges)

TÉLÉPHONES :
Saxe : 56-94, 60-24, 60-25

ADRESSE TÉLÉGRAPHIQUE :
Nieuport-Issymoulineaux

Appendix 2

LES PRINCIPES FONDAMENTAUX DU COMBAT AÉRIEN

Par Oscar RIBEL

'REMIER MONITEUR DANS UNE ÉCOLE DE P

La cinquième arme a pris dans la guerre européenne une part considérable, dont, au temps de paix, les plus chauds partisans de l'aviation militaire ne prévoyaient pas toute l'importance. Si l'on songe qu'en 1907, les plus jolies performances aériennes n'atteignaient pas un kilomètre en distance et 30 mètres en hauteur, on reste émerveillé devant les résultats obtenus en moins de dix ans. Les pronostics optimistes des plus clairvoyants ont été au-dessous de la réalité. Qui aurait osé soutenir, au temps où Farman essayait timidement ses ailes à Issy-les-Moulineaux, que, neuf ans plus tard, se livreraient dans l'espace des combats héroïques entre escadrilles adverses de trente ou quarante unités chacune, et parfois davantage ?

Les combats aériens ont permis aux Français et aux Anglais de développer toutes leurs qualités de courage, de sang-froid et de hardiesse. Ils ont rencontré dans les aviateurs allemands des adversaires moins habiles, moins entraînés qu'eux, mais dont il faut reconnaître la bravoure indéniable.

L'aviation de chasse est différemment organisée chez les belligérants. On sait qu'en France, nous avons plusieurs types d'avions affectés à des services distincts. Les uns, notamment, sont destinés aux reconnaissances et aux réglages d'artillerie ; les autres, aux opérations de bombardement. Tous sont protégés par une escorte d'appareils de chasse, rapides et puissamment armés. Les Allemands, le plus souvent, emploient indistinctement tous leurs appareils pour les différentes opérations de la guerre aérienne. Ceux qui sont étudiés pour

BIPLAN NIEUPORT APPARTENANT A LA CATÉGORIE DES AVIONS DE CHASSE

C'est le plus redoutable adversaire, et aussi le plus redouté, des meilleurs avions allemands sur le front.

le bombardement et le réglage d'artillerie sont également capables de se défendre efficacement. Seuls, des Fokkers et des Walvets, montés par des pilotes de valeur, sont exclusivement destinés à combattre les avions ennemis.

L'aviation française, au point de vue technique, est équivalente à l'aviation allemande.

Nos pilotes sont scientifiquement supérieurs aux pilotes allemands.

Le nombre des « as » français s'accroît sans cesse ; presque tous montent des avions Nieuport ou Spad dont les victoires, à ce jour, se chiffrent par centaines.

Nous ne pouvons naturellement pas indiquer la méthode qu'emploie chacun de ces « as » pour chasser l'avion ennemi. Presque tous leurs succès, répétons-le, sont dus à la virtuosité dont ils font preuve dans l'accomplissement de vols acrobatiques. Un exemple entre mille, que l'on nous permettra de citer parce qu'il est bien connu dans les escadrilles du front, nous suffira à montrer l'intérêt qu'a tout pilote à savoir *boucler la boucle:*

Au cours d'un vol de reconnaissance effectué dans l'Est, le sous-lieutenant Navarre se trouva inopinément entouré par cinq ou six avions allemands. Trois ou quatre autour de lui, un au-dessus, un en dessous, lui interdisaient d'aller à droite, à gauche, de monter ou de descendre. Il semblait impossible qu'il pût échapper au sort funeste qui lui était destiné.

Cependant, sans perdre un instant son admirable sang-froid, notre « as », à la grande surprise de ses adversaires, retournait son appareil, effectuant un looping parfait qui le ramenait derrière le groupe assaillant. Fonçant alors droit sur les avions les plus proches, il déchargeait sur eux le ruban de sa mitrailleuse et en abattait deux successivement ! Les autres, surpris, n'insistaient pas et fuyaient à tire-d'ailes vers leurs lignes, poursuivis par l'intrépide Navarre qui, depuis, a eu des destins obscurs.

LE « LOOPING » DANS LA GUERRE AÉRIENNE

Attaqué par quatre ou cinq avions allemands, le biplan français (1) est complètement entouré. Il réussit à se dégager par un « looping the loop » qui le ramène derrière le groupe assaillant, qu'il attaque à son tour (2).

Les « as » allemands sont bien moins nombreux que les nôtres. Le meilleur d'entre eux, le capitaine Boelke, s'est tué le 28 octobre 1916 après avoir mis *hors de combat* son quarantième adversaire.

Ne sont comptés à l'actif de nos pilotes que les avions ennemis abattus à l'intérieur de nos lignes ou tombés en flammes en territoire occupé. Les Allemands, eux, n'hésitent pas

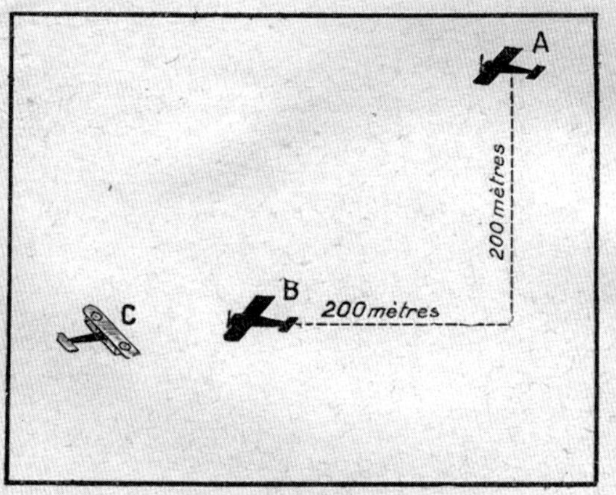

LA TACTIQUE FAVORITE DES WALVETS

Les Walvets patrouillent deux par deux: A à 200 mètres au-dessus et à 200 mètres derrière B. Si un avion C est rencontré, B engage le combat avec lui, la tâche de A consistant à surveiller la zone du combat afin de déjouer toute surprise de la part d'un nouvel adversaire qui pourrait survenir.

à compter comme appareil mis hors de combat tout avion qui, pour une cause quelconque, est obligé d'abandonner la lutte. Si nous adoptions la même base d'appréciation, il est certain que Guynemer, entre autres, aurait mis hors de combat une bonne soixantaine au moins d'avions ennemis.

La liste des « as » allemands est moins longue que la nôtre ; on y relève les noms de Boelke, Immelman, Wintgens, Hoehndorff, Frankl, Mulzer, Buddecker, Mohler, etc...

Les Allemands ont une conception de la chasse aérienne sensiblement différente de la nôtre. A un correspondant du *World* qui l'interviewait, Boelke fit la déclaration suivante :

« On dit que les aviateurs allemands ne vont jamais sur les lignes adverses et qu'ils restent sans cesse au-dessus de leur territoire. Pour les chasseurs, la réflexion est juste ; cela tient d'abord à ce que plusieurs dispositifs de nos nouveaux Fokkers doivent rester secrets et ensuite à ce que notre mission consiste uniquement à empêcher les avions d'observation ennemis de faire leur travail. C'est pourquoi nous préférons de beaucoup les attendre là où ils doivent venir. »

Le point de vue allemand est peut-être intéressant en ce sens qu'en essayant de triompher de son adversaire chez soi, on peut ainsi faire un prisonnier, si l'équipage n'est pas tué, et l'appareil peut être utilisé, s'il n'est pas détruit. Si, au contraire, l'ennemi est vainqueur, l'avion abattu ne risque pas de tomber entre ses mains et d'être examiné par lui, dans ses moindres détails, à son grand profit.

Toutefois, l'aviateur français a une conception du combat aérien autrement noble et autrement efficace. Il n'hésite pas à se poster au-dessus des lignes allemandes pour empêcher les avions d'y accomplir leur tâche, qui est de voir ce qui se passe chez nous. L'aviateur français engage parfois le combat à vingt ou trente kilomètres à l'arrière du front allemand ; dès qu'un appareil ennemi est signalé au loin, il se porte à sa rencontre et l'oblige à rebrousser chemin, s'il ne peut réussir à l'abattre. Au cours de nos offensives de la Somme et de Verdun, nos avions ont ainsi établi, en avant du front, une véritable barrière aérienne qu'aucun aviateur allemand n'a été capable de franchir, et cela pendant plusieurs jours.

La rapidité et la vitesse ascensionnelle sont les qualités essentielles d'un avion de chasse. L'aviateur doit pouvoir, à son gré, survoler l'adversaire, afin de foncer sur lui, au moment opportun, et l'atteindre par son feu dans ses œuvres vives. Les Fokkers, les Walvets, les L.V.G., que l'on rencontre le plus souvent sur

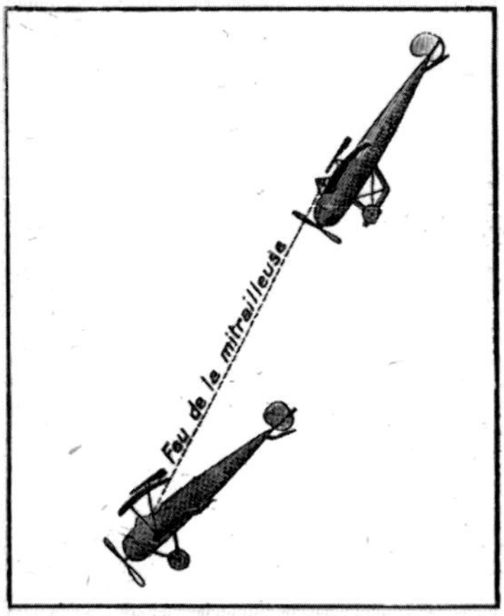

LA POURSUITE PIQUÉE

Dans le sens vertical, l'inclinaison de la mitrailleuse vers l'objet visé est obtenue par la propre inclinaison d'un aéroplane. L'assaillant pointe sur son adversaire en plongeant parfois de 60° et plus.

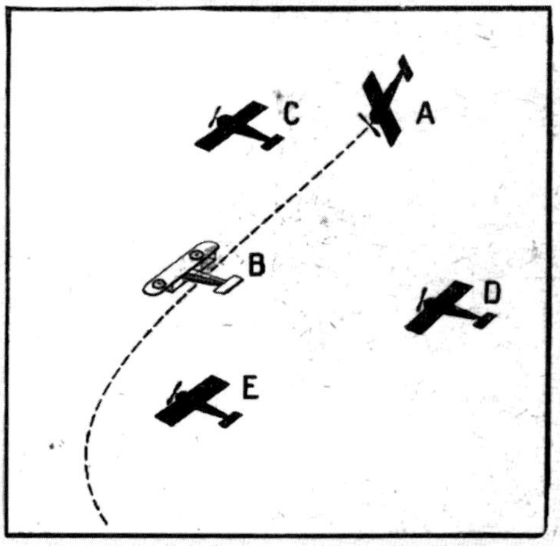

LA TACTIQUE DU FAMEUX BOELKE

La mission des avions C D E *est d'encercler l'adversaire* B ; *à un moment donné, l'avion* A, *qui jusque là s'était dissimulé à la vue de son adversaire, fonce sur lui en le mitraillant.*

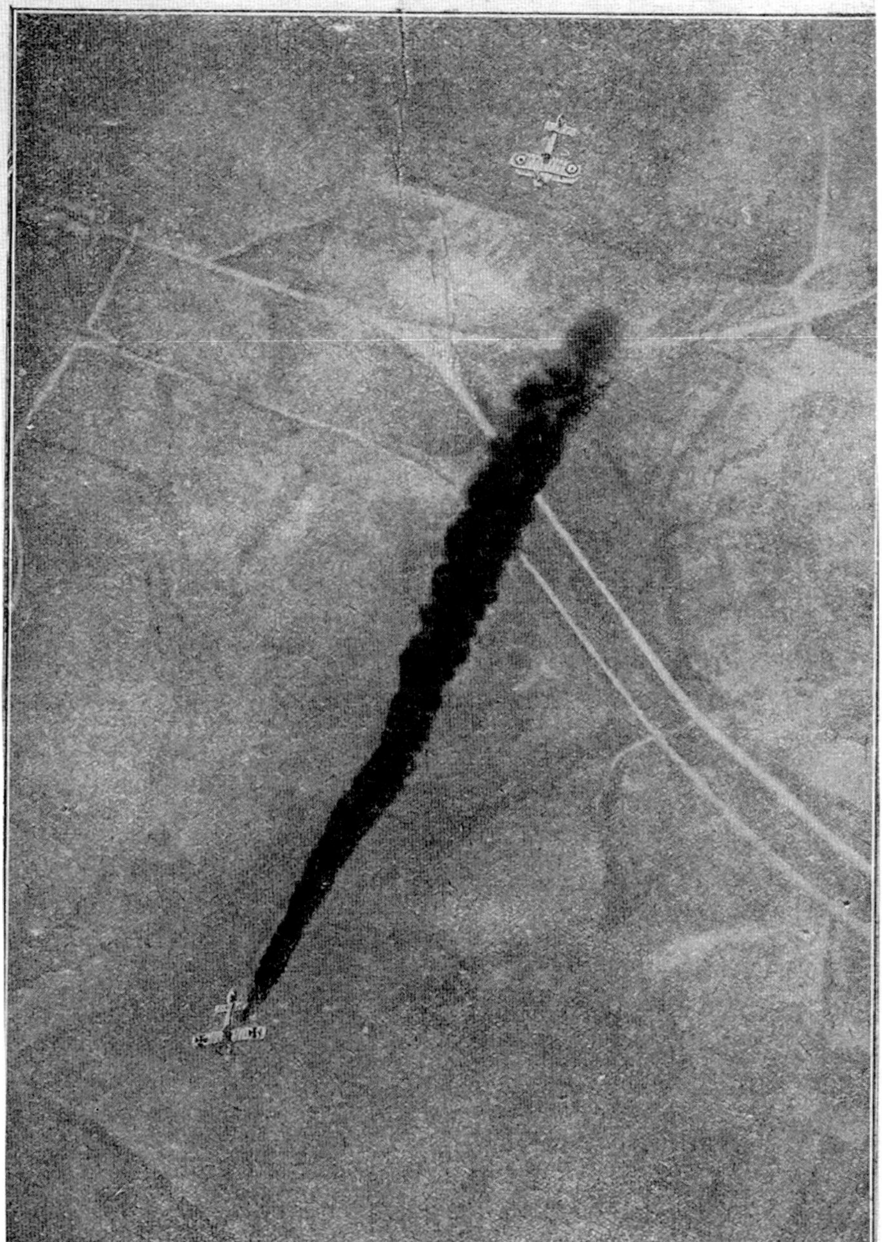

UN FOKKER S'ABATTANT EN FLAMMES DANS LES LIGNES FRANÇAISES

'appareil allemand a été atteint par une balle qui a traversé son réservoir d'essence; sa descente vertigineuse s'accompagne d'une longue traînée de fumée noire (photo originale).

notre front, sont animés d'une vitesse très grande que l'on estime supérieure à 150 kilomètres à l'heure. La montée de ces appareils s'effectue aussi très rapidement, et la hauteur à laquelle ils peuvent pratiquement s'élever au cours d'un combat est voisine de 4.000 mètres. D'une façon générale, les pilotes allemands chargés des opérations de chasse, surtout ceux qui montent des Walvets, se présentent au combat de la manière suivante : soit qu'ils volent au-dessus de leurs propres lignes, soit qu'ils affrontent celles de leurs adversaires, les avions germains patrouillent toujours en groupe ou tout au moins deux par deux. Si un appareil ennemi survient, le premier avion allemand est chargé de soutenir la lutte ; l'autre, qui se tient à deux cents mètres en arrière et à deux cents mètres plus haut, a seulement pour mission de surveiller la zone du combat sans intervenir directement dans la bataille. Cependant, si un second adversaire arrive à la rescousse, à son tour il l'attaque et s'efforce de lui faire rebrousser chemin. Naturellement, si son co-équipier est vaincu, il n'insiste pas et regagne ses lignes à toute allure. Souvent aussi, la manœuvre présente plus d'ampleur ; les avions

LA TACTIQUE D'IMMELMAN

L'avion A fonçant droit sur son adversaire B tire sur lui presqu'à bout portant. S'il le manque, il s'enfuit (A¹) et ne revient pas à la charge.

MITRAILLEUSE LEWIS MONTÉE SUR UN BIPLAN DE CHASSE NIEUPORT

L'engin est solidement fixé sur le plan porteur supérieur de l'appareil et parallèlement à celui-ci.

volent en groupe se protégeant mutuellement. Si un avion ennemi isolé est rencontré, il est vite entouré et il ne peut trouver son salut que dans la rapidité de son vol.

Les vitesses considérables auxquelles se déplacent les aéroplanes de chasse ont pour résultat d'accroître singulièrement les dangers de rupture des ailes. Un avion qui vole à 180 kilomètres à l'heure, qui monte à plus de 2.000 mètres en sept minutes, qui descend presque verticalement de cette hauteur, est soumis à des efforts énormes qui, peu à peu, disloquent ses organes essentiels. Un avion prenant un autre avion en chasse le poursuit dans les positions les plus extraordinaires et pique sur lui, incliné parfois à 90°. Dans ces conditions, la poussée de l'air peut amener le bris complet des ailes et la chute immédiate de l'appareil.

Les différentes parties des avions allemands sont généralement conçues avec un coefficient de sécurité bien suffisant. A plusieurs reprises cependant, on a pu constater de graves accidents survenus au cours d'un vol et dus à un vice de construction. Tout récemment encore, sur le front de Verdun, un aviateur français poursuivant un avion allemand fut, à son tour, pris en chasse par un petit biplan Rumpler. Au moment où notre pilote, après avoir triomphé de son adversaire, se préparait à faire face au nouvel assaillant, celui-ci s'effondra soudain, piquant droit vers le sol, les ailes brisées et relevées au-dessus du fuselage.

Plusieurs avions Rumpler ont subi le même sort au cours de différents combats aériens ; le constructeur a ainsi involontairement — et il faut l'en remercier — contribué au succès de nos pilotes.

Les « as » allemands combattent généralement en groupe, c'est-à-dire que les avions qui les accompagnent se chargent d' « occuper » l'adversaire, tandis qu'eux se préparent à l'abattre. Boelke avait adopté la tactique suivante, que rapporte M. Jacques Mortane : « Il partait avec une escadrille de cinq ou six bons pilotes montés sur des Rolands, des Walvets ou des Fokkers. Lui était de

DISPOSITIF DE GARROS PERMETTANT LE TIR A TRAVERS L'HÉLICE

Chaque pale du propulseur est munie d'une pièce métallique, sorte de coin en acier situé juste en face du canon de la mitrailleuse. Si une balle vient à frapper l'hélice, elle rencontre ce coin d'acier qui la fait dévier de sa trajectoire et la rejette sur le côté. Chaque balle déviée est un projectile perdu, mais l'hélice n'est nullement endommagée par le coup qu'elle reçoit.

DISPOSITIF DE TIR A TRAVERS L'HÉLICE INSTALLÉ SUR UN FOKKER

Le pilote commande le fonctionnement de la mitrailleuse 3 *au moyen d'une transmission Bowden, en abaissant le levier* 4 *au moment du tir. Sur l'arbre du moteur est disposé un excentrique* 12 *qui, par l'intermédiaire d'une came et d'une combinaison de ressorts et leviers* 1 *et* 2, *accroche le mécanisme de la mitrailleuse chaque fois qu'une pale d'hélice vient à passer devant le canon de l'arme. Lorsque le saillant de l'excentrique* 12 *vient à rencontrer le galet* 14, *la came est soulevée et la détente de la mitrailleuse est libérée; dès que le galet est passé sur le saillant, le mécanisme est bloqué de nouveau. Les douilles vides sont rejetées par le tube* 13. *La hauteur du siège du pilote est réglable par les glissières* 5 *et* 6. *Il a devant lui un levier de commande* 10 *dont la partie inférieure* 8 *est pourvue d'un dispositif* 9 *qui permet de bloquer à volonté le gouvernail d'altitude de l'avion pendant le tir. Le blocage du gouvernail est assuré par un Bowden* 7 *qui aboutit à l'extrémité supérieure du levier de commande;* 11, *capot de l'appareil moteur;* 15, *réservoir à essence.*

préférence sur un Fokker, mais parfois on le rencontrait sur un Roland ou sur un petit Aviatik. Lorsqu'à l'horizon se dessinait le profil caractéristique d'un avion allié, le groupe allait à sa rencontre. La mission des collaborateurs de Boelke consistait à encercler l'adversaire et à l'empêcher de fuir». Ils le mitraillaient, puis, soudain, arrêtaient leur tir : c'était l'instant où Boelke faisait son entrée en scène, fonçait sur l'ennemi et l'attaquait furieusement avec les mille cartouches de sa mitrailleuse.

Boelke s'acharnait au combat, contrairement à la plupart de ses compatriotes, qui s'attardent rarement à lutter avec un adversaire qui n'a pas été descendu aux premières balles. C'est ainsi que le lieutenant Immelman, qui fut l'un des meilleurs aviateurs allemands, se contentait de foncer droit sur l'avion ennemi, en déchargeant sur lui sa mitrailleuse. Lorsqu'il en était hors de portée et qu'il n'avait pas réussi à l'abattre, il s'enfuyait à son tour sans revenir à la charge, ce qui n'était pas très héroïque.

En général, les avions allemands volent très haut, et, comme nous l'avons vu, s'aventurent le moins possible au-dessus des lignes françaises, d'ailleurs bien gardées, durant les périodes d'offensive, par nos escadrilles de chasse.

L'état atmosphérique joue un grand rôle dans les batailles aériennes. Les jours calmes, sans le moindre vent, où le ciel est couvert de gros nuages gris, sont extrêmement favorables aux attaques par surprise. Les nuages font l'office d'écran et permettent à l'aviateur de se dissimuler jusqu'au moment qui lui semble opportun pour foncer droit sur son adversaire surpris.

Les aviateurs allemands apprécient beaucoup une méthode qu'ils ont inaugurée et qui paraît leur avoir quelquefois reussi. Quand la zone nuageuse est très basse, un de leurs avions évolue en dessous, à deux ou trois cents mètres du sol. Cet appareil sert en quelque sorte d'appât. C'est généralement un avion peu rapide, d'un modèle ancien et mal armé. Il constitue pour ses adversaires une proie relativement facile. Aussitôt qu'il est aperçu par un avion français, il est vite pris en chasse par celui-ci, qui n'hésite même pas à le poursuivre assez loin à l'intérieur des lignes ennemies. Mais au moment où le combat va s'engager dans des conditions favorables à notre pilote, surgissent inopinément autour de lui trois ou quatre avions allemands, ceux-là du plus récent modèle et formidablement armés. Volant au-dessus des nuages, ils ont suivi les deux antagonistes, dissimulés à la vue de leur ennemi pour n'entrer en scène que lorsque ce dernier a été attiré à vingt ou trente kilomètres de sa base. Le nombre des assaillants, la difficulté d'être secouru à temps, rendent alors extrêmement précaire la situation de l'aviateur français.

Un combat aérien ne se termine pas nécessairement par la destruction complète ou par-

DISPOSITIF DE TIR A TRAVERS L'HÉLICE DE LA SOCIÉTÉ NIEUPORT-MARCHI

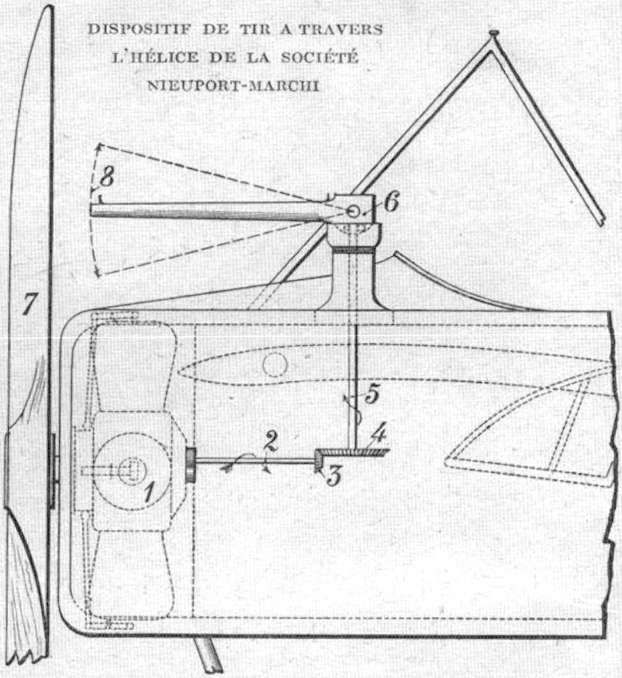

Le moteur 1 actionne l'arbre 2 qui, à son tour, entraîne un second arbre 5 au moyen des engrenages 3 et 4. A l'extrémité supérieure de l'arbre 5 est disposé un cliquet ou un excentrique qui, à intervalles variables, agit sur la détente de la mitrailleuse 6. La vitesse de l'arbre 5 est réglée avec celle du moteur, de façon que la pression du cliquet sur la détente de la mitrailleuse n'ait lieu qu'après le passage d'une pale de l'hélice 7 devant le canon de l'arme. Dans le sens vertical, la mitrailleuse peut pivoter sous un angle 8 sans que le réglage du mécanisme se trouve modifié.

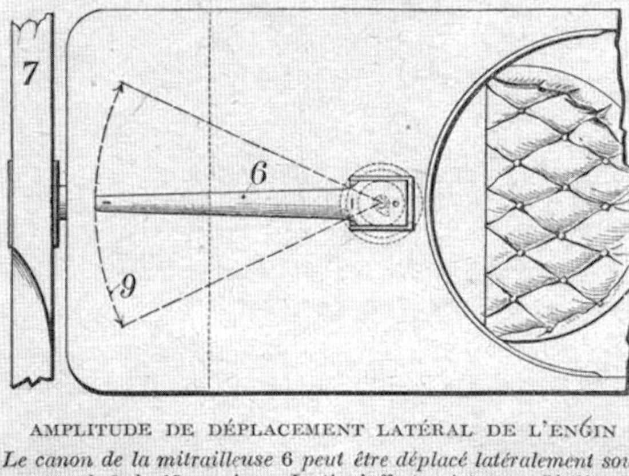

AMPLITUDE DE DÉPLACEMENT LATÉRAL DE L'ENGIN

Le canon de la mitrailleuse 6 peut être déplacé latéralement sous un angle 9 de 45° environ. Le tir s'effectue à travers l'hélice 7.

LES PRINCIPES DU COMBAT AÉRIEN 405

UN PILOTE FRANÇAIS EXAMINANT LA MITRAILLEUSE D'UN BIPLAN L. G. V. CAPTURÉ

L'appareil allemand est armé de deux mitrailleuses que manœuvre l'observateur : l'une sur le plan porteur, qu'il tire debout ; l'autre sur le fuselage, qu'il tire assis.

tielle de l'un des adversaires et sa mise hors de combat définitive ou momentanée. Il est arrivé quelques fois qu'un aviateur allemand, attaqué par l'un de nos « as » ait eu nettement conscience de son infériorité. L'issue du combat ne lui paraissant pas douteuse, il a préféré se rendre plutôt que d'être descendu, avec quelques balles dans le corps. Dans ce cas, l'observateur — s'il y en a un à bord — lève les bras, tandis que le pilote continue à conduire son appareil, suivi de très près par le vainqueur. Celui-ci accompagne l'ennemi jusqu'au parc d'aviation le plus proche et atterrit à ses côtés. Voilà !

C'est de cette façon que le regretté lieutenant Lafon « cueillit », en plein ciel, un Fokker du plus récent modèle qu'il conduisit ensuite au centre d'aviation du Plessis - Belleville. Cette capture fait d'autant plus honneur à l'officier français qu'il n'avait aucune arme à son bord, pas même un revolver.

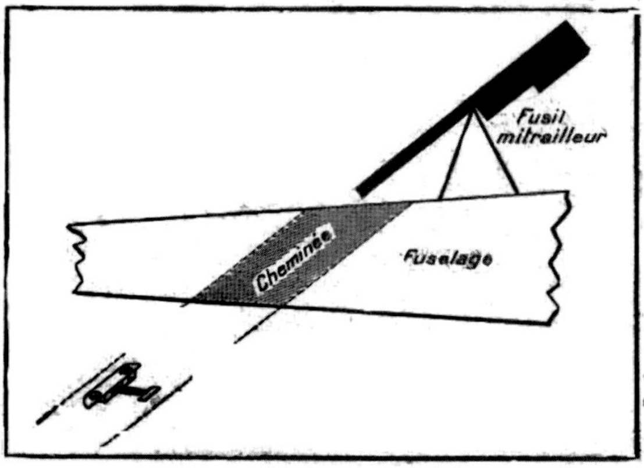

LA CHEMINÉE DU FUSELAGE D'UN BIPLAN L. G. V.

Le fusil-mitrailleur qui, sur les appareils allemands, remplace souvent la mitrailleuse arrière, peut être pointé à travers le fuselage, grâce à une sorte de cheminée cylindrique inclinée à 45°.

Avant la guerre, la question de l'armement des avions n'avait été que très superficiellement étudiée, en France du moins. Au début des hostilités, seuls quelques appareils étaient pourvus d'une mitrailleuse. La plupart des aviateurs ne disposaient que d'un mousqueton pour se défendre éventuelle-

406 LA SCIENCE ET LA VIE

OBSERVATEUR D'AVION ENNEMI TIRANT A TRAVERS LE FUSELAGE DE SON APPAREIL SUR L'ADVERSAIRE QUI LE POURSUIT

On comprend l'avantage de ce dispositif, qui permet de mettre à mal un poursuivant, même quand celui-ci se trouve au-dessous de soi.

ment contre les attaques des pilotes ennemis.

A l'heure actuelle — et nos ennemis en savent quelque chose— nos avions sont très efficacement armés, tant pour l'attaque que pour la défense. Tous ont au moins une mitrailleuse et certains en ont deux et même trois.

De la position de la mitrailleuse à bord de l'avion dépend en grande partie le succès d'un combat. On comprend que les Allemands aient étudié ce problème avec une

MONTAGE SUR TOURELLE ROTATIVE D'UNE MITRAILLEUSE ACTIONNÉE PAR L'OBSERVATEUR

Ce dispositif assure un vaste champ de tir sur l'arrière. L'amplitude du déplacement horizontal de la mitrailleuse dépasse 180°, et le tir peut être également dirigé vers le haut et vers le bas. Le fuselage, suffisamment profond, permet au mitrailleur de se dissimuler à la vue de son adversaire.

attention toute particulière. Sur leurs appareils, la mitrailleuse occupe le plus souvent l'une des cinq positions suivantes :

1° Sur le plan supérieur (mitrailleuse fixe, tir au-dessus de l'hélice) ;

2° Le long du fuselage de l'aéroplane (mitrailleuse fixe, tir à travers l'hélice) ;

3° A l'arrière des plans porteurs (mitrailleuse mobile sur tourelle rotative) ;

4° A l'avant de la carlingue (mitrailleuse mobile à champ de tir très étendu, appareil mono-moteur, hélice propulsive) ;

5° A l'avant et à l'arrière de la carlingue (mitrailleuses mobiles, appareil bi-moteur, hélices tractives, carlingue centrale.)

La première disposition est adoptée sur certains petits biplans rapides de nos ennemis ; elle est semblable, à peu de chose près, au système qui figure sur nos Nieuports. La mitrailleuse est fixée sur le plan supérieur, parallèlement au fuselage ; son fonctionnement est généralement commandé par un flexible Bowden aboutissant à une poignée placée à portée du pilote.

L'inclinaison verticale de la mitrailleuse vers l'objet visé est obtenue par la propre inclinaison de l'aéroplane. Son orientation horizontale est assurée de la même façon. En supposant que l'aéroplane poursuivi soit situé juste au-dessous de l'avion poursuivant, celui-ci devrait donc se placer dans la verticale et foncer sur son adversaire incliné à 90° pour l'atteindre par le feu de sa mitrailleuse. En réalité, les choses ne se passent pas exactement de cette façon ; l'avion assaillant n'attend pas d'être au-dessus de son adversaire pour le mitrailler ; dès qu'il en est à moins de cent mètres, il pointe sur lui en ouvrant le feu, plongeant ainsi de 55° à 65°, ce qui représente déjà, par rapport à l'horizontale, un angle de chute considérable.

La difficulté d'atteindre le but est d'autant plus grande que le tireur et la cible sont tous deux mobiles et que l'orientation de l'aéroplane a lieu par des mouvements de très grande amplitude et relativement lents.

Le montage de la mitrailleuse sur le plan supérieur est généralement adopté sur les appareils dont le poste du pilote est placé derrière les ailes. Par conséquent, pour avoir le plus de chances de toucher l'aviateur lui-même, son adversaire doit toujours s'efforcer de le dominer.

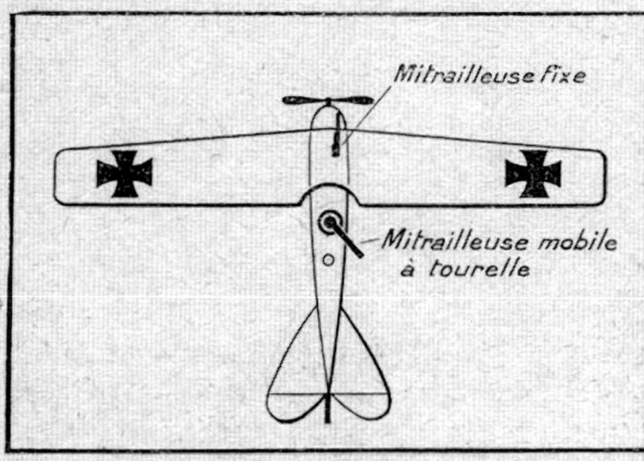

MONTAGE DE DEUX MITRAILLEUSES SUR UN NOUVEAU BIPLAN L. G. V.

La mitrailleuse avant, dont le tir a lieu à travers l'hélice, est actionnée par le pilote ; la mitrailleuse arrière, montée sur tourelle rotative, est commandée par l'observateur.

Le dispositif du tir dans l'hélice implique l'application des mêmes principes de vol ; on sait que l'inventeur de ce dispositif est Roland Garros, fait prisonnier par les Allemands avant d'avoir réussi à détruire son appareil.

Nos ennemis eurent vite fait de copier le dispositif ; il faut cependant admettre qu'ils le perfectionnèrent considérablement avant de l'appliquer sur leurs Fokkers, où il donna de très bons résultats.

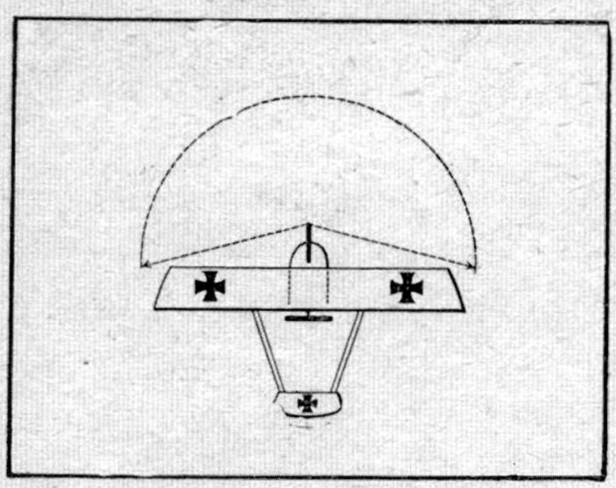

SCHÉMA DU MONTAGE D'UNE MITRAILLEUSE A CHAMP LIMITÉ

L'engin est fixé à l'avant de la carlingue sur un support peu élevé ; sa portée, dans le sens horizontal, est limitée par les parties débordantes de l'aéroplane.

Sur le Fokker, la mitrailleuse est également fixe ; elle est disposée au-dessus du capot, un peu désaxée à droite, presque face au pilote. Elle ne peut donc tirer que dans le cercle décrit par l'hélice. Par suite de la fixité de l'arme, c'est aussi avec l'avion tout entier que le pilote doit viser en le braquant sur son adversaire. D'où les difficultés considérables de visée que nous avons précédemment signalées.

L'idée originale du système de tir à travers l'hélice réside dans ce fait que le mécanisme de la mitrailleuse est automatiquement accroché pendant le passage de l'hélice devant le canon de l'arme. Ce canon est placé directement derrière l'hélice.

Le moteur est relié à la mitrailleuse par une came dont un réglage convenable assure l'accrochage du mécanisme de l'arme pendant un temps très court qui n'excède pas 1/500e de seconde. Dès que la pale du propulseur n'est plus dans la trajectoire du projectile, le système est libéré. Quand le pilote veut tirer, il presse sur un minuscule levier, placé au milieu de la double poignée du levier de commande et qui agit au moyen d'un Bowden sur la détente de la mitrailleuse.

La société d'aviation qui, en Italie, exploite la licence Nieuport, a fait breveter un dispositif de tir à travers l'hélice, presque identique à celui qui figure aujourd'hui sur les Fokkers. Il est basé sur la différence de vitesse qui existe entre le projectile de la mitrailleuse et l'hélice de l'aéroplane. En effet, le rapport entre la vitesse de la balle et celle de l'hélice est à peu près dans la proportion de 700 à 160. Il convient donc d'utiliser cet écart, afin de pouvoir régler la détente de la mitrailleuse avec le passage de l'hélice devant le canon de l'arme. (Voir la figure page 404).

Le dispositif de Garros était beaucoup plus rudimentaire. Il consistait simplement en de petites pièces d'acier suffisamment résistantes pour s'opposer à la pénétration des balles ; chaque pale d'hélice portait une de ces pièces, fixée juste en face du canon de la mitrailleuse. Si une balle venait à frapper le propulseur, la présence de la pièce métallique la faisait dévier de sa trajectoire et la rejetait vivement sur le côté sans qu'elle endommage les pales de l'hélice.

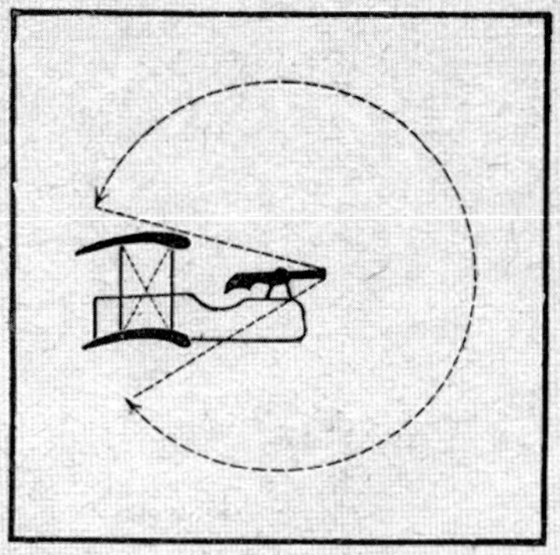

CHAMP DE TIR VERTICAL D'UNE MITRAILLEUSE SUR PIVOT

Dans le sens vertical, le tir de la mitrailleuse est plus étendu : il est seulement limité par la cellule de l'aéroplane.

Les biplaces allemands, comme les L. V. G., par exemple, sont pourvus de deux mitrailleuses : l'une, fixe, située sur le plan supérieur, l'autre, mobile, disposée sur le fuselage, derrière le poste de l'observateur. Montée sur tourelle rotative, cette mitrailleuse a une portée très grande (fig. p. 405).

La tourelle consiste en une couronne de bois qui tourne très librement sur le fuselage au moyen de galets et sur laquelle se trouve, dans un plan vertical, un parallélogramme métallique déformable, muni d'un ressort de rappel. Deux petites tiges permettent de bloquer facilement le support et la couronne. Cette disposition assure un vaste champ de tir, à l'arrière dans toutes les directions, et sur les côtés, vers le haut et vers le bas. Enfin, il est également possible de tirer en avant, par-dessus les ailes de l'avion.

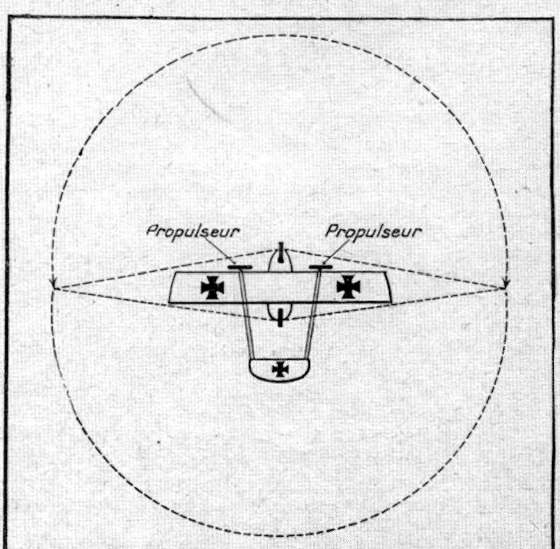

MONTAGE DE DEUX MITRAILLEUSES SUR UN BI-MOTEUR

Les deux mitrailleuses peuvent se déplacer à bord de l'avion de façon que leurs feux se croisent.

Souvent, la mitrailleuse arrière est remplacée par un fusil-mitrailleur. Pour supprimer le *champ mort* de cette arme, le fuselage est pourvu d'une sorte de cheminée, inclinée à 45° environ. Cette cheminée permet de viser et de tirer à travers le fuselage sur un avion ennemi, même s'il se trouve dissimulé aux yeux du mitrailleur par la partie arrière de l'aéroplane allemand. (Figure à la page 406)

Les mitrailleuses avant et arrière sont toutes deux manœuvrées par l'observateur. Sur un type plus récent, la mitrailleuse avant a été disposée entre les deux plans porteurs, le canon à côté du moteur et parallèlement à celui-ci. Elle est actionnée par le pilote, qui en a la commande à portée de sa main droite.

Certains avions allemands, au début, étaient pourvus d'une carlingue quelque peu semblable à celle de nos Farmans. La mitrailleuse était fixée à l'avant sur un support peu élevé ; cette disposition, qui laissait un champ mort considérable fut abandonnée par la suite. La mitrailleuse ne pouvait balayer qu'une zone restreinte, sa portée étant limitée par les parties débordantes de l'appareil, telles que bout d'aile, hélice, câbles, tendeurs, etc... On remédia dans une certaine mesure à cet inconvénient en surélevant le support de la mitrailleuse et même en lui substituant une tourelle rotative qui permettait de tirer dans toutes les directions, mais non sous tous les angles. Le remède était donc encore insuffisant ; aussi, à l'heure actuelle, l'avion lui-même a-t-il disparu à peu près complètement du front ennemi.

Il a été remplacé par un avion A. G. O. pourvu de deux moteurs, de deux hélices tractives et d'une carlingue centrale. Cette carlingue est munie de deux mitrailleuses mobiles à tourelle. L'une, pointée vers l'avant de l'appareil, balaye tout l'horizon ; l'autre, le canon braqué vers l'arrière, peut se déplacer latéralement de façon que ses feux se croisent avec ceux de la première.

Tous les avions allemands sont armés d'une ou deux mitrailleuses Maxim, Lewis ou Parabellum ; quelques-uns en possèdent trois. Ces armes ont été spécialement établies en vue de leur affectation aux services aériens ; certaines, comme le Parabellum, sont pourvues de ceintures de cartouches qui ne reçoivent pas moins de 1.000 projectiles chacune.

Si chaque pilote a sa manière propre de combattre, chaque type d'avion présente des points faibles et des qualités qu'il est bon de connaître avant de l'attaquer. Suivant, par exemple, que la mitrailleuse est disposée à bord de telle ou telle manière, l'assaillant doit attaquer soit par-dessus, soit par-dessous ou encore latéralement. Si le champ de tir de la mitrailleuse a des points morts, si certaines positions handicapent l'attaqué au profit de l'attaquant, celui-ci doit les connaître et mettre tout son savoir à profit.

C'est ainsi que le pilote qui combat un Aviatik est exposé à son feu à peu près dans toutes les directions, sauf dans le cône situé en avant de l'hélice ; en effet, sur les Aviatiks les plus courants, le passager qui est à l'avant dispose d'une mitrailleuse qu'il peut, à son gré, situer à droite ou à gauche du fuselage. Cette mitrailleuse est disposée sur un pivot monté sur des chariots. Ces chariots peuvent se déplacer, à la volonté du tireur, sur deux guides latéraux en forme de glissières, réunis au fuselage au moyen de supports ajourés. Une vis permet de fixer les chariots en un point quelconque des glissières. On peut tirer dans tous les sens.

ARMEMENT DÉFENSIF D'UN AVION DE BOMBARDEMENT

Bien que cet appareil, un biplan Voisin, ne soit pas destiné à des opérations de chasse, il est pourvu d'une mitrailleuse qui lui permet, le cas échéant, de repousser les attaques des avions allemands et même, parfois, d'abattre ceux-ci. En dépit de sa vitesse réduite, ce biplan a souvent triomphé des Fokkers.

L'aviateur qui attaque un L. V. G., dont nous avons examiné plus haut la disposition des deux mitrailleuses, peut se considérer à l'abri tant qu'il reste en avant, depuis l'horizontale jusqu'à la ligne passant de la tourelle au bord arrière des ailes inférieures.

Il s'ensuit que l'identification des aéroplanes ennemis est d'une grande utilité pour le pilote de chasse. Malheureusement la diversité des types d'avions employés par les Allemands et les modifications fréquemment apportées aux appareils en service, rendent cette identification assez compliquée.

Oscar Ribel.

34

R É S

	MOTEURS		ATTERRISSEURS			Type de Courbe	Flèche maxima	Angle Caisson Tête et Poutre	RÉGLAGE INCIDENCE DES PLANS					
									SUPÉRIEUR		INFÉRIEUR			
	Marque	HP	Nombre de Roues	Dimension des roues	Voie				Fus.	Ext.	Fus.	Ext.	Fus.	Ext.
X Biplan			2			N	46°	90°	2°30	2°30	4°	4°	4°	5°
X Monoplan	Rhône	80	2	d°		N			2°15	2°15	4°	4°	4°	5°
XI	Rhône	80	2	d°		N	34	86°30	2°30	2°30	4°	4°	4°	5°
XVI	Rhône	110	2	d°		N			2°30	2°30	4°	4°	4°	5°
XVII b	Clerget	130	2			N		86°40	2°50	2°50	4°	4°	4°	5°
XVII	Rhône	110		d°		N	34	87°40	2°50	2°50	4°	4°	4°	5°
XXIII	Rhône	120		d°		N		87°40	2°50	2°50	4°	4°	4°	5°
	Rhône	80	2			N		86°40	2°40	2°40	4°	4°	4°	5°
XXIV b	Rhône	120	2			N5			2°40	2°40	3°	3°	3°	4°
XXIV	Rhône	120		d°		N5	14	86°40	2°40	2°40	3°	3°	3°	4°
XXVII	Rhône	120	2	d°		N5			2°40	2°40	3°	3°	3°	4°
XII		110	2	700 × 100		N			3°30	3°30	4°	4°	4°	5°
XII b		130	2	d°		N	54	90°	3°	3°	4°	4°	4°	5°
	Rhône	110	2			N			3°	3°	4°	4°	4°	5°
XIV	Hispano	150	2	d°		N	53	90°	4°	4°	5°30	5°30	5°30	6°
80	Rhône		2		1 m 800	N	54	88°55	2°	2°	5°	5°	5°	6°
81	Rhône	80	2			N			2°	2°	5°	5°	5°	6°
82	Rhône	80	4	AV 650 × 80 AR 700 × 100	2 m 600	N	53	88°40	3°50	2°50	4°30	4°30	4°30	5°30
83	Rhône	80	2	700 × 100	1 m 800	N	46	90°	3°	3°	3°20	3°20	3°20	4°20

35

U M É

Surfaces	DIAMÈTRE DES CABLES Porteurs AV	Porteurs AR	Non porteurs AV	Non porteurs AR	HÉLICES Marque	Série	Béquilles	CARACTÉRISTIQUES SPÉCIALES	OBSERVATIONS
18 m 2	4	5	3	3	Régy	155		Pilote AV.	Les résistances équivalentes au diamètre des câbles sont les suivantes : 3 m/m 1100 k. 4 m m 1800 k. 5 m/m 2800 k. 6 m/m 4000 k. Les appareils type 17, 17 bis, 23, 21, 24, 24 bis et 27 comportent un câble de retenue dont les caractéristiques sont les suivantes : Diamètre : 3 m/m. Résistance : 800 k.
18					Chauvière	2219			
13	3	4	3	3	Levasseur	450			
13					Levasseur	482			
15					Levasseur	502			
15					Levasseur Eclair	484 4	Rigide		
	4	4	3	3					
15					Levasseur Régy Chauvière	549 354 2228			
15					Levasseur	450			
15					Levasseur	549			
15	4	4	3	3	Régy Chauvière	354 2228			
15							Souple	Pilote AV.	
23					Régy Eclair	274 2			
23	4	5	4	4	Eclair	20		Pilote AV.	
23					Régy Eclair	151 2	Rigide	Pilote AV.	
	1o/5	6	3	4					
30									
	2o/3	4	3	3	Eclair	8			
23							Souple	Pilote AR simple commande.	
	4	5	4	4					
23							Souple	Double commande.	
	1o/5	6	3	4	Régy	230			
30	2o/3	4	3	3		blindée.	Rigide	Double commande.	
18	4	5	4	4			Souple	Pilote AR simple commande.	